ISLAM
MUHAMMAD AND HIS RELIGION

The Library of Liberal Arts
OSKAR PIEST, FOUNDER

ISLAM
MUHAMMAD AND HIS RELIGION

Edited, with an introduction, by

ARTHUR JEFFERY

The Library of Liberal Arts

published by

THE BOBBS-MERRILL COMPANY, INC.

PUBLISHERS · INDIANAPOLIS · NEW YORK

The Bobbs-Merrill Company, Inc.
4300 West 62nd Street
Indianapolis, Indiana 46268

First Edition
Eighth Printing—1975
Library of Congress Catalog Card Number: 58–9958
ISBN 0–672–60348–9(pbk.)
ISBN 0–672–51058–8

PREFACE

Every editor of an anthology such as this knows that whatever his selections they will disappoint many of his fellow scholars who would have chosen other materials from the vast literature available. This selection, however, was not made merely by a non-Muslim scholar for other scholars; it was made for students of religion with the help of a practicing Muslim. The following pages contain only a fraction of the material selected as of primary religious importance for Muslims, limitations of space making it impossible to include all. The editor wishes to express his regrets to his Muslim associate for being obliged to omit or severely abridge many of the selections originally made.

What could be attempted here is to gather a number of selections from among the many relevant passages in the Qur'ān, the *Ḥadīth,* and later writings, which will serve to make clear the ordinary orthodox Muslim teaching about the Prophet, about his Book, about those things most truly believed, and about those means of grace most commonly practiced. For convenience of presentation it seemed best to begin with the Prophet and his Book, and then to assemble the selections under the conventional six articles of belief and five practical duties, concluding with some material illustrative of the devotional side of Islam.

Almost all the selections are from writers who set forth the old classical system of traditional Islam. It would be useful to compile another anthology of the literature of modernist movements, but as this book is intended to set forth to students what the religion of Islam has been through the centuries and still is today for the great majority of practicing Muslims, it seems wisest to omit from this collection the modernist interpretations of Islam which differ enormously from one another in their attempts to adapt Islam to the modern world.

The source of every selection has been indicated for those who may wish to consult the originals, and a glossary has been appended as a help to cross reference. All Qur'ānic quotations are from the Cairo text of 1344 A.H. (1925 A.D.), whose verse numbering is given, followed by that of Flügel where the latter differs: for example, "LVI, 77/76" means verse 77 of Sūra LVI in the Cairo text, which is verse 76 in Flügel's text, whose verse numbering is followed in most European translations and used in most European works on Islam.

Arabic words have been transliterated so as to give as nearly as possible the classical pronunciation. In the translations, words which are not in the original text but which are necessary in English to make the text intelligible have been put within square brackets, explanatory additions by the translator in parentheses.

Notes have been cut to the minimum, but bibliographical references are given to guide interested students to more elaborate treatments of the various matters discussed.

All who may use this anthology owe a debt of gratitude to Mr. E. Abdelnoor, who read over with the editor all the original texts for accuracy of translation, to Professor Horace Friess and Dr. Kenneth Cragg, who labored over earlier drafts to advise on how they could be cut to the present proportions, to the Committee on the History of Religions of the American Council of Learned Societies, and to the publisher of the series, to which this volume belongs.

A. J.

TABLE OF CONTENTS

INTRODUCTION

Islam is the religion which has developed from the preaching and life of Muḥammad, a citizen of the city of Mecca in Arabia, who early in the seventh century of the Christian Era appeared as a preacher of monotheism to his own people and founded a religious movement which today counts perhaps as many as 300,000,000 followers, mostly in the heat belt from Indonesia to Morocco.

The old Arabian paganism was at that time in a process of disintegration, but Judaism and Christianity were widely represented in the peninsula, and to a lesser extent Zoroastrianism and certain Gnostic sects. Several preachers of monotheism had arisen and each had gained a following, but it was Muḥammad who succeeded in syncretizing certain basic elements of Judaeo-Christian faith and practice with native Arabian beliefs and, by his own burning faith in his mission and indomitable courage in carrying out that mission, initiated what has become one of the world religions of our day.

Muḥammad seems to have thought of himself as in the succession of the Old Testament men of faith, sent on his mission by the one and only Lord of all. Like Noah, Jonah, and Elijah he preached a religious message in the name of this Supreme Lord, and like Moses he also issued legislation in His name, for like Abraham he was not only a maintainer of righteousness but the founder of a community of the righteous. Like neighboring religious communities, this community of his has, as its most precious and distinctive possession, a Book, a Scripture which sets forth his preaching and legislation for the community and the essential themes of his faith. Such material of this nature as his followers could gather together after his death and publish has come down to us as the Qur'ān.

The Qur'ān is thus the fundamental document for the religion of Islam and is regarded by the faithful as the Holy, Revealed, Eternal Word of God. After the Prophet's death, however, the growing community of his followers found that a great many problems of religion, and even more of community life, were arising for which there was no specific guidance in the Qur'ān. Guidance was therefore sought in the Traditions, *Ḥadīth,* as to what the Prophet had said and done, or was reported to have said and done. This vast accumulation of genuine, partly genuine, and quite spurious traditions was presently digested into the collections of *Ḥadīth,* six of which are considered to be the canonical collections.[1] But as these canonical collections were primarily concerned with material of a juristic nature, it follows that much material of importance for the religion of Islam had to be drawn from the other, uncanonical collections. It was well known to Muslims that much of the *Ḥadīth* material was spurious, but for the study of Islam even those traditions which the community invented and attributed to Muḥammad have their value, often as much value as those which may actually have come from him.

Muḥammad called his new religion "Islam," a word which means submission, that is, submission to the will of Allah, the Lord. One who accepts Islam and makes such submission is a Muslim. Such a person is termed a *mu'min* (believer), and one who does not accept Islam is a *kāfir* (unbeliever). To live in submission to Allah and in obedience to the teaching of the Prophet, a Muslim must follow a rule formulated for him as a good Muslim. Such a rule is provided in the *Sharī'a,* the Law, which is based in the first instance on the Qur'ān, in the second instance on the *Ḥadīth,* the Traditions, in the third instance on *Ijmā',* the consensus of the community, and in the fourth instance on *qiyās,* the application of analogical reasoning to the other three sources for the deduction of new rules. Obviously, the Prophet's intention was that the community should be a single community and the *Sharī'a* its common

[1] These six canonical collections of *Ḥadīth* are: the *Ṣaḥīḥ* of al-Bukhārī (d. 256 A.H., 870 A.D.), the *Ṣaḥīḥ* of Muslim (d. 261 A.H., 875 A.D.), the *Jāmi'* of at-Tirmidhī (d. 279 A.H., 892 A.D.), the *Sunan* of Abū Dāwūd (d. 275 A.H., 888 A.D.), the *Sunan* of Ibn Māja (d. 273 A.H., 886 A.D.), and the *Sunan* of an-Nasā'ī (d. 303 A.H., 915 A.D.).

rule of life. After his death, however, party strife broke out under his successors, the caliphs, three out of the first four of whom died by violence. Under the fourth caliph, 'Alī, the Prophet's cousin and husband of his daughter Fāṭima, the community was torn in two. The legitimists, who held that the succession should remain in the Prophet's family and that 'Alī should have been the first caliph, have developed into the Shī'a sects, which are still a minority group in Islam. The great mass of Muslims, however, form the Sunnī sect, ruled over at first by the caliphs of the Umayyad Dynasty reigning in Damascus, and then by the 'Abbasid Dynasty reigning in Baghdad, until the caliphate was taken over by the Turks.

In Sunnī Islam there were various attempts by learned jurists to work out a systematized formulation of the Law, the *Sharī'a*. Gradually four [2] such systematizations succeeded in imposing themselves on the community, so that today most Sunnī Muslims will be found following the *madhhab* (system) of one of these four, ordering their religious and community life according to the prescriptions worked out by the jurists of one of these schools. There is nothing binding in adherence to any one of these four, so that individuals can and do change for various reasons from one *madhhab* to another, just as among Christians a Baptist may become, if he wishes, an Episcopalian, or an Episcopalian a Baptist.

There were also attempts at an early period to work out some formulation of the beliefs and practices of Muslims. In the Qur'ān itself there were passages which briefly summarized the things a Muslim should believe, and somewhat more elaborate statements are to be found in the Traditions. These were too brief, however, to be sufficient and too bare to be satisfying to inquiring minds, especially where such minds had become aware of the existence of theological formulations in the hands of followers of other religions with whom they were in contact and not uncommonly in controversy: so ere long we find circulating, under the names of certain

[2] Those of Abū Ḥanīfa (d. 150 A.H., 767 A.D.), Mālik b. Anas (d. 179 A.H., 795 A.D.), ash-Shāfi'ī (d. 204 A.H., 820 A.D.), and Aḥmad b. Ḥanbal (d. 240 A.H., 855 A.D.).

famous divines, what may justly be called credal statements. These presently became the subject of discussion and commentary until in time there grew up an Islamic theology and a Muslim science of dogmatics. One result of this theological activity was that Islam, as other religions, developed its heretical sects, so that a part of the task of dogmatics is to distinguish orthodox belief and practice more precisely from various forms of heretical teaching.

The two schools in which orthodox Sunnī teaching found its final crystallization are those of the Ash'arites and of the Māturīdites.[3] Most of the standard theological treatises still studied in Muslim centers of learning come from one or the other of these schools. The simple general statement common to them both is that orthodox Islam consists of (a) *īmān* (faith) in six things most truly believed: in Allah, His angels, His books, His prophets, the Last Day, and the predestination of good and evil; together with (b) *dīn* (religious practices), or the five pillars of Islam: profession of faith, prayers, almsgiving, fasting, and pilgrimage to Mecca. For the content of these six articles of faith and five practical duties, the reader is referred to the appropriate sections of this anthology, where they are described.

Devotional life among Muslims has been fostered by the daily prayers, by frequenting mosques, by meditation, by the devotional reading of the Qur'ān, and by participation in annual feasts and fasts. Besides these practices, however, there grew up among the devotionally minded in Islam a distinctive Islamic mysticism. In its development of practical techniques for the devotional life, this trend finally embodied itself in the Dervish Orders which are widespread throughout the world of Islam, and on the intellectual side developed a somewhat complex but highly interesting mystical theology. Within the limited scope of this anthology, however, it was not possible to include material illustrative of the theological and philosophical developments in Islam.

ARTHUR JEFFERY

[3] These are the followers respectively of Abū'l-Ḥasan al-Ash'arī (d. 324 A.H., 935 A.D.) and Abū'l-Manṣūr al-Māturīdī (d. 333 A.H., 944 A.D.).

SELECTED BIBLIOGRAPHY

This bibliography supplements the references contained in the notes accompanying the source materials reproduced in this volume.

General Surveys

T. Arnold and A. Guillaume. *The Legacy of Islam.* 2nd ed. Oxford, 1948.

G. H. Bousquet et J. Schacht. *Oeuvres choisies de C. Snouck Hurgronje.* Leiden, 1957.

B. Carra de Vaux. *Les Penseurs de l'Islam.* 5 vols. Paris, 1921-1926.

I. Goldziher. *Vorlesungen über den Islam.* 2nd ed. by F. Babinger. Heidelberg, 1925.

M. Guidi. *Storia della religione dell'Islam,* Vol. II of P. Tacchi Venturi's *Storia delle Religioni.* Torino, 1949.

A. Guillaume. *Islam.* London, 1954.

R. Jockel. *Islamische Geisteswelt.* Darmstadt, 1954.

E. Kellerhals. *Der Islam: seine Geschichte, seine Lehre, sein Wesen.* Basel, 1945.

H. Lammens. *Islam, croyances et institutions.* Beyrouth, 1926; English tr., London, 1929.

A. Mieli. *La science arabe.* Leiden, 1939.

R. A. Nicholson. *A Literary History of the Arabs.* 2nd ed. Cambridge, 1930.

Johs Pedersen. *Islams Kultur.* Copenhagen, 1928.

O. Pfannmüller. *Handbuch der Islamliteratur.* Berlin, 1923.

J. Sauvaget. *Introduction à l'histoire de l'Orient musulman.* Paris, 1946.

J. Schacht. *Der Islam: mit Ausschluss des Qorans. Religionsgeschichtliches Lesebuch,* Nr. 16. Tübingen, 1931.

A. S. Tritton. *Islam.* London, 1951.

The World of Islam

P. J. André. *Islam et les races.* 2 vols. Paris, 1922.

T. Arnold. *The Caliphate.* Oxford, 1924.

———. *The Preaching of Islam.* London, 1913.

C. Brockelmann. *Geschichte der islamischen Völker und Staaten.* München, 1939; English tr., New York, 1947.

E. G. Browne. *A Literary History of Persia.* 4 vols. London, 1902-1924.

G. E. von Grunebaum. *Islam: Essays in the Nature and Growth of a Cultural Tradition.* Menasha, 1955.

———. *Mediaeval Islam.* Chicago, 1947.

E. W. Lane. *Manners and Customs of the Modern Egyptians.* London, 1924.

B. Lewis. *The Arabs in History.* London, 1950.

L. Massignon. *L'Islam et l'Occident.* Paris, 1947.

W. Muir. *The Caliphate, its Rise, Decline and Fall.* Edinburgh, 1924.

A. Pellegrini. *L'Islam dans le monde.* Paris, 1937.

G. Simon. *Die Welt des Islams und ihre Berührungen mit der Christenheit.* Gütersloh, 1948.

E. Westermarck. *Pagan Survivals in Mohammedan Civilisation.* London, 1933.

E. Zambaur. *Manuel de généalogie et de chronologie pour l'histoire de l'Islam.* Hannover, 1927.

The Prophet

R. Bell. *The Origin of Islam in its Christian Environment.* Edinburgh, 1926.

R. Blachère. *Le problème de Mahomet. Essai de biographie critique du fondateur de l'Islam.* Paris, 1952.

M. Gaudefroy-Desmombynes. *Mahomet, l'homme et son message.* Paris, 1957.

H. Grimme. *Mohammed.* 2 vols. Münster, 1892.

H. Holma. *Mahomet, Prophète de l'Islam.* Paris, 1945.

D. S. Margoliouth. *Mohammed.* London, 1939.

C. A. Nallino. *Vita di Maometto.* Roma, 1946.

Theology

Tor Andrae. *Der Ursprung des Islams und das Christentum.* Uppsala, 1926.

D. M. Donaldson. *The Shi'ite Religion.* London, 1933.

W. Goldsack. *Selections from Muhammadan Traditions.* Madras, 1923.

I. Goldziher. *Muhammedanische Studien.* 2 vols. Halle, 1888-90.

A. Guillaume. *The Traditions of Islam.* Oxford, 1924.

M. Horten. *Einführung in die höhere Geisteskultur des Islam.* Bonn, 1914.

Miguel Asin Palacios. *Abenhazam de Córdoba y su Historia crítica de las ideas religiosas.* Madrid, 1927-32.

J. W. Sweetman. *Islam and Christian Theology.* 3 vols. London, 1945-55.

Law

G. Bergsträsser. *Grundzüge des islamischen Rechts.* Leipzig, 1935.

T. W. Junyboll. *Handleiding tot de Kennis van de Mohammedaansche Wet.* 3rd ed. Leiden, 1925.

L. Milliot. *Introduction à l'étude du droit musulman.* Paris, 1953.

L. Ostrorog. *The Angora Reform.* London, 1927.

O. Pesle. *Les fondaments du droit musulman.* Casablanca, 1944.

D. Santillana. *Instituzioni di Diritto musulmano.* 2 vols. Roma, 1926-38.

J. Schacht. *The Origins of Muhammadan Jurisprudence.* Oxford, 1950.

E. Tyan. *Histoire de l'organisation judicaire en pays d'Islam.* 2 vols. Paris, 1938-43.

G. Vesey-Fitzgerald. *Muhammadan Law: an Abridgment.* Oxford, 1931.

Religious Life

A. J. Arberry. *The Doctrine of the Sufis.* Cambridge, 1935.

J. K. Birge. *The Bektashi Order of Dervishes.* London, 1937.

G. H. Bousquet. *Les grandes pratiques rituelles de l'Islam.* Paris, 1949.

D. M. Donaldson. *Studies in Muslim Ethics.* London, 1950.

M. Gaudefroy-Desmombynes. *Les institutions musulmanes.* Paris, 1946. (There is an English translation of an earlier edition.)

G. E. von Grunebaum. *Muhammadan Festivals.* New York, 1951.

A. von Kremer. *Geschichte der herrschenden Ideen des Islams.* Leipzig, 1868.

R. Levy. *The Social Structure of Islam.* Cambridge, 1957.

D. B. Macdonald. *The Religious Attitude and Life in Islam.* Chicago, 1912.

A. Mazaheri. *La vie quotidienne des Musulmans.* Paris, 1951.

E. Sell. *The Faith of Islam.* 4th ed. Madras, 1920.

Margaret Smith. *Rabi'a the Mystic and her Fellow-Saints in Islam.* Cambridge, 1928.

E. F. Tscheuschner. *Mönchsideale des Islam.* Gütersloh, 1933.

Modernism

C. C. Adams. *Islam and Modernism in Egypt.* London, 1933.

H. E. Allen. *The Turkish Transformation.* Chicago, 1935.

G. Antonius. *The Arab Awakening.* Philadelphia, 1939.

Kenneth Cragg, *The Call of the Minaret.* New York, 1956.

Angelo Ghirelli. *El Renacimiento musulmán.* Barcelona, 1948.

H. A. R. Gibb. *Modern Trends in Islam.* Chicago, 1947.

——— (ed.). *Whither Islam?* London, 1932.

R. Hartmann. *Die Krisis des Islam.* Leipzig, 1928.

M. Laissy. *Du panarabisme à la Ligue arabe.* Paris, 1949.

R. le Tourneau. *L'Islam contemporain.* Paris, 1950.

L. Stoddard. *The New World of Islam.* 2nd ed. London, 1922.

S. G. Wilson. *Modern Movements among Moslems.* New York, 1916.

ISLAM

MUHAMMAD AND HIS RELIGION

I. THE PROPHET

If it is true, as we are often told, that Christianity is Christ, there is also a sense in which it is true that Islam is Muḥammad. It was from his preaching in seventh-century Arabia that the religion got its start. Its Scripture, the Qur'ān, bears the impress of his mind, with its enthusiasms and its limitations, from the first page to the last. The *sunna* enshrined in the corpus of Traditions, both canonical and uncanonical, is from one point of view nothing more than an attempt to get Muḥammad's personal authority as backing for every detail of public or private conduct. In this sense it is an attempt to provide the faithful Muslim with material for an *imitatio Muhammedis* more far-reaching in its consequences than any *imitatio Christi* has ever been. There are thus two figures of Muḥammad, the Muḥammad of history and the Muḥammad of faith, the historical preacher who lived and labored in seventh-century Arabia and the mythical figure of the Prophet which lives in the faith of his community.

The historical Muḥammad is said to have been born about 570 A.D. in the city of Mecca of a poor and humble but well-connected family. Left an orphan at an early age, he was cared for by relatives, and as a youth seems to have worked as a camel-herdsman. In his youth he may possibly have gone with some of his kindred on caravan journeys to the markets of the north. Certainly he went later with the caravan of a wealthy Meccan widow, who, when he was twenty-five, married him and became the mother of all his children who survived. In about his fortieth year he went through the religious experience from which he emerged with a conviction that he had a prophetic mission to his own people. There was at first amused tolerance and then some persecution in Mecca, so that in the year 622 he left for Madina on that well-known "flight" which became the starting point for the Muslim era, whose lunar years A.H. (*anno Hegirae*) contrast with our solar years A.D. Once established in Madina, Muḥammad became less a preacher and prophet than a community leader and man of state, and we witness that curious change of character which develops steadily until his death from a wasting fever in 632.

The earliest Muslim *Life* of the Prophet that has come down to us is one by Ibn Hishām (d. 219 A.H. = 834 A.D.). There is a German translation of this by Gustav Weil, *Das Leben Mohammeds,* 2 vols. (Stuttgart, 1864), and an English translation by A. Guillaume (London, 1955). Aloys Sprenger's *Das Leben und die Lehre des Mohammed,* 2nd ed., 3 vols. (Berlin, 1839), and Sir William Muir's *Life of Mohammad,* ed. T. H. Weir (Edinburgh, 1923), are full-dress biographies of the Prophet still worth reading. Of more critical studies perhaps the best are D. S. Margoliouth's *Mohammed and the Rise of Islam* (London, 1905); Tor Andrae, *Mohammad,* translated by T. Menzel as *Mohammed, the Man and His Message* (New York, 1936); F. Buhl and H. H. Schaeder, *Das Leben Muhammeds* (Heidelberg, 1955). An attempt at a more favorable evaluation of Muḥammad has been made by W. Montgomery Watt in two volumes, *Muhammad at Mecca* (Oxford, 1953) and *Muhammad at Medina* (Oxford, 1956).

For some account of the curious development of the mythical Muḥammad, the older book by S. W. Koelle, *Mohammed and Mohammedanism* (London, 1889), may be consulted, and in particular the critical study by Tor Andrae, *Die Person Muhammeds in Lehre und Glauben seiner Gemeinde* (Stockholm, 1918).

MUḤAMMAD IN THE QUR'ĀN

EARLY MECCAN PASSAGES

XCVI, 1-5. This passage is traditionally regarded as the earliest revelation.

Recite, in the name of thy Lord who has created,
Created man from clots of blood.
Recite, seeing that thy Lord is the most generous,
Who has taught by the pen,
Taught man what he did not know.

LIII, 1-18.

By the star when it falls,
Your companion has not gone astray, nor has he been misled,
Nor is he speaking out of his own inclination.
It is nothing other than a revelation that is revealed [to him].

One mighty in power taught him,
One possessed of strength. He stood erect
When he was at the highest [point of the] horizon.
Then he drew near and descended,
So that he was two bows' lengths off, or even nearer,
And he revealed to his servant what he revealed.
[His] heart did not falsify what it (or he) saw.
So will ye dispute with him about what he saw?
Why, indeed, he saw him coming down another time
At the sidra tree of the boundary,
Beside which is the garden of resort,
When there covered the sidra tree what covered it.
[His] gaze neither turned aside nor did it go beyond,
For, indeed, he was seeing one of the greatest signs of his Lord.

The usual interpretation of the foregoing passage is that Gabriel was the one mighty in power and the one possessed of strength, although these epithets are applied elsewhere to Allah and many modern scholars are of the opinion that this passage refers to a vision of Allah Himself coming to call the Prophet to his mission. Pious fancy has embroidered all the details of this passage, but we are probably to understand that Muḥammad is telling of two occasions when he had this vision, once out in the open where the figure appeared on the horizon and then drew nearer, and once when he was at a certain garden in the vicinity of Mecca at a time when the sidra trees were in full bloom. On each occasion he was able to gaze directly at the figure, and on each occasion there was given him a revelation.

LXXXI, 15-29.

So I swear by the planets
Which swiftly move and conceal themselves;
By the night when it draws on;
By the morning when it comes in.
It is indeed the speech of a noble messenger,
One possessed of power, established beside the Lord of the Throne,
Obeyed there, faithful.
And your companion is not jinn-possessed,
For, indeed, he saw him on the clear horizon,
Nor was he niggardly concerning the unseen.
It is not the speech of a stoned satan.
So where are you [objectors] going?

It is naught but a reminder to mankind,
To whosoever among you is willing to go straight,
Though ye will not so will save if Allah, Lord of Mankind, wills.

This passage is early but has clearly been revised. Richard Bell, in *The Qur'ān* (Edinburgh, 1938-39), II, 638, thinks it was revised in the Madinan period, when Muḥammad had learned about Gabriel and his connection with revelation, in order to make the noble messenger no longer Muḥammad himself but Gabriel.

LXXIV, 1-7.

O thou who wrappest thyself in a mantle,
Arise! Warn!
And thy Lord, magnify [Him]
And thy garments, purify [them]
And the wrath [to come], flee [from it]
And do not do favors to seek increase,
But for thy Lord wait patiently.

LXXIII, 1-10.

O thou enwrapped one,
Rise up [for prayer] at night, save a little,
Half of it—or shorten that somewhat,
Or increase it—and prepare carefully the lesson (Qur'ān)
For we are going to cast on thee a weighty discourse.
Verily the early part of the night is [the best for getting] a strong impression and a just work,
During the day thou hast, indeed, long [hours of] toil.
So commemorate the name of thy Lord and devote thyself to Him, with complete devotion.
Lord of the East and of the West, there is no other deity save Him, so take Him as thy trustee (*wakīl*),
And be patient under what they are saying, and make a graceful withdrawal from them.

XCIII, 1-11.

By the bright morn,
And by the night when all is still,
Thy Lord hath not left thee, nor come to dislike thee,
So the latter [situation] will be better for thee than the former,

And anon thy Lord will assuredly give thee [thy desire], so that thou wilt be well content.
Did He not find thee an orphan and shelter thee?
Did He not find thee erring and guide thee?
Did He not find thee poor and enrich thee?
So as for the orphan, treat [him] not harshly,
And as for the beggar, do not drive [him] away,
And as for thy Lord's bounty, tell [of it].

LXXXVII, 1-9.

Glorify the name of thy Lord, the Most High,
Who created and then fashioned,
Who determined and then guided,
Who brought forth the pasture-land,
Then made it blackened stubble.
We shall cause thee to recite, and thou wilt not forget
Except what Allah wills. He, indeed, knows what is published abroad and what one conceals,
And We shall make it easy for thee, very easy.
So remind, if the reminder profits [anyone].

LATER MECCAN PASSAGES

LII, 29-34.

So warn, for thou art not, by the grace of thy Lord, a soothsayer, nor one jinn-possessed.
Or are they saying: "A poet, for whom we may wait expectantly the uncertainties of fate"?
Say: "Wait! for I am with you among those who wait expectantly."
Is it that their minds bid them to this? or are they an iniquitous folk?
Or are they saying, "He has forged it"? Nay, they will not believe.
So let them bring a discourse like it, if they are those who speak the truth.

XV, 6-15.

And they said: "O thou to whom the reminder has been sent down, thou art indeed one jinn-possessed.
Why dost thou not bring us the angels, if thou art of those who tell the truth?"

We do not send the angels down save with the truth, and [these folk] then would not be granted respite.
We it is, indeed, who have sent down the reminder, and it is We who shall keep watch for it.
We, indeed, have sent [messengers] before thee among the sects of the former peoples,
And never would a messenger come to them but they would be making jest of him.
Likewise We make way for it in the hearts of sinners.
They do not believe in it, though, indeed, the customary [rule of life] of the former peoples has come to an end.
Were We to open for them one of the gates of heaven so that they could continuously mount up into it
They would say: "Our sight has been made drunken; nay, but we are a people [who have been] ensorcelled."

XV, 87-89.

We, indeed, have given thee seven from the *Mathānī* [1] and the mighty Qur'ān.
Let not thine eyes look longingly on what We have given divers of them to enjoy, and grieve not over them, but lower thy wing to those who believe, and say: "As for me, I am the clear warner."

XV, 94-99.

So declare what thou art bidden, and turn from the polytheists.
Verily We will attend to the scoffers for thee,
Those who set up another deity along with Allah. Anon they will know.
We know, indeed, that thou dost feel a straitening of thy breast at what they are saying,
But give glory, with praise of thy Lord, and be one of those who do obeisance,
And worship thy Lord till the certainty come to thee.

XXVI, 213-220.

So do not call on any other deity along with Allah, lest thou be among those to be punished.
But warn thy kindred who are the nearest,

1 A word about which there have been innumerable theories. See Richard Bell, *The Qur'ān* (Edinburgh, 1938-39), I, 247.

And lower thy wing to whoever of the believers may follow thee.
Then, if they oppose thee, say: "I, indeed, am innocent of what ye do,"
And rely upon the Sublime, the Compassionate,
Who sees thee when thou standest,
And [sees] thy turning thyself among those who are prostrating in obeisance.
He, indeed, is the One who hears and knows.

XXV, 7/8-10/11.

They say: "What is there to this messenger? He eats food and walks in the market places. Why was not an angel sent down to him to be a warner along with him?
Or some treasure cast to him? or a garden given him from which he may eat?" The wrongdoers also say: "Ye follow naught but a man ensorcelled."
See how they strike out similitudes for thee. Yet they are in error and not able [to find] a way.
Blessed be He, who, if He will, may appoint for thee something better than that—gardens below which rivers flow, —and may appoint for thee palaces.

MADINAN PASSAGES

IV, 105/106-108, 113.

We have sent down to thee the Book with the truth that thou mayest judge between the people by what Allah has shown thee, so do not be a contender on behalf of the traitors,
But seek Allah's forgiveness. Verity, Allah is forgiving, compassionate. And do not dispute on behalf of those who are betraying themselves. Verily, Allah loves not one who has been traitorous, guilty.
They conceal themselves from the people, but they do not conceal themselves from Allah, for He is with them when they brood over words that are unseemly. Allah comprehends what they are doing.

. . . .

Had it not been for the kindness and mercy of Allah to thee, a party of them would well-nigh have led thee astray, but they lead only themselves astray, and do thee no harm at all. Allah has sent down to thee the Book and the Wisdom, and has taught thee what thou didst not know. Allah's kindness to thee is great.

XXVIII, 85-88.

Verily, He who imposed on thee the Qur'ān will assuredly bring thee back to a point of return. Say: "My Lord knows best who brings guidance, and who it is who is in obvious error."

Thou wert not hopeful that the Book would be sent forward to thee save as [an act of] mercy from thy Lord, so be not a protection for the unbelievers,

And do not let them turn thee aside from Allah's signs, after these have been sent down to thee, but summon [folk] to thy Lord, and be not of the polytheists.

Call not thou on any other deity along with Allah. There is no deity save Him. Everything will perish save His face. His is the jurisdiction, and to Him will ye be sent back.

III, 144/138.

Muḥammad is naught but a messenger. Messengers before Him have passed away, so should he die or be killed will ye turn back on your heels? No one who turns back on his heels will ever harm Allah at all, and Allah will recompense those who are grateful.

III, 145/139.

It is not for any soul to die except by Allah's permission, written, fixed. To him who desires the reward of this world We shall give thereof, and to him who desires the reward of the next world We shall give thereof, and We shall recompense those who are grateful.

V, 15, 16/18, 19/22.

O People of the Book, now indeed has Our messenger come to you, making clear for you much from the Book that ye had been concealing, and dispensing with much. Now, indeed, has there come to you from Allah a light and a clear Book

By which Allah will guide whosoever follows His good pleasure into ways of peace, and it will bring them forth out of darkness into the light, by His permission, and will guide them into a straight path.

O People of the Book, now indeed has Our messenger come to you making [matters] clear to you, after a break in the succession of messengers, lest ye should say: "There has not come to us either bringer of good tidings or warner." So a bringer of good tidings and a warner has now come to you, and Allah is powerful over everything.

XLVIII, 26-28.

When those who have disbelieved set fierce zeal in their hearts, the fierce zeal of paganism, then did Allah send down His tranquillity (*sakīna*) upon His messenger and upon the believers, causing them to cleave to the work of piety, to which they were the best entitled and most worthy. Allah is knowing about everything.

Allah had indeed given His messenger a proper vision in truth, [saying]: "Ye shall assuredly enter the sacred mosque safely, if Allah wills, [some of you] with your heads shaven, [others with hair] short-cropped, without being afraid." He knew what ye did not know, and He had appointed even before that an opening up not far off.

It is He who has sent His messenger with guidance and the religion of truth, to render it victorious over all religions. Allah suffices as a witness.

VII, 157/156-158.

Those who follow the messenger, the *ummī*[2] Prophet, whom they find mentioned in the *Tōrah* and the *Injīl* which they have, who bids them do what is approved and forbids them doing what is disapproved, who makes

2 Muslim orthodoxy has taken this word to mean "unlettered," in the sense that Muḥammad could neither read nor write. Probably, however, it means only that he had received no formal instruction in Scriptural matters, i.e., was a layman. Others think that it means rather "national," i.e., he was the Prophet of the Arab *umma* (community). The *Tōrah* is the Old Testament and the *Injīl* the Gospel.

allowable for them things that are good and prohibits them things that are foul, who takes from them their burden and the fetters which have been upon them. So those who have believed in him, assisted him, aided him and followed the light which was sent down with him, these are the ones who will prosper.

Say: "O people, I am Allah's messenger to you all, [the messenger of] Him to whom belongs the kingdom of the heavens and the earth. There is no deity save Him. He causes to live and causes to die, so believe in Allah and in His messenger, the *ummī* Prophet, who himself believes in Allah and his words, and follow him, maybe ye will be guided."

XLIX, 1-8.

O ye who have believed, do not put yourselves forward in the presence of Allah and His messenger, but show piety toward Allah. Verily, Allah is One who hears, One who knows.

O ye who have believed, raise not your voices above the Prophet's voice, and do not yell at him as ye do to one another, lest your works become of no avail while ye perceive it not.

Verily, those who lower their voices in the presence of Allah's messenger, they are those whose hearts Allah has tested for piety. Theirs is forgiveness and a mighty recompense.

Verily, those who call to thee [O Muḥammad] from behind the apartments [of thy wives] are mostly such as have no intelligence.

Could they wait patiently till thou comest forth to them, that would be better for them. Yet Allah is forgiving, compassionate.

O ye who have believed, if some rascal come to you with a tale, get [the matter] clear, lest out of ignorance ye afflict folk, and yourselves then repent of what ye have done.

Know that among you is Allah's messenger. Were he to obey you in many a matter ye would fall into distress. But Allah has made the faith dear to you, has beautified it in your hearts, and has made unbelief and profligacy and rebelliousness distasteful to you. These are the rightly guided,

A kindness from Allah and a favor; and Allah is knowing, wise.

XXXIII, 28-33, 36.

O Prophet, say to thy wives: "If ye are desirous of this worldly life and its adornment, then come along, I will give you your enjoyment, and divorce you kindly;

But if your desire is for Allah and His messenger and the future abode, then Allah, indeed, has prepared for those among you who do good works an excellent recompense."

O wives of the Prophet, whosoever from among you commits manifest lewdness, doubled twice over will the punishment be for her, and that will be easy for Allah.

But whosoever from among you is obedient to Allah and to His messenger, and does righteous works, her reward will We give her twice over, and for her have We prepared a noble provision.

O wives of the Prophet, ye are not like any other women. If ye show piety, then do not use provocative speech, so that he in whose heart is disease becomes lustful, but speak suitable speech.

Sit sedately in your houses and do not flaunt abroad with the flaunting of the former paganism; observe prayer, pay the legal alms (*zakāt*), be obedient to Allah and to His messenger. Allah desires only to remove the filthiness [of paganism] from you, O people of the house, and to purify you completely.

And remember what is recited to you in your houses of Allah's signs and the Wisdom. Allah, indeed, is kindly, well-informed.

. . . .

It is not for any believing man or believing woman, when Allah and His messenger have decided an affair, to have any choice in their affair, and whosoever opposes Allah and His messenger has manifestly strayed into error.

XXXIII, 45/44-48/47.

O Prophet, We have sent thee as a witness, as bringer of good tidings and as a warner,

As a summoner to Allah, by His leave, and a light-giving lamp.

So give the believers good tidings that they have from Allah a great bounty,

And do not obey the unbelievers and the hypocrites, but take quietly their insulting [words], putting thy trust in Allah, for Allah suffices as a trustee.

XXXIII, 50/49-57.

O Prophet, We have made allowable to thee those wives of thine to whom thou hast given their dowries, and those of whom thy right hand has taken possession (i.e., slave girls) from the booty Allah has given thee, and thy nieces on the paternal or the maternal side who have emigrated with thee, and any believing woman who may give herself to the Prophet, if the Prophet wants to take her in marriage—this is a special [privilege] for thee as distinguished from [other] believers. We know what We have laid upon them as incumbent duty with regard to their wives, and what their right hands have taken possession of, in order that there may be no blame on thee. Allah is forgiving, compassionate.

Thou mayest put aside whomsoever of them thou willest, and thou mayest take to thyself whomsoever thou willest, and shouldst thou have a desire for one of those thou hast set aside there is no blame on thee. That is the most suitable way to keep them cheerful, so that they grieve not, but all of them be content with what thou hast given them. Allah knows what is in your hearts, for Allah is knowing, forbearing.

Women beyond that are not allowable to thee, nor [is it allowable] that thou shouldst exchange them for other wives, even though their beauty attracts thee, except those of whom thy right hand has taken possession. Allah is watchful over everything.

O ye who have believed, do not enter the Prophet's houses except when permission is given you for a meal, [and do not enter] without watching to see if he is ready. But, when ye are summoned, enter, and when ye have taken food, disperse. And [do not enter] familiarly into conversation, for that on your part has been insulting to the Prophet, so that he is ashamed for you, though Allah is not ashamed of the truth. When ye ask them (i.e., the Prophet's wives) for something, ask them from behind a curtain. That is purer both for your hearts and theirs. It is not for you to insult Allah's messenger, nor ever to take in marriage his wives after him. That, in Allah's eyes, would be a serious thing.

Whether ye let a thing appear, or whether ye hide it, Allah knows about everything.

There is no blame on them (i.e., the Prophet's wives) with regard to their fathers, their sons, their brothers, their brothers' or their sisters' sons, or their women, or those of whom their right hands have taken possession. So [O ye wives] show piety to Allah. Allah is witness of everything.

Allah and His angels give blessings on the Prophet. O ye who have believed, give blessings on him and give him salutation of peace.

Verily, those who insult Allah and His messenger, them has Allah cursed in this world and the next, and has got ready for them a humiliating punishment.

MUḤAMMAD'S CALL

From at-Ṭabarī's *Ta'rīkh ar-rusul wa'l-mulūk* (Leiden, 1881), I, 1147-1152.

Aḥmad b. 'Uthmān, who is known as Abū'l-Jawzā', has related to me on the authority of Wahb b. Jarīr, who heard his father say that he had heard from an-Nu'mān b. Rāshid, on the authority of az-Zuhrī from 'Urwa, from 'Ā'isha, who said: The way revelation (*waḥy*) first began to come to the Apostle of Allah—on whom be Allah's blessing and peace—was by means of true dreams which would come like the morning dawn. Then he came to love solitude, so he used to go off to a cave in Ḥirā' [1] where he would practice *taḥannuth* [2] certain nights before returning to his family. Then he would come back to his family and take provisions for the like number [of nights] until unexpectedly the truth came to him.

1 A mountain in the environs of Mecca.

2 This is probably intended to represent the Hebrew word *tiḥinnōth*, "prayers."

He (i.e., Gabriel) came to him, saying: "O Muḥammad, thou art Allah's Apostle (*rasūl* [3])." Said the Apostle of Allah—upon whom be Allah's blessing and peace: "Thereat I fell to my knees where I had been standing, and then with trembling limbs dragged myself along till I came in to Khadīja,[4] saying: 'Wrap ye me up! Wrap ye me up!' [5] till the terror passed from me. Then [on another occasion] he came to me again and said: 'O Muḥammad, thou art Allah's Apostle,' [which so disturbed me] that I was about to cast myself down from some high mountain cliff. But he appeared before me as I was about to do this, and said: 'O Muḥammad, I am Gabriel, and thou art Allah's Apostle.' Then he said to me: 'Recite!'; but I answered: 'What should I recite?'; whereat he seized me and grievously treated me three times, till he wore me out. Then he said: 'Recite, in the name of thy Lord who has created' (Sūra XCVI, 1). So I recited it and then went to Khadīja, to whom I said: 'I am worried about myself.' Then I told her the whole story. She said: 'Rejoice, for by Allah, Allah will never put thee to shame. By Allah, thou art mindful of thy kinsfolk, speakest truthfully, renderest what is given thee in trust, bearest burdens, art ever hospitable to the guest, and dost always uphold the right against any wrong.' Then she took me to Waraqa b. Naufal b. Asad [to whom] she said: 'Give ear to what the son of thy brother [has to report].' So he questioned me, and I told him [the whole] story. Said he: 'This is the *nāmūs* [6] which was sent down upon Moses the son of Amram. Would that I might be a stalwart youth [again to take part] in it. Would that I might still be alive when your people turn you out.' 'And will they turn me out?' I asked. 'Yes,' said he, 'never yet has a man come with that

[3] *Rasūl* is literally "messenger," but, like the New Testament *apostolos*, as a messenger of God it technically means an Apostle.

[4] His first wife, an elderly and wealthy Meccan widow who had married him some years earlier.

[5] See Sūra LXXIII, 1.

[6] This is from the Syriac transliteration of the Greek word *nomos*, "law," which is used in the Septuagint and the New Testament for the Mosaic law, i.e., the Torah.

with which you come but has been turned away. Should I be there when your day comes I will lend you mighty assistance.'

"Now the first Qur'ān [passage] to come down to me after 'Recite' (XCVI, 1) was: 'Nūn. By the Pen and what they write. By bounty of thy Lord thou art not jinn-possessed.[7] Verily for thee is an uninterrupted reward. Verily thou art at a mighty task, so thou wilt see and they will see' (LXVIII, 1-5); then 'O thou who wrappest thyself in a mantle, Arise! Warn!' (LXXIV, 1, 2), and 'By the bright morn, and by the night when all is still' (XCIII, 1, 2)."

Yūnus b. 'Abd al-A'lā has related to me, on the authority of Ibn Wahb, who said that Yūnus had related to him from Ibn Shihāb [az-Zuhrī], from 'Urwa, from 'Ā'isha, who related to him as above, save that he did not mention [the last part about] 'the first Qur'ān to come down to me after' etc.

Muḥammad b. 'Abd al-Malik b. Abī ash-Shawārib has related to me on the authority of 'Abd al-Wāḥid b. Ziyād, from Sulaimān ash-Shaibānī, from 'Abdallah b. Shaddād, who said: Gabriel came to Muḥammad—upon whom be Allah's blessing and peace—and said: "O Muḥammad, recite." He replied: "What shall I recite?" Thereat he grievously afflicted him and said: "O Muḥammad, recite." "What shall I recite?" he answered. Again he grievously afflicted him, and said: "O Muḥammad, recite." "But what shall I recite?" he replied. He said: "Recite in the name of thy Lord who has created, created man from blood clots," and so on till he came to the words "taught man what he did not know" (Sūra XCVI, 1-5). Then [Muḥammad] went to Khadīja and said: "O Khadīja, the only conclusion I can come to is that I have been afflicted with madness." "Nay, never," she replied. "By Allah, thy Lord would never do that to thee, for never hast thou done anything unseemly." Then Khadīja went to Waraqa b. Naufal and told him the story. "If you speak truly," said he, "your

[7] The *jinn* are invisible beings, intermediate between men and angels, who hover around in the spaces between earth and heaven, and who may, under certain circumstances, enter into humans and "possess" them. See *majnūn* in Glossary.

husband is a prophet (*nabī*), who will assuredly meet with harsh treatment at the hands of his people, but should I live till then I will certainly put my faith in him."

After that Gabriel was slow in coming to him again, so Khadīja said to him: "It seems to me that your Lord must have come to dislike you"; but then Allah—mighty and majestic is He—sent down to him: "By the bright morn, and by the night when all is still. Thy Lord hath not left thee, nor come to dislike thee" (XCIII, 1-3).

Ibn Ḥumaid has related to me on the authority of Salma, from Muḥammad b. Isḥāq, who said: Wahb b. Kaisān, client of the Zubair family, has related to me that he heard 'Abdallah b. az-Zubair say to 'Ubaid b. 'Umair b. Qatāda al-Laithī: Relate to us, O 'Ubaid, how it was when the Apostle of Allah—upon whom be Allah's blessing and peace—first began his prophetic career, when Gabriel—upon whom be peace—came to him. 'Ubaid replied—and I was there when he began relating to 'Abdallah b. az-Zubair and the folk who were with him: The Apostle of Allah—upon whom be Allah's blessing and peace—used to retreat to Ḥirā' one month every year. That was part of the *taḥannuth* the Quraish [8] used to practice in the pre-Islamic period. *Taḥannuth* means *tabarrur* (i.e., to practice exercises of piety). Abū Ṭālib [9] said: He was an ascender, going up to Ḥirā', and descending again.

Now the Apostle of Allah—upon whom be Allah's blessing and peace—used to retreat there annually for that one month and feed such needy persons as came to him. Then when the Apostle of Allah—upon whom be Allah's blessing and peace—had finished his month's retreat, the first place he would visit on his return from his retreat, before he even entered his house, was the Ka'ba,[10] which he would circumambulate seven times, or as often as Allah willed, and then would return to

[8] The Quraish were the tribe in power at Mecca in Muḥammad's day.

[9] He was the uncle who cared for Muḥammad after the death of his parents. In the histories verses are at times ascribed to him, as here.

[10] The shrine in the city of Mecca and the center of the pilgrimage rites.

his house. This went on until it was the month in which Allah—mighty and majestic is He—desired to show him the favor He had willed for him, that year in which He sent him forth [as a prophet]. It was the month of Ramaḍān, and the Apostle of Allah—upon whom be Allah's blessing and peace—went out to Ḥirā', as he had been wont to do, for his retreat, taking his family with him. Now when it was the night on which Allah was going to honor him with a call to apostleship, and thereby show mercy to mortals, Gabriel, by Allah's command, came to him.

Said the Apostle of Allah—upon whom be Allah's blessing and peace: "He came to me while I was asleep, bringing a silken cloth (*namaṭ min dībāj*) on which was some writing. He said: 'Recite'; but I answered: 'What shall I recite?' Then he so grievously treated me that I thought I should die, but he pushed me off and said: 'Recite.' I answered: 'But what shall I recite?'; saying this only to guard myself against his doing again to me the like of what he had done to me. He said: 'Recite, in the name of thy Lord who has created,' and so on as far as 'taught man what he did not know' (XCVI, 1-5). So I recited it, and that ended the matter, for he departed from me. Thereupon I awoke from my sleep, and it was as though he had written it on my heart.

"Now it so happened that [at that time] no creature of Allah was more loathsome to me than a poet or a man possessed by jinn,[11] the sight of neither of whom could I bear. So I said: 'That one—meaning himself—has become either a poet or a man jinn-possessed. The Quraish will never say this about me. I shall go to some high mountain cliff and cast myself down therefrom so that I may kill myself and be at rest.' I went off with this in mind, but when I was in the midst of the mountains I heard a voice from heaven saying: 'O Muḥammad, thou art Allah's Apostle, and I am Gabriel.' At

[11] It was the belief of the ancient Arabs that poets, soothsayers, diviners, etc., were inspired by a familiar spirit from among the jinn. This is discussed by Ignaz Goldziher in the first essay in his *Abhandlungen zur arabischen Philologie* (Leiden, 1896).

that I raised my head to the skies, and there was Gabriel in clear human form, with his feet on the edges of the skies,[12] saying: 'O Muḥammad, thou art Allah's Apostle, and I am Gabriel.' I stood there gazing at him, and that kept me from what I had intended doing. I neither advanced nor retreated, but I began to turn my face from him to the whole expanse of the skies, but no matter in what direction I looked there I saw him. So I stood there, neither advancing forward nor retreating backward, while Khadīja (who had accompanied him to Ḥirā') sent her messengers to look for me. They even reached Mecca and returned to her while I was still standing in my place.

"Then [Gabriel] departed from me, and I went off making my way back to my family. I went straight to Khadīja and seated myself on her thigh [as though] to seek refuge there. She said: 'O Abū'l-Qāsim,[13] where were you? By Allah, I sent my messengers to seek you, but they reached Mecca and returned to me.' I said to her: 'That one (i.e., himself) has become either a poet or a man jinn-possessed.' 'I place you for refuge with Allah from such a thing, O Abū'l-Qāsim,' she replied. 'That Allah would not do that with you I am sure from what I know of how truthfully you speak, how trustworthy you are, how good your character, and how mindful you are of your kinsfolk. What is it, O son of my uncle? Could it be that you have seen something?' 'Yes,' I answered, and then I related to her what I had seen. She replied: 'Rejoice, O son of my uncle, and hold fast. By Him in whose hand is Khadīja's soul, I hope [this experience means] that you are to be the prophet of this people!' "

Then she arose, put on her outer garments, and went off to Waraqa b. Naufal, who was her cousin on the paternal side. This Waraqa had become a Christian, had read the Scriptures,

[12] In those days the earth was conceived of as a flat disc and the heavens like an upturned bowl over it, so the edges of the skies (*ufuq*, "horizon") was where heaven and earth met at the rim of the disc.

[13] Qāsim was the name of his eldest son by Khadīja, so she is here addressing him by his *kunya*, "Father of al-Qāsim."

and had listened to the people of the Law (*Tōrah*) and the Gospel (*Injīl*). To him she set forth what the Apostle of Allah —upon whom be Allah's blessing and peace—had told her about all he had seen and heard. Said Waraqa: "Quddūs! Quddūs! [14] By Him in whose hand is Waraqa's soul, if you are telling me the truth, O Khadīja, [it means that] there has indeed come to him the great *Nāmūs,"* and by *Nāmūs* he meant Gabriel, upon whom be peace, "who used to come to Moses, so he will assuredly be the prophet of this people. Tell him so, and have him stand firm." So Khadīja returned to the Apostle of Allah—upon whom be Allah's blessing and peace—and informed him of what Waraqa had said, and that eased somewhat the anxiety he had felt.

Now when the Apostle of Allah—upon whom be Allah's blessing and peace—had finished his retreat and departed, he did what he was accustomed to do, and went to the Ka'ba to circumambulate. As he was going around it Waraqa b. Naufal met him, for he also was circumambulating the shrine. Said [Waraqa]: "Tell me, O son of my brother, about what you saw and heard." So the Apostle of Allah—upon whom be Allah's blessing and peace—informed him. Thereupon Waraqa said: "By Him in whose hand is my soul, thou art assuredly to be the prophet of this people, for there has indeed come to thee the great Nāmūs that came to Moses. Thou wilt be treated as a liar, wilt be injured, wilt be driven out, wilt be fought against. Should I live to see that, I will lend Allah aid that He will acknowledge." Then he lowered his head and kissed the top of his (i.e., Muḥammad's) head. At that the Apostle of Allah—upon whom be Allah's blessing and peace—went to his house, encouraged by the words of Waraqa, so that some of the anxiety he had felt was relieved.

[14] *Quddūs* is "very holy," and as used here is probably a reminiscence of the Tersanctus.

THE BEATITUDES AND MALEDICTIONS OF THE PROPHET

The Traditions include a collection of utterances attributed to Muḥammad, each of which begins with the word *Ṭūbā*, a borrowing from the Syriac meaning "good fortune, happiness, blessedness," so that each utterance begins "Blessedness be to . . . ." *Ṭūbā* is here translated by the more familiar "Blessed is . . . ." They are given in as-Suyūṭī's *al-Jāmiʿ aṣ-ṣaghīr* (Cairo, 1352 A.H. = 1933 A.D.), II, 100-103 (Nos. 5286-5311).

Blessed is Damascus, for the angels of the Merciful One spread their wings over it.

Blessed is Damascus, for the Merciful One spreads His mercy over it.

Blessed are the Strangers,[1] for they are pious folk among evil folk. Many will be those who disobey them, far more than those who obey them.

Blessed are the sincere [worshipers of Allah]. Such [folk] are lamps of guidance from whom every temptation of darkness has been removed.

Blessed are those who race one another to the shadow of Allah, who when they are given what is right accept it, when asked for [what is right] grant it, and who judge others with the same judgment as that by which they judge themselves.

Blessed are the divines; [2] blessed are the worshipers; but woe to the people of the market places.

Blessed is the life that will follow the [coming of the] Messiah. The sky will be permitted to distill [its rains] and the

[1] In Ibn al-Athīr's *Nihāya* (Cairo, 1322 A.H. = 1904 A.D.), III, 171, these "Strangers" are explained to mean the believing Muslims, who in the first days of Islam were few in number and like strangers on the earth, and who in the Last Days, when piety decreases and evil increases, will again be the believing "remnant," few in numbers and low in consideration among the evildoers of that age.

[2] *Al-ʿUlamāʾ*, lit., "the learned ones," a title given those who have special training in the Islamic religion and law; and so "divines" in the same sense as we refer to "the Puritan divines."

earth to give forth its vegetation, so that even if you sow your grain on rocks it will come up. [In those days] a man will pass by a lion and it will do him no harm, will tread on a serpent and it will not hurt him, nor [in those days] will there be any grudge, any envy, any hatred.

Blessed is he who has met me and believed in me, and blessed is he who has not met me and yet has believed in me.

Blessed is he who when on Holy War in the way of Allah makes frequent mention of Allah, for he shall have for every word thereof seventy thousand good works [put to his credit], every good work of which will multiply itself tenfold, along with the increase he already has with Allah and the capital of merit to that measure.

Blessed is he whom Allah has caused to dwell at one of the two *'arūs,* cities, namely, Ascalon and Gaza.

Blessed is he who has become a Muslim and is content with a sufficient livelihood.

Blessed is he who spends the night as one who is on pilgrimage and the day as a campaigner [against the infidels]. [I mean] a man in modest circumstances and a father of children, who exercises restraint, being content with but little of this world, who enters to his family laughing and comes out from them laughing. By Him in whose hand is my soul, such men are pilgrims and are campaigners in the way of Allah.

Blessed is he who abandons ignorance, does good [to others], and acts with equity.

Blessed is he who acts with humility without lowering his position, holds himself in low esteem without assuming a state of misfortune, spends the wealth he has gathered without doing so in wicked ways, seeks the society of men of learning and wisdom, and has mercy toward the weak and the unfortunate. Blessed is he who holds his own self vile, who does good with what he earns, who sees that his inner life is excellent and his outward life honorable, who protects others from any evil from himself. Blessed is the one who acts conformably to his knowledge, spends in charity the excess of his wealth, and abstains from excess of speech.

Blessed is he whom Allah has provided with a sufficiency and who is content therewith.

Blessed is he who has seen me and believed in me. His is a single blessing, but he who has not seen me and yet has believed in me has sevenfold blessing.

Blessed is he who has seen me and believed in me, but thrice blessed is he who has not seen me and yet has believed in me.

Blessed is he who has seen me and has believed in me, but blessed, and again blessed, and still again blessed is he who has believed in me even though he has not seen me.

Blessed is he who has seen me and has believed in me; blessed is one who has seen one who has seen me; and blessed is one who has seen one who has seen one who has seen me and then has believed in me. Blessed are they and good is the place to which they are going.

Blessed is he who has seen me, and he who has seen one who has seen me, and he who has seen one who has seen one who has seen me.

Blessed is he whose own faults keep him too busy to notice the faults of others, who spends in charity the excess of his property, abstains from excess of speech, keeps to the *Sunna* and turns not from it to *Bid'a*.[3]

Blessed is he who has lived long and has seen to it that his works were good.

Blessed is he who has kept control over his tongue, kept himself to his house, and wept for his sins.

Blessed is he who has been guided to Islam and if his livelihood was sufficient has been content therewith.

Blessed is he on whose record sheet is found much seeking of forgiveness.

Blessed is he who on the Day is raised from the dead fully loaded with the Qur'ān, the duties of religion and knowledge.

[3] *Sunna* is the "custom," i.e., the way of life based on the pattern of life given in the deeds and words of Muhammad. *Bid'a* is "innovation," i.e., introducing ways for which there is no authority in the *sunna* of the Prophet.

Just as Tradition has preserved a collection of the beatitudes of the Prophet, his utterances beginning "Blessed is . . . ," so it has preserved a parallel collection of utterances beginning *la'ana 'llah*, "may Allah curse," which corresponds to our familiar "accursed be . . . ." For the practical religious life of Islam these maledictions have proved more significant than the beatitudes. From as-Suyūṭī's *al-Jāmi' aṣ-ṣaghīr* (Cairo, 1352 A.H. = 1933 A.D.), II, 348-351 (Nos. 7252-7284).

Accursed be the [mourning] woman who scratches her face, rends her shift, and cries: "Woe and alack-a-day!"

Accursed be wine. [Accursed be] he who drinks it, he who pours it, he who sells it, he who purchases it, he who presses it, he who draws it, he who carries it, the one to whom it is borne, and he who makes profit from it.

Accursed be the one who bribes and the one who accepts a bribe in a case under judgment.

Accursed be the one who bribes and the one who accepts a bribe and the go-between in a matter of bribery.

Accursed be usury, both he who takes it and he who gives it, he who writes it and he who witnesses to it, if they know about it. [Accursed be] the woman who wears false hair, or who adds false hair to her own, the female tattooer and the woman who lets herself be tatooed, the female depilator and the woman who has herself depilated.

Accursed be the man who dresses in women's garments and the woman who dresses in men's garments.

Accursed be the woman who apes the man.

Accursed be az-Zuhra, for she was the one who seduced the two angels Hārūt and Mārūt.[4]

[4] These two angels are mentioned in Sūra II, 102/96 as teachers of sorcery and magic arts. The story is that when Adam and Eve had to be driven out of their paradise some of the angels said to Allah: "We told you so," whereupon Allah responded that under like conditions they would have done no better. Three angels accepted the challenge and came down to live on earth by day but at night mounted up to heaven again. One of them soon gave up, but Hārūt and Mārūt continued until they were presently seduced by a fair woman named az-Zuhra, who as her price learned from them the secret of how they mounted up from earth to heaven at night. Allah changed her into a star and set her in the

Accursed be a thief. He steals the egg, so his hand is cut off, and he steals the rope, so his hand is cut off.[5]

Accursed be the scorpion. It spares not the place of worship, nor any other place, so kill it whether it be in a sacred or a profane spot.

Accursed be the scorpion. It spares neither the prophet nor the ordinary man in its stinging.

Accursed be the [mourning] woman who lacerates [her face].

Accursed be those who [in mourning] rend their things and tear their hair.

Accursed be the women who practice masculinity and the men who practice femininity.

Accursed be the sanctioner and the one for whom the sanction is made.[6]

Accursed be the male or female grave robber.

Accursed be the males who play the female and the women who play the male.

Accursed be the malingering woman who, when her husband calls her to his bed, says "Presently! Presently!" till sleep overcomes him.

Accursed be the ignoble woman who, when her husband wants to come to her, says: "My sickness is upon me."

Accursed be the professional wailing woman and the singing girl.

Accursed be the female tattooers and those whom they tattoo, the female depilators and those whom they depilate, the women who space their teeth for beauty's sake, and those who [in any other way] alter Allah's creation.

Accursed be the woman who wears false hair, and the

---

firmament, where she is Venus (*az-Zuhra*), while the punishment of the two angels was that they were to hang head downward till Judgment Day in a well somewhere near Babylon. It is to them that wizards and sorcerers go to learn their magic arts. See *EI*, s.v. "Hārūt."

5 The cutting off of the hand for theft is prescribed in Sūra V, 38/42.

6 The reference is to the matter of a man making lawful for another something which is religiously unlawful.

woman who adds false hair to her own, the woman who tattoos and the one who submits to tattooing.

Accursed be he who takes usury, and he from whom it is taken, and he who witnesses to it, and he who writes it down.

Accursed be the women who go on visitation to graves, and the men who set up thereon places of worship and lamps.

Accursed be he who slanders my companions.

Accursed be he who seats himself in the midst of a circle of people.

Accursed be he who brands anyone on the face.

Accursed be he who separates a mother from her child or a brother from his brother.

Accursed be he who curses his parents. Accursed be he who offers sacrifice to any other than Allah. Accursed be he who gives hospitality to an innovator.[7] Accursed be anyone who changes the waymarks of the land.

Accursed be he who mutilates animals.

Accursed be he who worships the coin of the realm (lit., dinars and dirhams).

MUḤAMMAD'S CHARACTER

This is the section "On the Prophet's Disposition and Characteristics" from the *Mishkāt al-Maṣābīh*, one of the most popular and widely used compendiums of Tradition. The translation has been made from the Indian lithograph with Urdu translation and commentary (Lahore, 1321 A.H. = 1903 A.D.), II, 187-194. At the end of each Tradition in the *Mishkāt* the compiler has indicated the collection or collections from which the Tradition has been taken, but these are omitted in the present translation.

From Anas, who said: For ten years did I act as servant to the Prophet—upon whom be Allah's blessing and peace—and never once did he say "Uff"[1] to me, nor [did he ever say

[7] That is one who introduces innovations contrary to the *sunna* or religious custom. See *bid'a* in Glossary.

[1] An exclamation expressing disgust or displeasure. Its use is forbidden in Sūra XVII, 23/24.

querulously], "Why did you do [such and such]?" or "Have you not done [such and such]?" From Anas, who said: The Apostle of Allah—upon whom be Allah's blessing and peace—was the best natured of men. One day he sent me on an errand, but I said: "By Allah, I will not go," though it was in my soul to go [and accomplish] what the Apostle had commanded me. I went out, and presently I passed by some boys who were playing in the street, and there was the Apostle of Allah—upon whom be Allah's blessing and peace—who caught me by the nape of my neck from behind. I looked at him and he was laughing and saying: "O little Anas, did you go where I bade you?" I answered: "Yes, I am going now, O Apostle of Allah."

From Anas, who said: I was once walking with the Apostle of Allah—upon whom be Allah's blessing and peace—who was wearing a cloak of Najrānī cloth with a coarse hem, when a nomad Arab came up to him and tugged his cloak so hard that the Prophet of Allah—upon whom be Allah's blessing and peace—was jerked right on to the man's chest and I could see that the side of the Apostle's shoulder was marked by the [coarse] hem of the cloak, so hard was the tug. The man said: "O Muḥammad, command [that there be given] me some of the wealth of Allah that you have." The Apostle of Allah—upon whom be Allah's blessing and peace—turned to him, then he laughed and gave command that he be given something. From Anas, who said: The Apostle of Allah—upon whom be Allah's blessing and peace—was the best of men, the most liberal of men, the bravest of men. One night the people of Madina were stricken by a sudden terror so that folk hurried to the sound [of the terrified voices], but the Apostle—upon whom be Allah's blessing and peace—had outstripped them, getting ahead of them to where the sound [of the voices] was, and was saying: "Be not afraid. Be not afraid." He was on an unaccoutred horse belonging to Abū Ṭalḥa, without any saddle, but with a sword on his shoulder, and he said: "I found it [a fast horse, swift moving] as a river."

From Jābir, who said: Never was the Apostle of Allah—

upon whom be Allah's blessing and peace—asked for anything to which he answered "No." From Anas [who said]: A man asked the Prophet—upon whom be Allah's blessing and peace—for all the small cattle that were [in the vale] between two hills, and he gave them to him. The man went to his people and said: "O people, become Muslims, for, by Allah, Muḥammad gives a gift without fearing poverty." From Jābir b. Muṭ'im [who said that] while he was journeying with the Apostle of Allah—upon whom be Allah's blessing and peace—as they were coming back from Ḥunain,[2] the nomad Arabs were pressing around him begging of him [some of the plunder], till they pushed him into a *samūra*[3] bush which tore off his cloak. The Prophet—upon whom be Allah's blessing and peace—stopped and said: "Give me my cloak. Did I have as many cattle as this bush has thorns I should divide them among you, and you would not find me parsimonious, nor a liar, nor a cowardly fellow."

From Anas, who said: When the Apostle of Allah—upon whom be Allah's blessing and peace—used to pray the morning prayers, the Madinese servants would bring their vessels with some water in them, and not a vessel would be brought but he would dip his hand into it.[4] Sometimes they would be brought to him on cold mornings, but nevertheless he would dip his hand into them. From Anas, who said: There was a certain slave girl [belonging to one] of the people of Madina who used to take the hand of the Apostle of Allah—upon whom be Allah's blessing and peace—and lead him off wherever she wished. From Anas [who said]: There was a woman who had something wrong with her mind who said: "O Apostle of Allah, I have need of you." He answered: "O Mother of So-and-So, look out any lane you please where I may fulfill your

[2] The battle of Ḥunain was fought in the year 8 A.H. (630 A.D.) and resulted in the defeat by the Muslims of the hostile Hawāzin tribe.

[3] The *samūra* is the gum acacia, sometimes called the Egyptian thorn.

[4] The commentary suggests that his dipping in of his hand was to confer on the water curative properties or otherwise make it a channel of blessing.

need for you." Then he would go aside alone with her into any one of the paths till her need was satisfied. From Anas, who said: The Apostle of Allah—upon whom be Allah's blessing and peace—was never dissolute in speech, nor was he a curser or a reviler. When he had to reprove someone he would say: "What is the matter with him? May he have dust on his forehead."

From Abū Huraira, who said: Someone said one day: "O Apostle of Allah, curse the polytheists"; but he answered: "I was not sent as a curser. I was sent only as a mercy." From Abū Sa'īd al-Khudrī, who said: The Prophet—upon whom be Allah's blessing and peace—was more modest than a virgin in her apartment. When he saw anything of which he disapproved we could recognize this from his face. From 'Ā'isha, who said: Never did I see the Prophet—upon whom be Allah's blessing and peace—laughing boisterously so that I could see his uvula; he used only to smile. From 'Ā'isha, who said: The Apostle of Allah—upon whom be Allah's blessing and peace—never used to chatter uninterruptedly as you do. He used to converse slowly so that had anyone wanted to count his words they could have numbered them.

From al-Aswad, who said: I asked 'Ā'isha what the Prophet—upon whom be Allah's blessing and peace—used to do at home. She said: "He used to be at the service of his family," i.e., he would act as their servant,[5] and when the prayer times came around he would go out to prayers. From 'Ā'isha, who said: Whenever the Apostle of Allah—upon whom be Allah's blessing and peace—was given the choice between two matters, he would invariably choose the easier of them, provided it was not something sinful, for no one was further than he was from that. Nor did the Apostle of Allah—upon whom be Allah's blessing and peace—ever exact punishment for anything done to himself, but if there was any violation of the respect due to Allah he would exact punishment for that.

[5] The commentary explains that he would mend sandals or clothes, milk the goats, and perform other such domestic tasks normally performed by servants.

From 'Ā'isha, who said: Never did the Apostle of Allah—upon whom be Allah's blessing and peace—strike anyone with his own hand, neither his wives nor his servants, though he fought vigorously in the way of Allah. Never was there any wrong done to himself for which he took vengeance on the one who did it, but when there was the slightest violation of the respect due to Allah he would avenge that for Allah.

From Anas, who said: I began to serve the Apostle of Allah—upon whom be Allah's blessing and peace—when I was a boy of eight, and I served him for ten years, yet never did he scold me for anything ruined by my hand, and, indeed, if anyone of his household scolded me he would say: "Let him be. If a thing has been decreed to happen it will happen." From 'Ā'isha, who said: The Apostle of Allah—upon whom be Allah's blessing and peace—was neither dissolute nor immoderate in speech. He was not one who talked loudly in the streets, nor did he return evil for evil, but rather he would pardon and forgive. From Anas, who related of the Prophet—upon whom be Allah's blessing and peace—that he was accustomed to visit the sick, follow the bier [at a funeral], would accept an invitation even from a slave, and would ride on an ass. "Indeed," he said, "I saw him on the day of Khaibar[6] riding on an ass whose bridle was of palm fiber."

From 'Ā'isha, who said: The Apostle of Allah—upon whom be Allah's blessing and peace—used to patch his own sandals, stitch his own garments, and work around the house just as any one of you works around his house. She also said: He was a cheerful man who would delouse his own clothes, milk his own she-goat, and wait upon himself. From Khalīfa b. Zaid b. Thābit, who said: Some folk came to [my father] Zaid b. Thābit, saying to him: "Relate to us some Traditions about the Apostle of Allah—upon whom be Allah's blessing and peace." He replied: "I was a neighbor of his, and it so was that when a revelation came to him he would send for me and I would write it down for him. If we happened to be

[6] That is, the day in the year 7 A.H. (628 A.D.) when the powerful Jewish settlement in the oasis of Khaibar was destroyed.

talking about this world he would talk about it with us, or if we were talking about the next world he would talk about it with us, or even if we were only talking about food he would talk about that with us. All this I relate to you about the Apostle of Allah—upon whom be Allah's blessing and peace."

From Anas [who said]: When the Apostle of Allah—upon whom be Allah's blessing and peace—shook hands with a man he would not be the first to withdraw his hand, and when he was facing a man he would not turn his face away till the other turned his, nor was he ever seen with his knees crossed in front of one of his guests. From Anas, who said: The Apostle of Allah—upon whom be Allah's blessing and peace—would never store up anything for the morrow. From Jābir b. Samura, who said: The Apostle of Allah—upon whom be Allah's blessing and peace—was a taciturn man (lit., a man of long silences). From Jābir, who said: The Apostle of Allah—upon whom be Allah's blessing and peace—was very correct and sedate of speech.

From 'Ā'isha, who said: The Apostle of Allah—upon whom be Allah's blessing and peace—did not chatter uninterruptedly as you do, but he used to speak with proper pauses so that those who sat with him could memorize it. From 'Abdallah b. al-Ḥārith b. Jaz', who said: Never did I see anyone who smiled more than the Apostle of Allah—upon whom be Allah's blessing and peace. From 'Abdallah b. Salām, who said: The Apostle of Allah—upon whom be Allah's blessing and peace—when he sat down to converse would often lift his gaze to the skies.[7]

From 'Amr b. Sa'īd, from Anas, who said: Never have I seen anyone who was more affectionate with children than the Apostle of Allah—upon whom be Allah's blessing and peace. His son Ibrāhīm was put out to nurse in the upper part of Madina and he used to go up there, taking us along with him, enter the house, which was always smoky because the foster father was a blacksmith, and take [the child] up and kiss him.

[7] The commentator suggests that this was because he was watching to see if Gabriel might be coming with some revelation from Allah.

Then he would return home. 'Amr said: When little Ibrāhīm died the Apostle of Allah—upon whom be Allah's blessing and peace—said: "Ibrāhīm was my son. He died while still at the breast, but he will have two foster mothers in Paradise who will finish off the period of suckling for him."

From 'Alī [who said]: There was a Jew who was called Master[8] So-and-So, to whom the Apostle of Allah—upon whom be Allah's blessing and peace—owed some dinars. He demanded them of the Prophet—upon whom be Allah's blessing and peace—who said to him: "O Jew, I do not have any money to give you." He replied: "Then I shall not let you go, O Muḥammad, till you pay me." "Very well," said the Apostle of Allah—upon whom be Allah's blessing and peace—"I shall sit here with you." So he sat with him and performed there the midday prayers, afternoon prayers, evening prayers, night prayers, and morning prayers on the next day. The companions of the Apostle of Allah—upon whom be Allah's blessing and peace—were meanwhile speaking harshly to [the Jew] and threatening him, and the Apostle of Allah—upon whom be Allah's blessing and peace—was aware of what they were doing. They said: "O Apostle of Allah, shall a Jew hold you a prisoner?" He answered: "My Lord has forbidden me to do wrong to any man who has a compact [with me], or indeed to any other man." When the day had advanced the Jew said: "I testify that there is no deity save Allah, and I testify that thou art the Apostle of Allah. Half of my wealth I bestow in the way of Allah. By Allah, I did not do what I did with you save to see [if you corresponded to] your description in the Torah [where it is written]: 'Muḥammad the son of 'Abdallah, whose birthplace is Mecca, his place of emigration Ṭaiba (i.e., Madina), his kingdom Syria. He is not churlish nor rude in speech, does not talk loudly in the streets, does not use foul speech or obscene language.' I testify that there is no deity save Allah, and that thou art the Apostle of Allah. Here is my

[8] *Ḥabr* is a Hebrew word that has been borrowed into Arabic. Its plural is used in the Qur'ān as a title for the learned men among the Jews, so that in this Tradition it may mean a rabbi.

wealth, dispose of it as Allah may show thee." Now this Jew was very wealthy.

From 'Abdallah b. Abī Aufā, who said: The Apostle of Allah—upon whom be Allah's blessing and peace—used to make long prayers but short sermons. He was not too proud to walk with widows or the poor, and would fulfill their need. From 'Alī [who said]: Abū Jahl said to the Apostle of Allah—upon whom be Allah's blessing and peace: "I do not say that you are false, but that you make a false claim about these [revelations] you bring." At that, Allah, Most High, sent down with regard to them [the words] (VI, 33): "It is not thee they treat as false, but the wrongdoers gainsay the signs of Allah." From 'Ā'isha, who said: The Apostle of Allah—upon whom be Allah's blessing and peace—said: "O 'Ā'isha, had I so desired, mountains of gold would have journeyed with me. There came to me an angel whose waist measured to the Ka'ba [9] and who said: 'Your Lord gives you greeting and says that if you so wish you may be a prophet who is a king.' I looked at Gabriel —on whom be peace—and he signed to me to be humble." In the line of transmission from Ibn 'Abbās it says that the Apostle of Allah—upon whom be Allah's blessing and peace—turned to Gabriel as though asking his advice, and Gabriel gave him a sign with his hand that he should be humble, so he replied that he wished to be a prophet who was a servant. Said 'Ā'isha: After that the Apostle of Allah—upon whom be Allah's blessing and peace—would never eat in a reclining position, but would say: "I shall eat as a servant eats, and sit as a servant sits."

[9] The Ka'ba is the central shrine at Mecca. It was a holy place in pagan Mecca and is still circumambulated during the Muslim pilgrimage ceremonies.

MUḤAMMAD'S ASCENSION

Each year throughout the Muslim world, on the night of the 27th day of the month Rajab, is celebrated the festival called *Lailat al-Mi'rāj*, i.e., the Night of the Prophet's Ascension. The Qur'ānic basis for this is Sūra XVII, 1: "Glory be to Him Who took His servant by night from the sacred temple [at Mecca] to the more remote temple, whose precincts We have blessed, to show him some of Our signs." On this night mosques are lit up and special services of celebration held at which it is customary to read certain little chapbooks which give more or less elaborate accounts of the famous Night Journey. The brief account of the *Mi'rāj* given here is that found in the well-known compendium of Traditions, al-Baghawī's *Maṣābīḥ as-Sunna* (Khairiyya edition; Cairo, A.H. 1318 = 1900 A.D.), II, 169-172.

[It is related] from Qatāda, quoting from Anas b. Mālik—with whom may Allah be pleased—from Mālik b. Ṣa'ṣa'a, who said that the Prophet of Allah—on whom be Allah's blessing and peace—related to them [the story of] the night on which he was taken on his heavenly journey, saying: While I was in al-Ḥaṭīm [1]—or maybe he said, While I was in al-Ḥijr—lying at rest, one came to me,[2] split all between here and here—i.e., from the hollow of his throat to his pubic hair—and drew out my heart. Then there was brought a golden basin filled with faith in which he washed my heart and my bowels and then they were returned [to their place]. According to another line of transmission [the Prophet] said: Then he washed my stomach with water of Zamzam,[3] and filled it with faith and wisdom. Then a white riding beast was brought, somewhat smaller than a mule yet bigger than an ass, whose every bound

[1] The Ḥaṭīm is a semicircular, low, and thick wall to the northwest of the Ka'ba at Mecca. The Ḥijr is the space between this wall and the Ka'ba itself.

[2] Lit., "a comer came," a common way of expressing the coming of some supernatural visitor. From what follows we may assume that it was the archangel Gabriel.

[3] This is the sacred well in the precincts of the shrine at Mecca from which the pilgrims drink as an act of piety and thereby partake of its blessedness.

carried him as far as his eye could reach. Him I mounted and Gabriel set off with me till we came to the lowest heaven, which he asked should be opened. "Who is this?" he was asked. "Gabriel," he replied. "And who is that with you?" "Muḥammad," said he. "And has he had revelation sent him?" "Assuredly," said he. "Then welcome to him. How blessed a coming." Thereat [the gate] was opened, and when I had cleared it, lo! there was Adam. [Gabriel] said: "This is your father Adam, greet him." So I gave him greeting, which he returned, saying: "Welcome to you, O righteous son, righteous prophet." Then Gabriel mounted up with me till we came to the second heaven, which he asked should be opened. "Who is this?" he was asked. "Gabriel," he replied. "And who is that with you?" "Muḥammad," said he. "And has he had revelation sent him?" "Assuredly," said he. "Then welcome to him. How blessed a coming." Thereat [the gate] was opened, and when I had cleared it, lo! there were John [the Baptist] and Jesus, who were cousins on their mothers' side. Said [Gabriel]: "These are John and Jesus, give them greeting." So I greeted them and they returned it, saying: "Welcome to the righteous brother, the righteous prophet." Then he ascended with me to the third heaven, which he asked should be opened. "Who is this?" he was asked. "Gabriel," he replied. "And who is that with you?" "Muḥammad," said he. "And has he had revelation sent him?" "Assuredly," said he. "Then welcome to him. How blessed a coming." Thereat [the gate] was opened, and when I had cleared it, lo! there was Joseph. [Gabriel] said: "This is Joseph, greet him." So I gave him greeting, which he returned, saying: "Welcome to the righteous brother, the righteous prophet." Then he ascended with me till we came to the fourth heaven, which he asked should be opened. "Who is this?" he was asked. "Gabriel," he replied. "And who is that with you?" "Muḥammad," said he. "And has he had revelation sent him?" "Assuredly," said he. "Then welcome to him. How blessed a coming." Thereat [the gate] was opened, and when I had cleared it, lo! there was Idrīs (Enoch). Said [Gabriel]: "This is Idrīs, give him greeting."

So I greeted him, and he returned it, saying: "Welcome to the righteous brother, the righteous prophet." Then he ascended with me to the fifth heaven, which he asked should be opened. "Who is this?" he was asked. "Gabriel," he replied. "And who is that with you?" "Muḥammad," said he. "And has he had revelation sent him?" "Assuredly," said he. "Then welcome to him. How blessed a coming." When I had cleared [the gate], lo! there was Aaron. Said [Gabriel]: "This is Aaron, give him greeting." So I greeted him, and he returned it, saying: "Welcome to the righteous brother, the righteous prophet." Then he ascended with me to the sixth heaven, which he asked should be opened. "Who is this?" he was asked. "Gabriel," he replied. "And who is that with you?" "Muḥammad," said he. "And has he had revelation sent him?" "Assuredly," said he. "Then welcome to him. How blessed a coming." When I had cleared [the gate], lo! there was Moses. Said [Gabriel]: "This is Moses, give him greeting." So I greeted him, and he returned it, saying: "Welcome to the righteous brother, the righteous prophet." When I passed on he wept, and one asked him why he wept. "I weep," said he, "because of a youth who has been sent [as an Apostle] after me, more of whose community will enter Paradise than of my community." Then [Gabriel] ascended with me till we reached the seventh heaven, which he asked should be opened. "Who is this?" he was asked. "Gabriel," he replied. "And who is that with you?" "Muḥammad," said he. "And has he had revelation sent him?" "Assuredly," said he. "Then welcome to him. How blessed a coming." When I had cleared [the gate], lo! there was Abraham. Said [Gabriel]: "This is your father Abraham, so greet him." I gave him greeting, which he returned, saying: "Welcome to the righteous son, the righteous prophet."

Then I ascended to the Sidrat al-Muntahā, whose fruits were the size of Hajar [4] waterpots and its leaves like elephants'

[4] Hajar is the district of Arabia which includes Baḥrain over on the Persian Gulf. The *Sidrat al-Muntahā,* i.e., "lote tree of the boundary," is said to be a celestial tree which marks the boundary beyond which creatures may not ascend. It is mentioned in Sūra LIII, 14.

ears. Said [Gabriel]: "This is the Sidrat al-Muntahā." There I beheld four streams, two within and two without, so I asked: "What are these, O Gabriel?" "The two within," he answered, "are the two rivers of Paradise, but the two without are the Nile and the Euphrates." Then I was taken up to the Frequented Fane,[5] where a vessel of wine, a vessel of milk, and a vessel of honey were brought to me. I took the milk, whereat he said: "This is the *fiṭra*[6] of you and your community." Then there was laid on me the religious duty of performing fifty prayer services daily, and I departed. As I passed by Moses he asked: "With what have you been commanded?" "With fifty prayer services each day," I replied. "But your community," said he, "will never be able to perform fifty prayer services a day. By Allah, I have had experience with people before you, and I had to strive hard with the Children of Israel. Return to your Lord and ask Him to lighten it for your community." So I went back and He remitted ten. Then I returned to Moses, but he said the like [of what he had said before], so I went back and He remitted ten more. When, however, I got back to Moses he said the like again, so I returned and He remitted another ten. When I returned to Moses he again said the like, so I went back and was commanded ten prayer services each day and night. When I got back to Moses he said as he had said before, so I went back and was bidden perform five prayer services daily. When I got back to Moses, he said: "And with what are you commanded now?" "I am bidden," I replied, "perform five prayer services day and night." "Your community," said he, "will never be able to perform five prayer services daily. I have had experience with people before you, and have had to strive hard with the Children of Israel. Go back to your Lord and ask

[5] This is the celestial Ka'ba, the navel of the celestial world, situated directly above the earthly Ka'ba.

[6] A *fiṭra* is a natural, inborn disposition. The meaning here is that the Muslim community will be a "middler" community, like milk, which has neither the intoxicating qualities of wine nor the cloying sweetness of honey.

Him to lighten it for your community." "I have been asking of my Lord," I replied, "till I am ashamed. I am content and I submit." Then as I passed on a Crier cried: "I have settled My ordinance, and have made things easy for My servants."

Thābit has related on the authority of Anas—with whom may Allah be pleased—quoting the Prophet—on whom be Allah's blessing and peace—who said: Burāq was brought to me. He was a riding beast, white and standing higher than an ass but not so high as a mule, who at each bound placed his hoof at a point as far as his eye could see. On him I rode till I came to the Bait al-Maqdis,[7] where I tied him to the ring at which the Prophets used to tie him. Then I entered the shrine and prayed a prayer of two *rak'as*. As I went out Gabriel came to me with a vessel of wine and a vessel of milk. I took the milk, whereat Gabriel said: "You have chosen the *fiṭra*." Then we ascended up to the heavens. In the third heaven I saw Joseph, to whom had been given one half of all beauty, and he welcomed me and wished me every good thing. In the seventh heaven I saw Abraham with his back propped against the Frequented Fane which every day is entered by seventy thousand angels who never return to it. Then I was taken to the Sidrat al-Muntahā, whose leaves are like elephants' ears and its fruits like waterpots, and which is changed when by Allah's command there covers it what covers it,[8] and whose beauty none of Allah's creatures is capable of describing. There Allah revealed to me what He revealed,[9] laying on me the religious duty of performing fifty prayer services each day and night. Then I went down to Moses. Said he (i.e., Muḥammad): I ceased not going to and fro between Moses and my Lord, till finally He said: "O Muḥammad, it shall be five prayers each day and night, but each prayer service I will count as ten, so that will make it fifty prayer services. The fact

[7] The common name for the Temple at Jerusalem.

[8] This is a reference to Sūra LIII, 16: "when there covered the Sidra tree what covered it," a verse of uncertain meaning.

[9] This is from the same Sūra LIII where v. 10 reads: "and He revealed to His servant what He revealed."

is that when a man intends a good deed but does not perform it I write it to his account as a good deed, but if he performs it I write it as ten good deeds. Also when a man intends an evil deed but does not perform it I write to his account nothing, but if he performs it I write it as one evil deed in his account."

[It is related] from Ibn Shihāb, relating from Anas—with whom may Allah be pleased—who records that Abū Dharr used to relate that the Apostle of Allah—upon whom be Allah's blessing and peace—said: When I was in Mecca [one night] the roof was split asunder above me and Gabriel descended. He slit open my breast which he washed out with Zamzam water. Then he brought a golden basin filled with wisdom and faith which he emptied into my breast and then closed it up. Then, taking me by the hand, he mounted up with me to the heavens. When we came to the lowest heaven Gabriel said to the chamberlain of that heaven: "Open!" When he had opened we went up into the lowest heaven and there was a man sitting with a lot of black specks to his right and a similar lot of black specks to his left. Whenever he looked to his right he laughed, but whenever he looked to his left he wept. He said [to me]: "Welcome to the righteous son, the righteous prophet." I asked Gabriel who this was, and he answered, "This is Adam, and those black specks to his right and his left are the souls [10] of his progeny. Those to the right of him will go to Paradise and those on his left to Hell. So when he looks to his right he laughs and when he looks to his left he weeps."

Said Ibn Shihāb—with whom may Allah be pleased: Ibn Ḥazm has informed me that Ibn 'Abbās and Abū Ḥayya the Anṣārī used to tell how the Apostle of Allah—on whom be Allah's blessing and peace—said: "Then he ascended with me till I came forth at a level place where I could hear the

[10] *Nasam,* the plural of *nasama,* "a breath," which is the Arabic equivalent of the Hebrew *neshāma* used in Gen. 2:7 for God breathing into man the "breath" of life.

scratching of the pens."[11] Ibn Ḥazm and Anas have reported that the Prophet—upon whom be Allah's blessing and peace—said: Then Allah laid as a religious duty on my community the performance of fifty prayer services. I made my way back till I passed Moses, who kept me going to and fro to get them reduced till finally I went back to Him and He said: "They are five, but they are fifty, for with Me no sentence changes."[12] I returned to Moses, who said: "Go back to your Lord," but I replied: "I am ashamed before my Lord." Then I was taken off to the Sidrat al-Muntahā, which was covered with such colors as I know not [how to describe], and I was let in to Paradise where there were pomegranate blossoms of pearl and whose soil was of musk.

[It is related] that 'Abdallah [b. Mas'ūd] said that when the Apostle of Allah—upon whom be Allah's blessing and peace—was taken by night he was brought finally to the Sidrat al-Muntahā, which is in the seventh heaven, and is the farthest limit to be reached by anything that ascends from earth, for it catches such, and also the limit reached by anything that falls from above, for that also it catches.[13] He said that the verse "when there covered the sidra tree what covered it" (LIII, 16) means golden moths. He also said that it was there that the Apostle of Allah—upon whom be Allah's blessing and peace—was given three things, viz., the five daily prayers, the concluding verses of Sūra II, and pardon for anyone of his community who refrains from giving Allah a partner.

Abū Huraira has related that the Prophet—upon whom be Allah's blessing and peace—said: You saw me in al-Ḥijr where the Quraish were asking me about my night journey, questioning me about things at the Jerusalem temple which I could not tell for certain, so that I was distressed as I had

[11] I.e., the pens of the celestial scribes.

[12] This is quoting Sūra L, 29/28.

[13] The verb *intahā* means "to come to an end," and so *al-muntahā* is taken to mean the limit beyond which things may not go.

never been before, when Allah—exalted be He—raised it up [before my eyes] so that I could look at it, and they could no longer ask me anything but I could inform them about it. Also you saw me in a group of Prophets, and there was Moses standing praying. There also was a man, thin and curly-haired as though he were one of the men of Shanū'a.[14] This was Jesus who was standing praying, and the one who most resembles him is 'Urwa b. Mas'ūd ath-Thaqafī. There also was Abraham standing praying, and the one who resembles him most is your companion—meaning himself. Then the time for prayers came and I acted as Imām for them. When we had finished prayers a voice said to me: "O Muḥammad, this is Mālik, the Chamberlain of Hell, so greet him." I turned to him and he offered me greeting.

MUḤAMMAD'S MEETING WITH HIS LORD

A favorite episode in the account of Muḥammad's Ascension is that which tells of the Prophet being taken into the presence of Allah. As Enoch walked with God, as Abraham was the friend of God, as Moses spoke with God face to face on Mt. Sinai, as Jesus had a son's relationship with his Father, so this story is intended to show how Muḥammad had an equally intimate acquaintance with his Lord. There are many versions of the story. That given here is from as-Suyūṭī's *al-La'ālī al-maṣnū'a* (Cairo, 1317 A.H. = 1899 A.D.), I, 39.

Now when I was brought on my Night Journey to the [place of the] Throne and drew near to it, a green *rafraf*[1] was let down to me, a thing too beautiful for me to describe to you, whereat Gabriel advanced and seated me on it. Then

[14] The Shanū'a were a South Arabian tribal group.

[1] The lexicons give as one meaning of *rafraf* "a narrow piece of silk brocade." It was an ancient idea that a human must be accompanied during ascent to celestial places. Gabriel had accompanied Muḥammad so far, but now he can go no further, so a kind of magic carpet is sent down to bring the Prophet the rest of the way into the Divine Presence.

he had to withdraw from me, placing his hands over his eyes, fearing lest his sight be destroyed by the scintillating light of the Throne, and he began to weep aloud, uttering *tasbīḥ, taḥmīd* and *tathniya* [2] to Allah. By Allah's leave, as a sign of His mercy toward me and the perfection of His favor to me, that *rafraf* floated me into the [presence of the] Lord of the Throne, a thing too stupendous for the tongue to tell of or the imagination to picture. My sight was so dazzled by it that I feared blindness. Therefore I shut my eyes, which was by Allah's good favor. When I thus veiled my sight Allah shifted my sight [from my eyes] to my heart, so with my heart I began to look at what I had been looking at with my eyes. It was a light so bright in its scintillation that I despair of ever describing to you what I saw of His majesty. Then I besought my Lord to complete His favor to me by granting me the boon of having a steadfast vision of Him with my heart. This my Lord did, giving me that favor, so I gazed at Him with my heart till it was steady and I had a steady vision of Him.

There He was, when the veil had been lifted from Him, seated on His Throne, in His dignity, His might, His glory, His exaltedness, but beyond that it is not permitted me to describe Him to you. Glory be to Him! How majestic is He! How bountiful are His works! How exalted is His position! How brilliant is His light! Then He lowered somewhat for me His dignity and drew me near to Him, which is as He has said in His book, informing you of how He would deal with me and honor me: "One possessed of strength. He stood erect when He was at the highest point of the horizon. Then He drew near and descended, so that He was two bows' lengths off, or even nearer" (LIII, 6-9). This means that when He inclined to me He drew me as near to Him as the distance between the two ends of a bow, nay, rather, nearer than the distance between the crotch of the bow and its curved ends. "Then He revealed to His servant what he revealed" (v. 10), i.e., what matters He had decided to enjoin upon me. "His

[2] For these technical terms see Glossary.

heart did not falsify what it saw" (v. 11), i.e., my vision of Him with my heart. "Indeed he was seeing one of the greatest signs of his Lord" (v. 18).

Now when He—glory be to Him—lowered His dignity for me He placed one of His hands between my shoulders and I felt the coldness of His finger tips for a while on my heart, whereat I experienced such a sweetness, so pleasant a perfume, so delightful a coolness, such a sense of honor in [being granted this] vision of Him, that all my terrors melted away and my fears departed from me, so my heart became tranquil. Then was I filled with joy, my eyes were refreshed, and such delight and happiness took hold of me that I began to bend and sway to right and left like one overtaken by slumber. Indeed, it seemed to me as though everyone in heaven and earth had died, for I heard no voices of angels, nor during the vision of my Lord did I see any dark bodies. My Lord left me there such time as He willed, then brought me back to my senses, and it was as though I had been asleep and had awakened. My mind returned to me and I was tranquil, realizing where I was and how I was enjoying surpassing favor and being shown manifest preference.

Then my Lord, glorified and praised be He, spoke to me, saying: "O Muḥammad, do you know about what the Highest Council is disputing?" I answered: "O Lord, Thou knowest best about that, as about all things, for Thou art the One who knows the unseen" (cf. V, 109/108). "They are disputing," He said, "about the degrees (*darajāt*) and the excellences (*ḥasanāt*). Do you know, O Muḥammad, what the degrees and the excellences are?" "Thou, O Lord," I answered, "knowest better and art more wise." Then He said: "The degrees are concerned with performing one's ablutions at times when that is disagreeable, walking on foot to religious assemblies, watching expectantly for the next hour of prayer when one time of prayer is over. As for the excellences, they consist of feeding the hungry, spreading peace, and performing the *Tahajjud* prayer at night when other folk are sleeping." Never have I heard anything sweeter or more pleasant than the melodious sound of His voice.

Such was the sweetness of His melodious voice that it gave me confidence, and so I spoke to Him of my need. I said: "O Lord, Thou didst take Abraham as a friend, Thou didst speak with Moses face to face, Thou didst raise Enoch to a high place, Thou didst give Solomon a kingdom such as none after him might attain, and didst give to David the Psalter. What then is there for me, O Lord?" He replied: "O Muḥammad, I take you as a friend just as I took Abraham as a friend. I am speaking to you just as I spoke face to face with Moses. I am giving you the *Fātiḥa* (Sūra I) and the closing verses of *al-Baqara* (II, 284-286), both of which are from the treasuries of My Throne and which I have given to no prophet before you. I am sending you as a prophet to the white folk of the earth and the black folk and the red folk, to jinn and to men thereon, though never before you have I sent a prophet to the whole of them. I am appointing the earth, its dry land and its sea, for you and for your community as a place for purification and for worship. I am giving your community the right to booty which I have given as provision to no community before them. I shall aid you with such terrors as will make your enemies flee before you while you are still a month's journey away. I shall send down to you the Master of all Books and the guardian of them, a Qur'ān which We Ourselves have parceled out (XVII, 106/107). I shall exalt your name for you (XCIV, 4), even to the extent of conjoining it with My name, so that none of the regulations of My religion will ever be mentioned without you being mentioned along with Me."

Then after this He communicated to me matters which I am not permitted to tell you, and when He had made His covenant with me and had left me there such time as He willed, He took His seat again upon His Throne. Glory be to Him in His majesty, His dignity, His might. Then I looked, and behold, something passed between us and a veil of light was drawn in front of Him, blazing ardently to a distance that none knows save Allah, and so intense that were it to be rent at any point it would burn up all Allah's creation. Then the green *rafraf* on which I was descended with me, gently rising and falling with me in 'Illiyūn [3] . . . till it brought me back to Gabriel, who took me from it. Then the *rafraf* mounted up till it disappeared from my sight.

[3] 'Illiyūn is said to be the highest of all celestial regions. It is mentioned in Sūra LXXXIII, 18-21.

II. THE QUR'ĀN

The Qur'ān is the scripture of Islam. It is called the Noble Qur'ān, the Glorious Qur'ān, the Mighty Qur'ān, but never the Holy Qur'ān save by modern, Western-educated Muslims who are imitating the title Holy Bible. It contains the substance of Muḥammad's deliverances during the twenty-odd years of his public ministry. It is clear that he had been preparing a book for his community which would be for them what the Old Testament was for the Jews and the New Testament for the Christians, but he died before his book was ready, and what we have in the Qur'ān is what his followers were able to gather together after his death and issue as the corpus of his "revelations." Orthodox Muslim theory, however, holds that this material was all there, arranged just as we have it today, in a heavenly archetype, whence it was revealed by Gabriel to Muḥammad bit by bit as circumstances warranted, was written down by scribes as it was proclaimed by Muḥammad, was collated by him and Gabriel with the heavenly original, and was all ready for publication by the Prophet's successors at his death.

In style it is in rhymed prose, closely resembling the form in which the pre-Islamic soothsayers of Arabia set forth their pronouncements. Its present arrangement is doubtless that given it by the committee appointed by the third caliph, 'Uthmān, to issue an official recension of the text. In this arrangement we find the whole divided into 114 chapters (*Sūras*) of varying lengths, generally the longer coming at the beginning and the shorter at the end, preceded by a prayer entitled the *Fātiḥa* (Opener) and closed by two little charms, known as *al-Mu'awidhdhatān*. None of the longer Sūras save Sūra XII deals with any one subject consistently, and in most of them will be found material coming from the most varied periods of the Prophet's ministry. The arrangement is clearly haphazard, though some modern Muslim writers make fantastic attempts to show a purposeful arrangement of the material in the Sūras. Since the Prophet's style of utterance changed markedly as he moved from period to period of his mission, it has been customary since the days of Weil [1] and Nöldeke [2] to class material in four periods: I. Early Meccan; II. Middle Meccan; III. Late Meccan; IV. Madinan. In Richard Bell's *The Qur'ān: Translated with a Critical Rearrangement of the Sūrahs* (Edinburgh, 1938-39) an attempt has been made by means of printing devices to show the structure of each Sūra and the periods to which the various units may be provisionally assigned.

There have been many translations of the Qur'ān into various languages, both of the East and the West. There is an excellent French version by Régis Blachère (Paris, 1949-50), and one in Dutch by J. H. Kramers (Amsterdam, 1956). In English the above-mentioned translation by Bell is by far the best for serious study, though for the general reader perhaps the most convenient is Rodwell's translation (available in Everyman's Library). Arberry's translation, in two volumes (London, 1955), makes an attempt to preserve the stylistic, rhythmic units of the original. The translations by Marmaduke Pickthall, by N. J. Dawood, and by the Indian Muslims Muḥammad 'Alī and Yūsuf 'Alī are not recommended.

For critical study of the Qur'ān the student should consult: T. Nöldeke, *Geschichte des Qorans*, 2nd ed. by F. Schwally, G. Bergsträsser, and O. Pretzl in 3 parts (Leipzig, 1909-38); Edward Sell, *The Historical Development of the Qur'ān* (London, 1909); Régis Blachère, *Introduction au Coran* (Paris, 1947); Richard Bell, *Introduction to the Qur'ān* (Edinburgh, 1952); W. St. Clair Tisdall, *The Original Sources of the Qur'ān* (London, 1911); I. Goldziher, *Die Richtungen der islamischen Koranauslegung* (Leiden, 1920); H. U. W. Stanton, *The Teaching of the Qur'ān* (London, 1919); Harris Birkeland, *The Lord Guideth: Studies on Primitive Islam* (Oslo, 1956).

1 *Historisch-kritische Einleitung in den Koran* (Frankfurt, 1845; 2nd ed., Leipzig, 1872).

2 *Geschichte des Qorans* (Göttingen, 1860).

THE QUR'ĀN ON ITSELF

III, 1-7/5.

A. L. M.[1] Allah, there is no deity save Him, the Living, the Self-subsistent. He has sent down upon thee the Book with the truth, confirming what is before it. He also sent down the Torah and the Evangel (*Injīl*) aforetime as guidance for people, and [now] has He sent down the *Furqān*.[2] As for those who disbelieve in Allah's signs, for them is severe punishment, for Allah is mighty, He who seeks vengeance. From Allah, indeed, nothing is hidden either in heaven or on earth. It is He who forms you in the wombs as He wills, and there is no deity save Him, the Mighty, the Wise. It is He who has sent down upon thee the Book, some of whose verses are clear, which are the mother (i.e., the essential matter) of the Book, but others are ambiguous. Now as for those in whose hearts is deviation, they follow what is ambiguous in it, seeking dissension, seeking its interpretation, whereas none knows its interpretation save Allah. Those well grounded in knowledge say: "We believe in it; it is all from our Lord." Yet none take warning save those of insight.

X, 37/38-40/41.

This Qur'ān is not something that could have been invented apart from Allah, but is a confirmation of what is before it, and is a distinct setting forth of the Scripture in which is no doubt, from the Lord of mankind. Or are they saying: "He

[1] These are so-called "mystic letters," which stand at the head of certain Sūras and whose meaning is known only to Allah. They are considered part of the revealed text.

[2] *Furqān* is one of the names of the Qur'ān. By Torah he means the Scripture in the hands of the Jews, and by Evangel the Scripture in the hands of the Christians, which are the things before it the Qur'ān is confirming.

has invented it"? Say: "Then produce a Sūra like it, and summon [to help you] anyone you are able apart from Allah, if ye are of those who speak the truth." Nay, but they have treated as false that which they could not comprehend, and whose interpretation has not yet come to them. Thus did those who were before them treat [the message] as false, and see what was the final end of the wrongdoers. Yet there are some among them who believe in it, though some do not believe in it, and thy Lord knows best about those who cause corruption.

XLIII, 1-4/3.

H. M. By the Book that makes clear. We have made it an Arabic Qur'ān that maybe ye will understand. And it, indeed, is in the Mother of the Book (i.e., the celestial archetype), in Our presence, high, wise.

LVI, 77/76-82/81.

It, indeed, is a noble Qur'ān, in a Book kept treasured. Let none touch it but the purified. It is something sent down from the Lord of mankind, so will ye with such a discourse be dissimulating, and make it your daily portion that ye treat it as false?

XXIX, 47/46-51/50.

Thus have We sent down to thee the Book, so those to whom We have given Scripture will believe in it, and among these [pagan people] are also some who will believe in it, for none but the unbelieving gainsay Our signs. Thou wast not reciting any Book before it, nor writing it with thy right hand, otherwise those who consider it worthless would have been suspicious. Nay, but it is evidential signs in the breasts of those given knowledge, and none but the wrongdoers gainsay Our signs. They say: "Why have not signs (i.e., miracles) been sent down to him from his Lord?" Say: "Such signs are with Allah alone, and I am only a plain warner." Is it not sufficient for them that We have sent down the Book upon thee to be recited to them? Surely in that there is a mercy and a reminder for folk who believe.

XLI, 41-44.

Verily, those who disbelieved in the Reminder when it came to them—and it, indeed, is a sublime Book, to which falsehood comes not either from before or from behind, something sent down from One who is wise, who is praiseworthy. Nothing is said to thee [O Muḥammad] but what had already been said to the messengers who preceded thee. Verily, thy Lord is the One who has [in His power] forgiveness but also painful punishment. Had We made it a foreign Qur'ān they would have said: "Why are its verses not made distinct? Is it foreign and Arabic?" Say: "To those who believe, it is a guidance and a healing, but for those who do not believe, in their ears it is a heaviness, and for them a blindness. Such as these are addressed from a place afar off."

LXXX, 11-16/15.

Nay, indeed! it is a reminder,
And whosoever wills remembers it.
[It is] in honored scrolls (or sheets),
Exalted, purified,
[Written] by the hands of scribes,
Honored, pious.

XLII, 51/50-53.

It was not for a human that Allah should speak to him save by revelation (*waḥy*) or from behind a veil, or that He should send an [angelic] messenger, who, by His permission, would reveal [to the Prophet] what He wills. He, indeed, is High, Wise. Thus have We revealed to thee [O Muḥammad] a spirit from Our affair (*amr*). Thou didst not know what Scripture was, nor the Faith (*al-Īmān*), but We have made it a light by which We guide whomsoever of Our servants We will. As for thee, thou wilt guide to a straight path, the path of Allah, to Whom belongs whatever is in the heavens and whatever is on earth. Is it not [the truth that] the trend of affairs is toward Allah?

ON THE ETERNAL NATURE OF THE WORD OF ALLAH

From an-Naisābūrī's *Gharā'ib al-Qur'ān* (printed on the margin of the Qur'ān commentary of Ibn Jarīr aṭ-Ṭabarī, Cairo, 1321 A.H. = 1903 A.D.), I, 43.

Some of the divines of this community have recorded their opinion that the Word (*kalām*) of Allah is eternal (*qadīm*), after having already given a pronouncement that these expressions which are spoken and are heard [when the Qur'ān is being read] are the Word of the Most High. Is it then that His Word—exalted be He—consists in these expressions? The Most High, indeed, has said (IX, 6): "If anyone from among the polytheists should seek asylum with thee, give him asylum that he may hear the word (*kalām*) of Allah," and it is obvious that what was to be heard belonged to these expressions. Or is it that it is pre-existent (*qadīma*), since speech (*kalām*) is one of the attributes of the Most High, and it is impossible that a phenomenal thing (*ḥādith*) [1] should have existed from eternity. Moreover, every phenomenal thing is subject to change, and for anything belonging to Allah's essence or His attributes to suffer change is impossible. For this reason some say that the Word which is composed of letters and sounds cannot be eternal because such have a beginning. How could this be otherwise when they are sounds produced one after the other by the reader? Were we to say that such are the very Word of Allah—exalted be He—we should have to say that that very attribute which has been existing from eternity in

[1] A thing which is *ḥādith* is a thing newly produced as a phenomenon belonging to a particular moment of time.

the essential nature (*dhāt*) of Allah is at the same time something that is taking place now in the body of this man [who is reading the Qur'ān], and that is obviously a mischievous statement. So others have sought to combine the two conceptions, and state that a thing may have an existence in essences (*a'yān*) but may also have an existence in memories (*adhhān*), an existence in phrases (*'ibārāt*), and an existence in writing (*kitāba*). Thus the Qur'ān can have an essential existence in which it is present in the essential nature of Allah—exalted be He—and so is eternal, undoubtedly so, and unaffected by anything that savors of defect, but at the same time it can have an existence in memory, as when the *ḥāfiẓ*[2] has learned the Qur'ān by heart, an existence in phrases, as when the reader pronounces it aloud with his tongue, and an existence in writing, as when it is set down in exemplars (*maṣāḥif*).[3] Now there is no doubt that the Qur'ān in respect to some of these forms of existence is phenomenal, but the Qur'ān only comes to be referred to figuratively as memorized, recited, written, since really its reference is to the Word of Allah which has its being in the eternal essential nature of Allah—exalted be He. So be it known that there is no need to demonstrate that every spoken sound takes its rise in a body, nor that every letter has to be formed by one who possesses bodily members, but maybe that is only in appearance, for speech [is an attribute] of the Eternal One, who is perfect and eternal, who speaks and hears and sees, though without any instrument or members, just as He perceives and knows without any faculty or organ. He who does not grasp that as he ought has not fully understood as he ought, so let him blame no one but himself. His word is a scripture (*Kitāb*) and His scripture is right, His statements (*qawl*) are decisive, His judgment is equitable, His light ap-

[2] The *ḥāfiẓ* is the professional Qur'ān reciter, a profession much in favor with blind men.

[3] A *muṣḥaf* (pl., *maṣāḥif*) is properly a codex, but it is the word now commonly used for the ordinary lithographed copies of the Qur'ān in daily use among Muslims.

pears, His existence is evident, the vision of Him [in the future world] is a certainty, and to disbelieve in all beside Him is faith. "All on earth will pass away, but the face of thy Lord, majestic and glorious, will remain" (LV, 26-27).[4]

ON THE MIRACULOUS NATURE (I'JĀZ) OF THE QUR'ĀN

From al-Bāqillānī, *I'jāz al-Qur'ān* (Cairo, 1349 A.H. = 1930 A.D.), pp. 13, 36-38.

How the Qur'ān is the Evidential Miracle for Muḥammad's Prophetic Office

What makes it necessary to pay quite particular attention to that [branch of Qur'ānic] science [known as] *I'jāz al-Qur'ān* is that the prophetic office of the Prophet—upon whom be peace—is built upon this miracle. Even though later on he was given the support of many miracles, yet those miracles all belonged to special times, special circumstances, and concerned special individuals. [The accounts about] some of these have been transmitted by many lines of tradition, testifying to knowledge of their occurrence. Others have been transmitted by a particular line of tradition, yet [that unique line] relates the evidence of a great many who testify that they witnessed [the miracle], so that were the matter other than what has been related these would deny it, or at least some would deny it, so that this group occupies essentially the position of the former, even though the original account is not from many lines of tradition. Some, however, depend on a single line of

4 All these concluding statements are reminiscences of Qur'ānic verses. Thus in III, 23/22 scripture is said to be the *Kitāb* of Allah; LXXVIII, 38 speaks of saying that which is right; XVI, 90/92 tells how Allah enjoins equity; IX, 32 declares that Allah will perfect His light though men try to put it out, and the vision of Allah in the future life is promised, since in LVII, 3 He is called "the Seen" (*aẓ-Ẓāhir* being taken to mean here "manifest").

tradition and happened in the presence of only a single person. [As against all this] the evidence of the Qur'ān is to a miracle of a general kind [witnessed] in common by men and jinn, and which has remained a miracle throughout the ages. . . .

Some Aspects of the Miraculous Nature of the Qur'ān

Not only our own friends but others have mentioned three particular aspects of the miraculous nature (*i'jāz*) of the Qur'ān.

One of them is that it contains information about the unseen, and that is something beyond the powers of humans, for they have no way to attain it. One example is the promise Allah, Most High, made to His Prophet—upon whom be peace—that his religion would triumph over the [other] religions. Thus He—mighty and exalted is He—said (IX, 33): "He it is who has sent His messenger with guidance and the religion of truth, that He might make it victorious over all religion, even though the polytheists dislike it," and this He did. Abū Bakr, the trusty one—with whom may Allah be pleased—when he sent out his troops raiding, used to remind them of Allah's promise to make His religion victorious, so that they should be hopeful of victory and feel certain of success. 'Umar b. al-Khaṭṭāb—with whom may Allah be pleased—also used to do likewise in his day, so that his army commanders were aware of it. So Sa'd b. Abī Waqqāṣ—on whom may Allah have mercy—and other army leaders like him, used to remind their companions of that, urging them on by it and making them hopeful. And they used to meet with success in their ventures, such that in the latter days of 'Umar—with whom may Allah be pleased—they had captured all [the lands] as far as Balkh and to the land of India. (Then he goes on with lists of the various places they had conquered, where other monarchs had ruled and other religions had been practiced.)

Allah—mighty and majestic is He—also said (III, 12/10): "Say to those who disbelieve: 'Ye will be overcome and will be gathered into Gehenna—how evil a bed,' " and this came true.

Also He said with reference to those [who fought] at Badr,[1] (VIII, 7): "And when Allah was promising you one of the two parties that they should be yours," He fulfilled to them what He had promised. It would be far too much [to set out] all the verses of the Qur'ān which contain information about the unseen. All we wanted was to draw attention to some which might stand for all.

The second aspect is that it is well known that the Prophet —upon whom be Allah's blessing and peace—was an *ummī*[2] who could not write, and who could not read very well. Likewise it was generally recognized that he had no knowledge whatever of the books of the earlier peoples, nor of their records, their histories, their biographies. Yet he produced summaries of what had happened [in history], told about mighty matters [of past days], and gave the important life histories from the creation of Adam—on whom be peace—up to his own mission. He makes mention in the Book, which he brought as his miracle, of the story of Adam—upon whom be peace—how he was created, what brought about his being turned out of the garden, then somewhat about his progeny and his condition, and his repentance. He also makes mention of the story of Noah—on whom be peace—what happened between him and his people, and how his affair turned out in the end. Likewise [he told] about Abraham—upon whom be peace—and about all the other prophets mentioned in the Qur'ān, and the kings and Pharaohs who lived in the days of the prophets —on whom be Allah's blessings.

Now we know for sure that he had no way to [obtain knowledge of all] this save that of being taught, and since it is known that he had no intimacy with antiquarians or those who stored up information [about such matters], and did not

1 The Muslim forces moved out to Badr to attack a Meccan caravan which Abū Sufyān was bringing back from Syria. The caravan eluded them, but they met the troops the Quraish had sent out from Mecca to protect their caravan. These are the "two parties." See Sir William Muir, *Life of Mohammed* (Edinburgh, 1912), ch. 12, and *EI*, s.v. "Badr."

2 An unlettered man.

go frequently to get teaching from them, and that he was not one who could read, so that he might have taken this from some book that could possibly have come to him, then the conclusion is that he did not obtain this knowledge save by aid from revelation. This is what Allah—mighty and majestic is He—has said (XXIX, 48/47): "Thou wast not reciting any book before it, nor writing it with thy right hand, otherwise those who consider it worthless would have been suspicious." He also said (VI, 105): "And thus do We change about the signs, and [We do so] that they may say: 'Thou hast been studying.'" We have already made clear that one who was accustomed to go repeatedly to receive instruction and busy himself at becoming intimate with those who had skill [in these matters] would not have been able to hide this from the people, nor would there have been any disagreement among them as to the way he was acting. It was well known among them who [those were who] had knowledge of these matters, even though such persons were seldom to be met, and who was in the habit of going to such for instruction. It was no secret who was the man most learned in each of these matters and who was being instructed [by him] in them, so if [Muḥammad] had been among the latter this would have been no secret.

The third aspect is that [the Qur'ān] is wonderfully arranged, and marvelously composed, and so exalted in its literary elegance as to be beyond what any mere creature could attain. This is in substance the opinion expressed by the learned theologians.

THE MUSLIM AND THE QUR'ĀN

From the *Sunan* of Ibn Māja (Cairo, 1349 A.H. = 1930 A.D.), I, 92-95.

On the Excellence of Him Who Learns and Teaches the Qur'ān

Muḥammad b. Bashshār has related to us, on the authority of Yaḥyā b. Sa'd al-Qaṭṭān, on the authority of Shu'ba and Sufyān, from 'Alqama b. Marthad, from Sa'd b. 'Ubaida, from Abū 'Abd ar-Raḥmān as-Sulamī from 'Uthmān b. 'Affān, who said that the Apostle of Allah—upon whom be Allah's blessing and peace—said: "The best man among you is he who learns the Qur'ān and teaches it." Shu'ba's version has "the best man among you," but Sufyān's has "the most excellent man among you."

Azhar b. Marwān has related to us, on the authority of al-Ḥārith b. Nabhān, on the authority of 'Āṣim b. Bahdala, from Muṣ'ab b. Sa'd, from his father, who said: "Said the Apostle of Allah—upon whom be Allah's blessing and peace: 'The choice one among you is he who learns the Qur'ān and teaches it,' then he took me by the hand and made me sit in this place of mine from which I recite."

Muḥammad b. Bashshār and Muḥammad b. al-Muthannā have related to us, saying: Yaḥyā b. Sa'īd has related to us, from Shu'ba, from Qatāda, from Anas b. Mālik, from Abū Mūsā al-Ash'arī, from the Prophet—upon whom be Allah's blessing and peace—who said: "The similitude of a true believer who recites the Qur'ān (i.e., recites it from memory) is that of a citron whose taste is good and whose smell is also good, whereas the similitude of a true believer who does not recite the Qur'ān is that of a date whose taste is good but which has no smell. Also the similitude of a hypocrite who recites the Qur'ān is that of sweet basil whose smell is good but whose taste is bitter, while the similitude of a hypocrite who does not recite the Qur'ān is that of the colocynth whose taste is bitter and which has no smell."

Bakr b. Khalaf Abū Bishr has related to us, on the authority of 'Abd ar-Raḥmān b. Mahdī, on the authority of 'Abd ar-Raḥmān b. Budail, from his father, from Anas b. Mālik, who states that the Apostle of Allah—upon whom be Allah's blessing and peace—said: "Allah has kinsfolk among men." They asked: "O Apostle of Allah, who are they?" He answered: "The Qur'ān people (i.e., those who memorize it). They are Allah's kinsfolk and His chief men." [1]

'Amr b. 'Uthmān b. Sa'īd b. Kathīr b. Dīnār al-Ḥimṣī has related to us, on the authority of Muḥammad b. Ḥarb, from Abū 'Umar, from Kathīr b. Zādān, from 'Āṣim b. Ḥamza, from 'Ālī b. Abī Ṭālib, who reports that the Apostle of Allah —upon whom be Allah's blessing and peace—said: "If any man recites the Qur'ān and memorizes it, Allah will cause him to enter Paradise, and will give him [the right to] intercede successfully for ten people of his household, all of whom deserve Hell Fire."

'Amr b. 'Abdallah al-Awdī has related to us, on the authority of Abū Usāma, from 'Abd al-Ḥamīd b. Ja'far, from al-Maqbarī, from 'Aṭā', the client of Abū Aḥmad, from Abū Huraira, who said that the Apostle of Allah—upon whom be Allah's blessing and peace—said: "Learn the Qur'ān, recite it and sleep, for the similitude of the Qur'ān and the one who learns it so that it remains with him is that of a leather bag stuffed with musk whose scent diffuses all around, while the similitude of him who learns the Qur'ān and then goes to sleep with it inside him is that of a leather bag of musk with its mouth tied up."

Abū Marwān Muḥammad b. 'Uthmān al-'Uthmānī has related to us, on the authority of Ibrāhīm b. Sa'd, from Ibn Shihāb, from 'Āmir b. Wāthila Abū'ṭ-Ṭufail, from Nāfi' b. 'Abd

[1] *Ahl* are the people of one's tent group, i.e., one's kin, and *khāṣṣa* are the chief men of a tribe. So he means that in Allah's case it is those who memorize the Qur'ān who count as His *ahl* and His *khāṣṣa,* i.e., are His nearest and dearest.

al-Ḥārith, that he met 'Umar b. al-Khaṭṭāb at 'Asifān.[2] Now 'Umar had appointed him [as governor] over Mecca, so 'Umar asked him: "Whom have you set as your representative over the people of this Wādī?" "I have appointed Ibn Abzī over them," he replied. "And who," he asked, "may Ibn Abzī be?" "A man from among our clients," he answered. "What!" said 'Umar, "you have appointed a client[3] over them as your representative?" He replied: "But he is a man who can recite the Book of Allah—exalted be He—one who knows about the duties incumbent [on Muslims], and is a *qāḍī* (i.e., one who exercises judicial functions in the community)." Said 'Umar: "How true is what your Prophet—upon whom be Allah's blessing and peace—said: 'Allah will by this Book exalt the position of some and lower by it that of others.' "

Al-'Abbās b. 'Abdallah al-Wāsiṭī has related to us, on the authority of 'Abdallah b. Ghālib al-'Abbādānī, from 'Abdallah b. Ziyād al-Baḥrānī, from 'Alī b. Zaid, from Sa'īd b. al-Musayyib, from Abū Dharr, who said: The Apostle of Allah—upon whom be Allah's blessing and peace—said to me: "O Abū Dharr, if you rise early and learn a verse of Allah's Book, that is better for you than the performance of a hundred *rak'as* in prayer, and if you rise early and learn a section of the knowledge,[4] whether that concerns things that have to be put into practice or does not, that is better for you than the performance of a thousand *rak'as* in prayer."

2 A large village on the route between Mecca and Madina.

3 A client among the Arabs was a man who had no real kinship in a tribe but who had placed himself under the protection of some full member and was thus only a "second sort" member of the group.

4 *Al-'ilm* is one of the names of the Qur'ān, some of whose passages deal with the practical duties of religion, but others with religious beliefs that have no concern with practice. For the meaning of *rak'a* see Glossary.

ON READING OR RECITING THE QUR'ĀN

From Jamāl ad-Dīn al-Qāsimī's *Maw'izat al-Mu'minīn min Iḥyā' 'Ulūm ad-Dīn* (Cairo, 1331 A.H. = 1912 A.D.), I, 99-102. The section is entitled *Kitāb Ādāb tilāwat al-Qur'ān,* where *ādāb* means literally "good breeding" and *tilāwat* may refer either to reading the Qur'ān or reciting it. This chapter is thus concerned with what is considered as right and proper to be observed by any well-bred person when reading or reciting the Scripture of Islam. The chapter deals with both the outward and the inward observances, but we have room for only the first half.

Allah has shown favor to His servants by [sending them] His Prophet as a messenger (*rasūl*) and His Book which has been revealed, "to which falsehood comes not, either from before or from behind" (XLI, 42) till it has spread abroad among thoughtful people. [He sent it as] a way of warning through the stories and the noteworthy things it contains, and by it He made clear the direction of the right path, the straight way, for in it He has set out the rules for distinguishing what is licit from what is illicit. Thus it is an illumination and a light whereby one may be safe from delusions and find healing for all that is in the breast. He who holds fast to it will assuredly be guided, and he who acts in accordance with it will assuredly have success. The Most High has said (XV, 9): "It is We who have sent down the Reminder,[1] and We shall keep watch for it." Now one of the ways whereby it is preserved, in the hearts and in the exemplars, is by our constantly reciting it and being assiduous in teaching it. [In doing so], however, we must be mindful to preserve the proper observances (*ādāb*), and to be careful of the stipulations, keeping watch over both inward attitudes and outward observances. This is what must now be explained and set forth.

[1] *Adh-Dhikrā* is one of the many names used in the Qur'ān for the message proclaimed by Muḥammad.

On the Excellence of the Qur'ān and of Its People, and on the Blameworthiness of Those Who Fall Short in the Reciting of It

He—upon whom be Allah's blessing and peace—has said: "Anyone who recites the Qur'ān and thinks that someone else has been given something superior to what he has been given is minimizing what Allah—exalted be He—has magnified." He—upon whom be Allah's blessing and peace—has also said: "The most excellent act of worship (*'ibāda*) in my community is the reciting of the Qur'ān." Again he—upon whom be Allah's blessing and peace—has said: "The best one among you is he who learns the Qur'ān and teaches it." Ibn Mas'ūd has said: "If knowledge is what ye desire, then read the Qur'ān much, for therein is the knowledge of the former peoples and the latter." 'Amr b. al-'Āṣ has said: "He who reads the Qur'ān has prophecy inserted between his sides, save only that no revelation has been given to him."

[On the other hand] there is censure of the Qur'ān recitation of those who are religiously neglectful in what he—upon whom be Allah's blessing and peace—has said: "He does not believe the Qur'ān who [in practice] takes as licit what it declares illicit." He—upon whom be Allah's blessing and peace—has also said: "Read in the Qur'ān what things it forbids you, and if [you consider that] it forbids you nothing, then you have not been reading it." Anas said: "How many a reciter of the Qur'ān there is who is cursed by the Qur'ān itself." Ibn Mas'ūd said: "The Qur'ān was sent down that they might labor at it, so they took to studying it as a labor in order that one of them might recite the Qur'ān from beginning to end without dropping a single letter, and thereby the labor dropped." One of the theologians has said: "Often a man will recite the Qur'ān and draw curses on himself without knowing it, for it says (XI, 18/21): 'Is not the curse of Allah on the wrongdoers?' and he is one who is wronging his own soul; [and it says]: 'Is not the curse of Allah on those who speak falsely?' [2] and he is one of them."

2 There is no such passage in the Qur'ān though the curse on those who speak falsely can be found in III, 61/54 and XXIV, 7.

External Things to be Observed in Reciting the Qur'ān

The *first* concerns the state of the reader (or reciter). He must have become ritually pure by the lesser ablution (*wuḍu'*)[3] and be of a quiet and serious mien. He may be either standing or sitting, but [must be] facing the direction of prayer (*qibla*[4]), his head lowered but not bowed, and be neither slovenly reclining nor sitting proudly. Should he recite without having performed the lesser ablution, or [recite] reclining on his mattress, that has its merit, but not so great. Allah, Most High, has said (III, 191/188): "Those who remember Allah standing, or sitting, or reclining, and meditate on the creation of the heavens and the earth," where He speaks favorably of all [three], but He gives precedence to the standing, then to sitting to make mention, and then the making mention while reclining.

The *second* concerns the amount to be read (or recited). The *Qurrā'*[5] had various practices whether of reading much or of limiting it. What has been transmitted [as to the practice] of 'Uthmān and Zaid b. Thābit, of Ibn Mas'ūd and Ubai b. Ka'b—with all of whom may Allah be pleased—is that they used to complete a recitation of the Qur'ān every week, dividing it up into seven portions (*aḥzāb*).

The *third* concerns correctness of reading (*tartīl*).[6] This is what is liked in the case of the Qur'ān because we shall thus make clear that the object of the reading is that we may think thereon, and correctness of reading helps in this. It is thus that Umm Salama[7]—with whom may Allah be pleased—de-

[3] For a description of the lesser and the greater ablutions see Edward Sell, *The Faith of Islam* (4th ed.; Madras, 1920), pp. 357-361.

[4] The *qibla* is the direction of the sacred shrine at Mecca.

[5] The *Qurrā'* (Readers) were the professional reciters of the Qur'ān. The four names immediately to be mentioned are those of Muslims prominent in the fixing of the early text of the Qur'ān.

[6] *Tartīl,* which originally referred to the clear and correct enunciation of the sounds, was later the word used for the cantillation customary in recitation of the Qur'ān.

[7] The widow of one of those who fell at the battle of Uḥud, and whom Muḥammad later took to wife.

scribes the recitation of the Apostle of Allah—on whom be Allah's blessing and peace—for she describes his reading as interpreting letter by letter. Ibn 'Abbās—with whom and with whose father may Allah be pleased—has said: "I had rather read the 'Cow' and the 'Family of 'Imrān' (Sūras II and III), reading them correctly and reflecting on them, than read the whole Qur'ān quickly through." It is, of course, obvious that reading correctly and seriously shows more honor and respect and is more likely to make a strong impression on the heart than rapid and hasty reading.

The *fourth* concerns weeping. This is what is liked as an accompaniment to the recitation (or reading), for it creates grief. This is that when one meditates on the threats and the threatenings, the covenants and the pacts there are in [the Qur'ān], then meditates on his own shortcomings in regard to its commands and its chidings, he will grieve, there is no doubt about that, and will weep.

The *fifth* is that he should observe what is due to its verses. Thus when he passes by a verse of *sajda* [8] let him make a prostration. Likewise when he hears someone else reach a *sajda* let him make a prostration when that reader prostrates, but let him not make a prostration unless he is in a state of ritual purity. It has been said that to do it perfectly he should say a *takbīr* [9] for putting himself in a sacral state, another *takbīr* for the inclination to make the prostration, then another *takbīr* at the straightening up [from the prostration position], and then say a *salām* (peace greeting).

The *sixth* is that he should say a *ta'awwudh* as he commences. That is, he should say: "I take refuge with Allah, the One who hears, the One who knows, from Satan the

8 There are several places in the Qur'ān, usually marked by a special sign on the margin of the text, called *sajadāt,* because the reader is expected to make a *sajda,* or prostration, whenever he comes to one of them. The nearest parallel is the "Selah" which occurs sporadically in the Psalter.

9 I.e., ejaculate *Allahu akbar,* "Allah is very great." This *takbīr* is customary at various points during the performance of the daily prayers.

stoned." If, during the recitation (or reading) he comes upon a verse of *tasbīḥ*,[10] let him say the *tasbīḥ* and the *takbīr*. Should he come upon a verse of supplication or of asking pardon, let him supplicate and ask for pardon. Finally, should he come upon any [verse expressing] request for something that is hoped for, or taking refuge [with Allah] from something that is feared, let him do the same either with his tongue or in his heart.

The *seventh* is that to read (or recite) privately is the best protection against hypocrisy and affectation. It is thus preferable in the case of anyone who fears these things for himself, but if one has no such fear, and if in public [recitation] there is nothing which would disturb anyone praying, then public [recitation] is preferable. This is because there is more labor in it, because it wakens the heart of the reader (or reciter), and makes him anxious to ponder over it. Moreover, raising the voice drives away sleepiness, increases one's interest in the reading, and lessens one's indolence. So whenever there is question of any of these things, public [recitation or reading] is preferable.

The *eighth* is making the recitation [or reading] as beautiful and orderly as possible, without adding any excessive embellishments which would change the proper arrangement. This is *sunna*,[11] for in the Traditions it says: "Adorn the Qur'ān by your voices," and another says: "He is not of us who never makes melody with the Qur'ān." Some think that by this [latter Tradition Muḥammad] meant singsong recitation, but others think he meant trilling and repeating the melody, which meaning the linguists think is the more likely. He—upon whom be Allah's blessing and peace—once listened to Abū Mūsā[12] reciting, and said: "This man has indeed been

[10] Lit., "glorification." To pronounce a *tasbīḥ* is to say *Subḥān Allah*, "Glory be to Allah."

[11] *Sunna* means "customary," i.e., the custom of the early Muslims following the known practice of the Prophet.

[12] Abū Mūsā al-Ash'arī (d. 44 A.H. = 664 A.D.), one of the early "collectors" of the Qur'ān.

given some of the psalms of David's family." It is related that the Companions of the Apostle of Allah—upon whom be Allah's blessing and peace—when they gathered together used to bid one of their number recite a Sūra of the Qur'ān.

ABROGATION

The Qur'ān is unique among sacred scriptures in teaching a doctrine of abrogation according to which later pronouncements of the Prophet abrogate, i.e., declare null and void, his earlier pronouncements. The importance of knowing which verses abrogate others has given rise to the Qur'ānic science known as *Nāsikh wa Mansūkh*, i.e., "the Abrogators and the Abrogated." The following Qur'ānic verses are the basis of the doctrine of abrogation.

Whatever verse We abrogate or cause [thee] to forget it, We bring one better than it or one like it. Dost thou not know that Allah is powerful over everything? (II, 106/100.)

We shall cause thee to recite, and thou wilt not forget except what Allah wills. He, indeed, knows what is published abroad and what one conceals. (LXXXVII, 6-7.)

And when we substitute a verse in place of a verse—and Allah well knows what He sends down—they say: "Thou art only an inventor." Nay, but most of them have no knowledge. (XVI, 101/103.)

Allah deletes what He wishes or confirms it, for with Him is the Mother of the Book.[1] (XIII, 39.)

On the meaning of abrogation. From Abū Ja'far an-Nahḥās, *Kitāb an-Nāsikh wa'l-Mansūkh* (Cairo, 1323 A.H. = 1905 A.D.), p. 7.

By derivation *naskh* has two meanings. One of them is "to replace," as when one says: "The sun has replaced the darkness," when it has made it pass away and [the sunshine] has taken its place. This sense occurs in Sūra XXII, 52/51: "So Allah abrogates what Satan has cast in." The other meaning is

[1] This *Umm al-Kitāb* is generally taken to mean the heavenly archetype of Scripture. Cf. Sūra LXXXV, 22; LXXX, 13-14.

"to copy," as when one says: "I have copied the document," i.e., I have taken it over from its exemplar. It is thus that we are to understand the abrogator and the abrogated (*an-nāsikh wa'l-mansūkh*). The signification is that a thing may have been lawful for a while, but then He made it unlawful, or it may have been unlawful and He made it lawful, or it may have been forbidden and He made it permissible, or permissible and He made it forbidden. That is, it concerns commands and prohibitions, binding and setting free, allowing and disallowing.

On the kinds of abrogation. From Ibn Salāma, *Kitāb an-Nāsikh wa'l-Mansūkh* (Cairo, 1315 A.H. = 1897 A.D.), pp. 9-10.

Abrogation in Allah's Book is of three kinds. One kind is where both text and prescription have been abrogated. Another is where the text has been abrogated but the prescription remains. Yet another is where the prescription has been abrogated but the text remains. An example of where both text and prescription have been abrogated is that related by Anas b. Mālik—with whom may Allah be pleased—where he says: In the days of the Apostle of Allah—upon whom be Allah's blessing and peace—we used to recite a Sūra comparable in size to Sūra IX, but all I remember of it is one verse: "Did man possess two valleys full of gold he would surely desire a third beside, and did he have three he would desire a fourth. Naught will fill man's belly save the dust, yet Allah turns to one who repents." It is also related of 'Abdallah b. Mas'ūd—with whom may Allah be pleased—that he said: The Apostle of Allah—upon whom be Allah's blessing and peace—recited to me a verse which I memorized and which I wrote in my exemplar. That night when I went back to my sleeping place I could not recall it at all, so I had recourse to my exemplar, but, behold, the place was blank. [Next day] I informed the Apostle of Allah—upon whom be Allah's blessing and peace—of this, and he said to me: "O son of Mas'ūd, that was abrogated yesterday." An example of where the text has been abrogated and where the prescription remains is what is related from 'Umar b. al-Khaṭṭāb—with whom may Allah be pleased—how he said: Were it not that I am unwilling to have people say that 'Umar has added to the Qur'ān something that belongs not to it, I would have myself written there the Verse of Stoning and seen that it stayed there. By Allah, we recited it from the Apostle of Allah—upon whom be Allah's blessing and peace—thus: "Turn not away from your parents, for that would be ingratitude on your part. If the old man and the old woman commit adultery, then stone them out of hand as a punishment from Allah, for Allah is Mighty, Wise." The text of this has been abrogated, but the prescription stands. Examples of where the prescription has been abrogated but the text remains are to be found in sixty-three Sūras. Instances are the saying of prayers facing toward the Jerusalem shrine, the former fastings, letting the polytheists be, and turning from the ignorant.[2]

A PRAYER AFTER COMPLETING A READING THROUGH OF THE QUR'ĀN

From Muhammad Ṭāhir al-Kurdī's *Tārīkh al-Qur'ān* (Mecca, 1365 A.H. = 1946 A.D.) pp. 207-208. *Allahumma* is a lengthened form of the name Allah, perhaps derived from *Elohim.*

Allahumma! make the Qur'ān a mercy for me and set it as a model for me, a light, a guidance, and a mercy.

Allahumma! cause me to recollect what I have forgotten of it, teach me what I am ignorant of about it, grant me the blessing of reciting it all day and all night, and make it a

[2] The earlier practice of facing Jerusalem in prayer, mentioned in II, 143/138, was abrogated by the command in II, 144/139 ff. to turn toward the sacred mosque in Mecca; the earlier practice of fasting like the Jews in Muḥarram ten days of 'Ashūrā' was abrogated by the command to fast the whole thirty days of Ramaḍān (II, 183/179 ff.); XLIII, 89, which orders that the polytheists be let alone, and VII, 199/198, which bids the Prophet turn away from the ignorant, are both said to be abrogated by the Verse of the Sword (II, 191/187), which orders their slaughter.

thing that pleads for me [on the Day of Judgment], O Lord of mankind.

Allahumma! set aright for me my religion which is my protection from evil; set aright for me my world in which I play out my life; set aright for me my future abode to which I must someday go; make life for me a thing which brings increase of every good, and death a thing which brings release from every ill.

Allahumma! make the latter period of my life its best one, my finest deeds those I do toward my end, and my best day the one on which I shall meet with Thee.

Allahumma! I beg of Thee a tranquil life, a quiet death, and a return to Thee without disgrace or shame.

Allahumma! I beg of Thee that I may make always the best of requests, the best of supplications, enjoy the best redemption, work the best works, receive the best reward, live the best life, and have the best death. Keep me steadfast [in my faith]. Make heavy my balance [at the weighing of good and evil deeds]. Keep true my belief. Exalt my station [in the hereafter]. Accept my prayers. Forgive my sins. I ask Thee for one of the high places in Paradise.

Allahumma! I beg of Thee to exalt [people's] remembrance of me, to remove my heavy burden, to set right my affair, to purify my heart, to keep my pudenda well under control, to light up my heart, and forgive my misdemeanors.

Allahumma! may the final outcome of all our affairs be good. Grant us protection from disgrace in this world and from punishment in the next.

Allahumma! portion out to us such fear of Thee as will keep us from disobeying Thee, such submissiveness to Thee as will cause us to reach Thy Paradise, and such assurance as will remove from us all grieving at the vicissitudes of this world. Grant us enjoyment in our hearing and in our seeing. Grant us provision for our daily lives and an heir to inherit from us. Grant us vengeance on those who have wronged us and to see victory over our enemies. Let us meet with no mishap in our religion. Let not this world become our greatest care or the limit of our knowledge. Place not in authority over us those who will show no mercy to us.

Allahumma! I beg of Thee all of Thy mercy that is needful, all Thy forgiveness which may be besought, security from all evil, rich provision of all piety, the enjoyment of Paradise and escape from Hell.

Allahumma! permit us not to fall into any sin without forgiving us, nor to be beset by any care without easing it for us, nor to contract any obligation without enabling us to fulfill it, nor to become involved in any matters of this worldly life or the next without seeing us through, O Thou most merciful of all who show mercy.

Allahumma! our Lord, cause good to come upon us in this world, and good in the next, and preserve us from the punishment of the Fire, and may Thy blessing be upon our prophet Muḥammad, on his family, and on his Companions, and great peace.

III. FORMULATIONS OF THE FAITH

Once the preaching of Muḥammad began to attract attention and the body of his followers to increase, there inevitably arose the need for some clear formulation of what this new religious teaching was and what was expected from converts who broke with the old paganism of their forefathers to follow it. Muḥammad claimed to be restoring the religion of Abraham (VI, 161/162; III, 65/58 ff.; II, 124/118 ff.), yet his religion was clearly not that of the Jews or the Christians, who also claimed to be the spiritual children of Abraham. In the Qur'ān we find certain directions about prayers, alms, fasting, and pilgrimage, and it seems highly probable that Muḥammad during the years in Madina gave his followers some definite formulation of the things they were to believe and the religious rites they were to practice. No such formulation appears, however, either in the Qur'ān or in the earliest strata of Tradition. What we do have is a number of brief and variant statements about some of the things that are part of true belief and part of the Muslim rule of life.

As the expansion of their empire brought Muslim people more and more into contact with other religious communities, the necessity for formulating more precisely what Islam was as contrasted with these other religions became urgent. This urgency was sharpened by—some would say was really initiated by—the rise of dissident groups within Islam itself, for one must know what true Islam is if one is to distinguish it clearly from what falsely claims to be Islam. There exists quite a number of early compendiums of belief and practice intended to explain in brief compass what Islam is. Commonly these are associated with some well-known historical occasion or attached to some famous name. Though the attribution may be false, these compendiums themselves are of great interest. Later there came into circulation more elaborate credal statements (*'aqā'id*, sing., *'aqīda*), and later still commentaries on these, theological treatises, and even catechisms.

See M. Keijzer, *De Leerstellingen van de mohammedaansche Godsdienst* (Gorinchem, 1854); M. T. Houtsma,

De Strijd over het Dogma in den Islam tot op el-Ash'ari (Leiden, 1875); B. D. Macdonald, *Muslim Theology* (London, 1903); Max Horten, *Die philosophischen Systeme der spekulativen Theologen im Islam* (Bonn, 1912); D. S. Margoliouth, *The Early Development of Mohammedanism* (London, 1914); A. J. Wensinck, *The Muslim Creed* (Cambridge, 1932); A. S. Tritton, *Muslim Theology* (London, 1947); L. Gardet and M. M. Anawati, *Introduction à la Théologie musulmane* (Paris, 1948). A credal statement from the Shī'ite division of Islam is to be found in W. McE. Miller's translation of al-Hillī's *Al-Bābū'l-Ḥādī 'ashar* (London, 1928), and another in A. A. A. Fyzee's translation of Ibn Bābawaih in *A Shī'ite Creed* (Oxford, 1942).

THE QUR'ĀN ON TRUE ISLAM

IV, 135/134-137/136.

O ye who believe, be ye those who stand fast for justice, witnesses for Allah, even though it be against yourselves, or [your] parents or kinsfolk, whether [the person concerned] be rich or poor, for Allah is nearer of kin to them both. So follow ye not desire so that ye are waverers. If ye incline to [the one party] or turn from [the other], Allah is well informed about what ye are doing.

O ye who believe, believe in Allah, and in His messenger, and in the Book which He has sent down to His messenger, and in the scripture which He sent down previously, for whosoever disbelieves in Allah, and His angels, and His Books, and His messengers, and the Last Day, he indeed has strayed far in error. Verily, those who believe, then disbelieve, then believe, then disbelieve, then increase in disbelief, it is not for Allah to forgive them or to guide them to a way.

II, 284-286.

Allah's is whatever is in the heavens and whatever is on earth. Whether ye disclose what is in your souls or conceal it, Allah will reckon with you for it. He forgives whom He wills, and He punishes whom He wills, for Allah is powerful over everything. The Apostle believes in what has been sent down to him from his Lord, as do the believers. Each believes in Allah, and in His angels, and His Books, and His messengers. We make no distinction between any of His messengers. And they say: "We hear and we obey. [May we have] Thy forgiveness, O our Lord, for to Thee is the journey back. Allah does not impose upon a soul more than it is capable [of bearing]. To its credit is what it has earned, and against it is what it has stored up. O our Lord, take us not to task should we forget, or should we make a mistake. O our Lord, lay not on us such a load as Thou didst lay on those who were before us. O our Lord, do not burden us with what is beyond our capacity, but pardon us, and forgive us, and have mercy on us. Thou art our Patron, so assist us against the unbelieving people."

ON FAITH AND PRACTICE

From the *Ṣaḥīḥ* of al-Bukhārī, ed. L. Krehl (Leiden, 1862), I, 21, 354-355.

On how Gabriel questioned the Prophet—upon whom be Allah's blessing and peace—about the faith (*Imān*) and about Islam, and what it is to do good, and about knowledge of the Hour, and on how the Prophet—upon whom be Allah's blessing and peace—explained it to him, and then said: "Gabriel has come to teach you your religion," thus making all this religion (*dīn*). Also how the Prophet explained the faith to the deputation from the 'Abd al-Qais,[1] and the saying of the Most High (III, 85/79): "Should anyone desire any other than Islam as a religion (*dīn*), it will not be accepted from him."

Musaddad has related to us on the authority of Ismā'īl b. Ibrāhīm, who said: Abū Ḥayyān at-Taimī has informed us

[1] The 'Abd al-Qais were a partly Christianized tribe of Arabs from Baḥrain who came to make their submission to Muḥammad in the year VIII of the Hijra.

from Abū Zur'a, from Abū Huraira, who said: The Prophet—upon whom be Allah's blessing and peace—was one day showing himself publicly to the people when a man came to him and asked: "What is the faith (*imān*)?" He answered: "The faith is that you should believe in Allah, in His angels, in the meeting with Him, in His messengers, and believe in the resurrection." "Then what," asked [the man,] "is Islam?" He answered: "Islam is that you should worship Allah, giving Him no partner, that you should observe prayers, pay the legal alms that are incumbent, and that you should fast during Ramaḍān." "And what," asked he, "is it to do good?" He answered: "To do good is to serve Allah as though you saw Him, for though you do not see Him, He assuredly sees you." "And when," he asked, "will the Hour be?" He answered: "He who is asked knows no more about that than the one who asks, yet I shall inform you of the signs thereof. [It is] when the handmaiden gives birth to her master, and when boorish camel-herds comport themselves arrogantly in fine houses. This is one of the five things which no one knows save Allah." Then the Prophet—upon whom be Allah's blessing and peace—recited (XXXI, 34): "Verily, with Allah is knowledge of the Hour." At that [the man] turned and went off. [The Prophet] called out: "Bring him back!" but they saw not a thing. Then he said: "That was Gabriel." He had come to him (i.e., to Muḥammad) to teach men their religion. Saith Abū 'Abdallah (i.e., al-Bukhārī himself): "He assigned all that to the faith (*īmān*)." [2]

Abū 'Āṣim aḍ-Ḍaḥḥāk b. Makhlad has related to us from

[2] Nothing follows here about either the deputation of the 'Abd al-Qais or the verse III, 85/79 mentioned in the rubric. The former, however, is mentioned in another Tradition a little later (Krehl ed., I, 22), where it tells how Muḥammad told this deputation that the faith consisted in testifying that there is no deity save Allah and that Muḥammad is his Apostle, in observing prayer, paying the legal alms, fasting during Ramaḍān, and giving up a fifth of all booty taken. He also forbade them to use four kinds of vessels used for winebibbing, and said, "Keep these prescriptions and hand them on to those who come after you."

Zakariyā' b. Isḥāq, from Yaḥyā b. 'Abdallah b. Ṣaifiy, from Abū Ma'bad, from Ibn 'Abbās, that when the Prophet—upon whom be Allah's blessing and peace—sent Mu'ādh to the Yemen he said [to him]: "Summon them to testify that there is no deity save Allah and that I am the Apostle of Allah. If they respond obediently to that, then teach them that Allah has made obligatory for them five prayers each day and night. If they respond obediently to that, then teach them that Allah has made obligatory for them charitable alms which is to be taken from the wealth of their rich folk and given to the poor among them."

Wuhaib has related to us from Yaḥyā b. Sa'īd b. Ḥayyān, from Abū Zur'a, from Abū Huraira, that one of the Bedouin came to the Prophet—upon whom be Allah's blessing and peace—saying: "Direct me to some work by the doing of which I shall enter Paradise." He replied: "You should worship Allah, associating nothing with Him, you should observe the prescribed prayers and pay the *zakāt* that has been made obligatory, and you should fast during Ramaḍān." Said [the man]: "By Him in whose hand is my soul, I shall add nothing to that." Then he turned away, and the Prophet—upon whom be Allah's blessing and peace—said: "If anyone would be happy to look on a man who will be of the people of Paradise, let him look on this fellow."

JA'FAR'S STATEMENT TO THE ABYSSINIAN KING

Muslim tradition tells of how some seven years before Muḥammad's own "flight" from Mecca to Madina, he advised a number of his followers to escape Meccan persecution by emigrating to Abyssinia, where they might live in safety under the Christian Negus of that country. Later piety has embellished the story of this sojourn in Abyssinia with numerous legends, one of which tells how Ja'far b. Abī Ṭālib, in an audience with the Negus, explained to him the new religion which was the cause of their being persecuted. In spite of its legendary character, it has great interest as an early apologia for Islam. From Ibn Hishām's *Sīrat Rasūl Allah,* ed. F. Wüstenfeld

(Göttingen, 1858-60), pp. 219-220. As much of the phraseology has been borrowed from the Qur'ān, the more important Qur'ānic passages have been indicated in parentheses.

O King, we were a people, ignorant pagan folk, worshiping idols (XIV, 35/38), eating what was found dead (II, 173/168), committing shameless profligacy (VI, 151/152), cutting ties of kinship (XLVII, 22/24), failing in our obligations to those under our protection (IV, 36/40), the strong among us devouring the weak. Thus we were till Allah sent to us an Apostle from among us (III, 164/158), whose genealogy, truthfulness, faithfulness, and abstemiousness we know. He summoned us to Allah, Whom we should recognize as unique, Whom we should worship, abandoning the stones and idols (XXII, 30/31) we and our fathers had been wont to worship instead of Him. He bade us speak truthfully, deal faithfully, observe kinship ties, treat well those under our protection, and refrain from forbidden things and bloodshedding (II, 84/78). He forbade us to commit shameless profligacy, to speak what is false (XXII, 30/31), to devour the property of orphans (IV, 2) and to slander chaste women (XXIV, 4). He bade us worship Allah, without associating anything with Him (IV, 36/40). He bade us pray, pay the legal alms, fast—and [Ja'far went on to] enumerate all the duties of Islam. So we trusted him, believed in him, and followed that which he brought from Allah. Thus we worshiped only Allah, not associating anything with Him, and we considered as not permissible what he had not permitted us, and as permissible what he had permitted us. As a result our people became inimical to us and persecuted us, in order to seduce us from our religion and turn us back from the worship of Allah to the worship of idols, and make us again consider permissible those abominations we had been wont to think permissible. So when they got the mastery over us and misused us, treating us with harshness and coming between us and our religion, we emigrated to your land, choosing you rather than anyone else, praying humbly for your protection, and hoping that near you we shall not be unjustly treated, O King.

THE PROPHET'S STATEMENT TO SALMĀN

Salmān the Persian was an early convert to Islam around whose name have clustered a great many legends. He is said to have been dissatisfied with the Zoroastrian faith of his youth and to have traveled to Syria in search of true religion, becoming a Christian there. Captured and sold as a slave to a Jew in Madina, he heard Muḥammad preach and became a Muslim. See the article "Salmān al-Fārisī" in *EI,* IV, 116-117, and L. Massignon, *Salmān Pak et les prémices spirituelles de l'Islam iranien* (Tours, 1934).

The famous statement of Muḥammad to Salmān about the beliefs and the practices of Islam was published as early as 1660 in Hottinger's *Historia Orientalis,* pp. 409-411.

It has been related from Mujāhid that Salmān told how the Prophet said: "If anyone of my community will memorize forty Traditions from me he will enter Paradise, and on the Day of Judgment Allah will assemble him along with the theologians and the Prophets." We said: "O Apostle of Allah, what are the forty Traditions?" He answered: "[They are those which explain the things you should believe and practice], viz.: (1) that you should believe in Allah; (2) and in the Last Day; (3) and in the angels; (4) and in Scripture; (5) and in the prophets; (6) and in resurrection after death; (7) and in the decreeing by Allah of both good and evil; (8) that you should bear witness that there is no deity save Allah and that I am Allah's Apostle; (9) that after proper lustration you should say the prayers with all the requisite bowings and prostrations; (10) that you should pay the legal alms; (11) that you should fast during Ramaḍān; (12) that you should go on pilgrimage to the House if that is possible for you; (13) that you should perform twelve *rak'as* of prayer every day and night following my custom and three *rak'as* of *witr;* [1] (14) that you should not take usury; (15) that you should not drink wine; (16) that you should not swear false oaths by Allah; (17) that you should not

[1] The *witr* is any prayer with an odd number of *rak'as,* but is usually the name for the extra prayer that pious Muslims say after the night prayer. For *rak'a* see Glossary.

call on Allah in testimony against anyone near or far; (18) that you should not give judgment swayed by your own desires; (19) that you should not defraud your brother [Muslim] whether behind his back or to his face; (20) that you should make no foul accusations against a chaste woman; (21) that you should spread no mischievous tales about anyone; (22) that you should not scoff at anyone in the community; (23) that you should not consider yourself safe from the wrath of Allah; (24) that you should not spread slanderous reports about what is going on among the people; (25) that you should express thankfulness to Allah for every favor; (26) that you should endure with patience all afflictions and adversities, and despair not of the mercy of Allah, knowing that what has befallen you could not have missed you and that what has passed you by could not have happened to you; (27) that you should not provoke the Lord's wrath in order to be well pleasing to creatures; (28) that you should not give preference to this world over the hereafter; (29) that when your brother Muslim asks for something you have you act not niggardly about it; (30) that in matters of religion you should observe him who is above you, but in matters of this world him who is below you; (31) that you should speak no lie; (32) that you should have no intercourse with Satan; (33) that you should forsake falsehood; (34) that you should not seize the property of orphans; (35) that when you hear a plea you should not pretend deafness; (36) that you should properly train your family and children in what will benefit them before Allah and bring them near to Him; (37) that you should do good to your neighbors and not prevent your compassion from reaching them; (38) that you should not curse any creature, but rather indulge much in *tasbīḥ, tahlīl, tamjīd* and *takbīr;*[2] (39) that you should constantly recite the Qur'ān under all circumstances save when you are ritually impure; (40) that you cease not to observe Friday, doing what will be pleasing to Him, that He may do with you what will be pleasing to you." This is the complete list.

2 For the meaning of these technical terms see Glossary.

WHO IS AND WHO IS NOT A TRUE MUSLIM

From 'Abd al-Qāhir al-Baghdādī, *Kitāb al-Farq bain al-Firaq* (Cairo, 1945), pp. 13-14.

In our opinion the true view is that the Islamic community comprises those who profess their belief in the createdness of the world, in the oneness of its Maker, in His existence from all eternity, in His attributes, His justice, His wisdom, in denying that He can be likened to anything, in the prophetic office of Muḥammad—upon whom be Allah's blessing and peace—and in his mission to all mankind, in the abiding validity of his religious law (*sharī'a*), that everything he brought is true, that the Qur'ān is the source of the prescriptions of the religious law, that the Ka'ba (at Mecca) is the *qibla* to which all must turn in prayer. Everyone who professes belief in all this, and does not assimilate it to any heretical ideas (*bid'a*) which would lead to unbelief, is a Sunnī monotheist.

Should he join to these beliefs we have mentioned any infamous heretical ideas, his case must come under consideration. Should he follow the heretical ideas of the Bāṭiniyya, the Bayāniyya, the Mughīriyya, or the Khaṭṭābiyya,[1] all of whom believe in the divinity of the Imāms, or of certain of the Imāms, or should he belong to the Ḥulūlī [2] sects, or to one of the

[1] The *Bāṭiniyya* are the esoteric sects who claim to derive special teaching from some hidden wisdom. The *Bayāniyya* are the Shī'a group who hold that the true Imamate was in the line of Muḥammad b. al-Ḥanafiyya, and passed from Abū Hāshim to Bayān b. Sim'ān. The *Mughīriyya* were the followers of al-Mughīra b. Sa'īd, who taught that Muḥammad b. 'Abdallah, the grandson of al-Ḥusain, had not been killed but had gone into occultation and would appear during the last days as the Mahdī. The *Khaṭṭābiyya* were the followers of Abū'l-Khaṭṭāb al-Asadī, who taught that the Imāms of the Shī'a sect incarnated the divine.

[2] The Hulūlī sects are said to have been ten in number, all of them with Shī'a connections, and all teaching that there has been a series of incarnations of the divine from Adam onward.

sects believing in metempsychosis,[3] or to the Khārijite sect [named] Maimūniyya,[4] who permit marriage with one's granddaughters on the male or female side, or to the Ibāḍite sect [named] Yazīdiyya,[5] who teach that in the Last Days the religious law of Islam will be abrogated, or if he takes as legitimate that which the Qur'ānic text declares illegitimate, or makes illegitimate what the text of the Qur'ān makes legitimate and does not admit of a different interpretation, then he is not of the Muslim community and has [no right to our] esteem.

If, however, his heresy should be of such a kind as that of the Mu'tazilites or the Khārijites, or the Rāfiḍites who hold to the Imāms, or the Zaidites,[6] or should it be of the heresies of the Najjāriyya, or the Jahmiyya, or the Ḍirāriyya, or the Mujassima,[7] then he belongs to the community in some respects, so that it is quite permissible for him to be buried in a Muslim cemetery, for him not to be denied his share in the spoils and the booty should he go raiding with the Muslims, nor be hindered from praying in the mosques. Yet in other respects he is not of the community. So it is not permissible to pray over him [when he dies], nor after him [if he leads public prayers], nor is it permissible [to partake of] an animal slaughtered by

3 The technical term used is *tanāsukh*, i.e., passing from one body to another.

4 They were the followers of one Maimūn b. Khālid (or b. 'Imrān).

5 They were the followers of one Yazīd b. Abī Unaisa of Baṣra. The Ibāḍites were of the Khārijite persuasion.

6 The *Mu'tazilites* were the rationalists in Islam (see *EI*, III, 787-793). The *Khārijites* were the "seceders" who left the orthodox body during the strife between 'Alī and Mu'āwiya, and developed certain peculiar doctrines of their own (see *EI*, II, 904-908). *Rāfiḍites* is but another name for the Shī'a groups. The *Zaidites* were also really a Shī'a group, but they followed Zaid b. 'Alī instead of Muḥammad al-Bāqir who became the fifth Imām of the orthodox Shī'a (see *EI*, IV, 1196-1198).

7 The *Najjāriyya* were the followers of Al-Ḥusain b. Muḥammad an-Najjār (*EI*, III, 819-820), the *Jahmiyya*, the followers of Jahm b. Ṣafwān (d. 128 A.H. = 746 A.D.), the *Ḍirāriyya*, the followers of Ḍirār b. 'Amr (*c.* 200 A.H. = 815 A.D.), and the *Mujassima* were the "corporealists," who, like the anthropomorphists, attributed corporeal qualities to Allah.

him. It is not lawful for him to marry a Sunnī woman, nor for a Sunnī man to take in marriage one of their women if she follows their beliefs.

THE ESSENCE OF ISLAM

From al-Malaṭī's *Kitāb at-Tanbīh,* in Sven Dedering (ed.), "Die Widerlegung der Irrglaubigen und Neuerer, von Abū'l-Ḥusain al-Malaṭī," *Bibliotheca Islamica* (Leipzig, 1936), IX, 110-111.

Ibn 'Umar has said: Islam is built upon five things: on confessing that there is no deity save Allah, performing prayers (*ṣalāt*), giving the legal alms (*zakāt*), going on pilgrimage to the House (i.e., the Ka'ba at Mecca), and fasting during [the month of] Ramaḍān. Thus did the Apostle of Allah hand it on to us, but beyond that there is holy war (*jihād*), which is an excellent thing. Said Ḥudaifa: Verily, I know people of two religions among the people of your religion, two religions which are due for hell fire, namely, folk who say that faith is a matter of words [and a man may be a true believer] even though he fornicates and murders, and those who say [that men can be true believers] even if they are patrons of error, claiming that there are not five daily prayers but only two, morning prayer and evening prayer.

'Abdallah al-Yashkurī said: I went to Kūfa to procure some mules, and I entered the mosque where there was a man of Qais named Ibn al-Muntafiq who was saying: Someone described to me the Apostle of Allah, and it was pleasing to me, so I went to Mecca to find him, but they said that he was at Munā. So I went to Munā to find him, but they said that he was at 'Arafāt. Finally I found him and approached him, getting so close that I could catch the bridle of his mount—or perhaps he said: till I could catch hold of the neck-rein of his mount—so that the necks of our two steeds crossed. I said: "There are two things about which I want to ask you. What will save me from Hell, and what will assure me entrance to Paradise?" He looked up at the sky, then he turned to face me, and said: "Even though you have put the matter in short, you are on to something that is immense and really needs a long answer. Nevertheless take this from me: You should worship Allah, associating nothing with Him, perform the prayers that have been prescribed, fast the month of Ramaḍān, act with people the way you would like them to act with you, do not be averse to folk coming to you but let the people do it, and let go the neck-rein of my riding beast."

It is related from al-Ḥasan that the Apostle of Allah said: "O sons of Adam, prayer prohibits immorality, yet you do not pray." Ibn 'Abbās quoted the verse (XXXV, 10/11): "To Him rises up the good word, and the righteous deed He will exalt," and said: The good word is the making mention of Allah, and the righteous deed is performing the prescribed religious duties (*farā'iḍ*). So whoever makes mention of Allah while performing the prescribed duties is carried on the remembrance of Allah and taken up to the heavens, but he who makes mention of Allah yet does not perform the prescribed duties has his words set in charge of his deeds, which is what he was well entitled to. Said the Apostle of Allah: "The first thing about which a man will have to give reckoning [at Judgment] will be the *farā'iḍ*. Should any deficiency be found in them [Allah will say]: 'Has My servant any voluntary deeds (*tatawwu'*)?' [1] If any such are found He will say: 'Fill up [the deficiency in the] *farā'iḍ* from the *tatawwu'*.' "

According to Ka'b the Apostle of Allah said: "Whoever performs the prayers, and gives the legal alms, and hears and obeys, has a middling sort of faith, but he who loves and hates only for Allah's sake, who gives and withholds only for Allah's sake, has attained a perfect faith." To the delegation that came from the 'Abd al-Qais, the Apostle of Allah said: "I command you four things, the first of which is faith in Allah. Do you know what faith in Allah is?" They replied: "Allah and His Apostle know better." He said: "It consists in testifying that

[1] I.e., deeds which religiously are good deeds but which are not among the prescribed duties of religion covered by the *farā'iḍ*. An example would be extra prayers beyond the prescribed five daily prayers.

there is no deity save Allah, performing the prayers, giving the legal alms, and giving the fifth of the booty." [2]

Said Ibn 'Umar: "There are three [necessary things] of which should a man have two but not have the third [his religion] will not be acceptable. [These three are] prayer, fasting, and the washing oneself pure from that which makes legally impure (*janāba*)."

Some of these formulations of Islamic beliefs are available in translations. Among the more accessible are the following.

Abū Ḥanīfa (d. 150 A.H. = 767 A.D.): The *Fiqh Akbar I, Fiqh Akbar II* and the *Waṣiyya* attributed to Abū Ḥanīfa are translated in A. J. Wensinck, *Muslim Creed* (Cambridge, 1932).

Al-Ash'arī (d. 324 A.H. = 935 A.D.): A short creed of his is translated in the Appendix to B. D. Macdonald's *Muslim Theology* (London, 1903), his longer *Ibāna* was translated by W. C. Klein (New York, 1940), and what professes to be his *Luma'* in R. J. McCarthy's *Theology of al-Ash'arī* (Beirut, 1953).

Aṭ-Ṭaḥāwī (d. 331 A.H. = 942 A.D.): His creed is translated by E. E. Elder in the *Macdonald Presentation Volume* (Princeton, 1933).

Al-Juwainī (d. 478 A.H. = 1085 A.D.): There is a French translation of his *Irshād,* along with the text, in J. D. Luciani's edition (Paris, 1938).

Al-Ghazzālī (d. 505 A.H. = 1111 A.D.): A short creed of his is in the Appendix to Macdonald's *Muslim Theology,* and his *Iqtiṣād* is translated in Miguel Asin's *El justo medio en la creencia* (Madrid, 1929).

An-Nasafī (d. 537 A.H. = 1142 A.D.): His credal statement is in Macdonald's Appendix mentioned above, and has been translated along with the exposition thereof by at-Taftāzānī (d. 791 A.H. = 1338 A.D.) by E. E. Elder in *A Commentary on the Creed of Islam* (New York, 1950).

As-Sanūsī (d. 895 A.H. = 1490 A.D.): His creed is translated in Max Horten's *Muhammedanische Glaubenslehre* (Bonn, 1916).

Al-Laqqānī (d. 1041 A.H. = 1631 A.D.): His *Jawharat at-Tawḥīd* is translated, along with the exposition of al-Bai-

[2] The reference is to the prescription in Sūra VIII, 41/42.

jūrī (d. 1277 A.H. = 1860 A.D.) in J. D. Luciani's *La Djaouhara, traité de théologie* (Alger, 1907).

Al-Faḍālī (d. 1236 A.H. = 1820 A.D.): His tractate is translated in Macdonald's Appendix, and in Max Horten's *Muhammedanische Glaubenslehre* (Bonn, 1916).

Al-Jazā'irī (d. 1339 A.H. = 1920 A.D.): His little catechism *al-Jawāhir* is translated in G. F. Pijper's *De Edelgesteenten der Geloofsleer* (Leiden, 1948).

IV. THE DOCTRINES OF ISLAM

ALLAH

The first and most important doctrine in the creed of Islam is the doctrine of God. The name Allah, as the Qur'ān itself is witness, was well known in pre-Islamic Arabia. Indeed, both it and its feminine form, Allāt, are found not infrequently among the theophorous names in inscriptions from North Arabia. The common theory is that it is formed from *ilāh,* the common word for a god, and the article *al-*; thus *al-ilāh,* "the god," becomes *Allah,* "God." This theory, however, is untenable. In fact, the name is one of the words borrowed into the language in pre-Islamic times from Aramaic. The old Arabian paganism both in North and in South Arabia was polytheistic, but under the influence of the surrounding culture a strong movement toward monotheism had developed. The legends about the Ḥanīfs are one evidence of this. Muḥammad was only one of several preachers of monotheism in the Arabia of his day.

It has frequently been pointed out how Muḥammad's concept of Allah in the Qur'ān falls far short of that of other monotheistic religions of the Near East, but he does emphasize Allah's uniqueness, and the moral attributes of Allah are there even though they are largely overshadowed by the attributes of transcendence. Thus it follows for orthodox Islam that the greatest of all sins is *shirk* or "association," i.e., giving to anyone or anything even the smallest share in Allah's unique sovereignty. Theology has lovingly, though rigorously, developed the doctrine of God, the technical term for which is *tawḥīd,* literally, "the making one." Muslims are *al-muwaḥḥidūn,* "those who maintain the Oneness."

In later theology the doctrine of God is commonly taken to cover three matters: (1) the being or essence of Allah; (2) the attributes of Allah; (3) the works of Allah. As to the essence of Allah nine things are to be believed, viz.: (a) His necessary existence; (b) His being from all eternity; (c) His being to all eternity; (d) His unsubstantiality; (e) His unembodiedness; (f) His essentiality; (g) His omnipresence: (h) His formlessness; (i) His uniqueness. As to His attributes, seven things are to be believed, viz., that He has: (a) life; (b) knowledge; (c) power; (d) will; (e) sensibility; (f) speech; (g) activity. As to His works, four things are His: (a) creation; (b) preservation; (c) revelation; (d) predestination.

On Allah and the doctrine of God see, besides D. B. Macdonald's articles "Allah" in *EI,* I, 302-310, and in Hasting's *Encyclopaedia of Religion and Ethics,* I, 326-327: J. W. Redhouse, "The Laudatory Epithets or Titles of Praise Bestowed on God in the Qur'ān or by Muslim Writers," in the *Journal of the Royal Asiatic Society,* XII (1880), 1-69; S. M. Zwemer, *The Moslem Doctrine of God* (New York, 1905); W. R. W. Gardner, *The Qur'-ānic Doctrine of God* (Madras, 1916); T. J. de Boer, *Die Entwicklung der Gottesvorstellung im Islam* (1913).

ALLAH IN THE QUR'ĀN

I, 1-7.

In the name of Allah, the Merciful, the Compassionate.
Praise be to Allah, Lord of mankind,
The Merciful, the Compassionate,
Master of the Day of Judgment.
Thee do we worship, and to Thee do we turn for help.
Guide us in the straight path,
The path of those to whom Thou hast been gracious,
Not that of those with whom Thou art angered, nor of those
who go astray.

II, 255/256.

Allah, there is no deity save Him, the Living, the Self-subsistent. Slumber takes Him not, nor sleep. His is whatever is in the heavens and whatever is on earth. Who is it will intercede with Him save by His leave? He knows what is before them and what is behind them, whereas they comprehend naught of His knowledge save what He wills. Wide stretches His Throne over the heavens and the earth, yet to guard them both wearies Him not, for He is the High, the Mighty.

CXII, 1-3.

Say: "The fact is, Allah is One; Allah is the Eternal. He did not beget and He was not begotten, and no one has ever been His peer."

XXIV, 34-46/45.

And indeed We have sent down to you evidential signs, and a parable from those who passed away before your time, and an admonition to such as show piety. Allah is the light of the heavens and the earth. The similitude of His light is that of a niche in which is a lamp, the lamp is in a glass, the glass is as it were a pearly star, lit from a blessed olive tree, neither eastern nor western, whose oil would well nigh light up though untouched by fire. It is a light upon a light. Allah guides to His light whom He will, and Allah strikes out parables for men, and Allah knows everything. In Houses (i.e., temples) which Allah has given permission to be erected, in them His name is remembered, glory being given to Him therein in the mornings and in the evenings, by men whom neither commerce nor bargaining divert from the remembrance of Allah, from observing prayer and paying the legal alms (*zakāt*), who fear a Day on which both hearts and sight will be disturbed.

[This is] that Allah may reward them for the best of what they have done, and increase His bounty to them, for Allah makes provision for whom He will without taking account. But those who have disbelieved, their works are like a desert mirage which the thirsty traveler thinks is water until, when he comes to it, he finds that it is nothing, but he finds Allah there beside him, Who pays him his account in full, and Allah is quick at reckoning accounts. Or [their works are] like darkness on a swollen sea where a wave covers him from above, a wave above which is a cloud, black darknesses one above another, [so that] when he stretches forth his hand he can barely see it. The one to whom Allah gives no light, for him there is no light.

Seest thou not that whosoever is in the heavens and the earth gives glory to Allah? Even the birds of the flocks each knows assuredly its prayer and its [form of] giving glory, and Allah is aware of what they do. Allah's is the kingdom of the heavens and the earth, and to Allah is the journey back. Seest thou not that Allah drives along a cloud, then unites it with another, then makes it a heap, so that you see the rain coming forth from its midst? He also sends down from heaven mountainous clouds in which is hail, wherewith He smites whom He wills and turns it away from whom He wills. The flashing of His lightning almost takes away the sight. Allah makes day and night interchange. In that surely there is a lesson for those who can see. Allah has created every beast from water. Some of them go on their bellies, some go on two legs, and some go on four. Allah creates what He wills. Verily, Allah has power over everything. We assuredly have sent down evidential signs, and Allah guides whom He wills to a straight path.

LIX, 22-24.

He is Allah, other than whom there is no deity; the One who knows both the hidden and the evident. He is the Merciful, the Compassionate. He is Allah, other than whom there is no deity, the King, the Most Holy One, the Peacemaker, the Faithful, the Guardian, the Sublime, the Mighty, the Proud. Glory be to Allah, [who is far] from what they associate [with Him]. He is Allah, the Creator, the Maker, the Fashioner. His are the most beautiful names. To Him gives glory whatsoever is in the heavens and the earth, for He is the Sublime, the Wise.

XIII, 2-4.

[It is] Allah who raised up the heavens without pillars that ye can see. Then He seated Himself on the Throne and brought into service the sun and the moon, each of which runs to a fixed term. He arranges the affair, setting out the signs distinctly, that maybe ye will be convinced of the meeting with your Lord. He it is who stretched out the earth and set on it mountain masses and rivers. Also He placed in it two pairs of all kinds of fruits. He makes the night obscure the day. Surely in that are signs for a people who take thought. And in the earth are plots set next to one another, and gardens of grapevines, cultivated fields, palm trees both clustered and unclustered, watered by a single source of water. Yet We give preference to some over others in [the matter of] food. Surely in that are signs to a people who have intelligence.

LXIV, 1-4.

Whatsoever is in the heavens and whatsoever is on earth gives glory to Allah. His is the sovereignty and His is the praise, and He is powerful over everything. He it is who created you. Some of you are unbelievers, and some are believers, but Allah is observant of what ye are doing. He created the heavens truly, and the earth. He not only fashioned you but excellent did He make your forms and to Him is the journey back. He knows whatever is in the heavens and the earth. He knows what ye keep secret and what ye make known. Indeed, Allah knows about the inmost things of the breasts.

LVIII, 7/8.

Hast thou not seen that Allah knows whatever is in the heavens and whatever is on earth? No three are ever in private conference but He is the fourth of them, nor five but He is their sixth, nor [any number] lower than that or higher, but He is with them wherever they may be. Then on the Day of Resurrection He will announce to them what they were doing, for Allah, indeed, knows about everything.

THE DOCTRINE OF GOD

From Jamāl ad-Dīn al-Qāsimī's *Maw'izat al-Mu'minīn min Iḥyā' 'Ulūm ad-Dīn* (Cairo, 1331 A.H. = 1912 A.D.) I, 10-12. This book contains a body of extracts from al-Ghazzālī's famous *Revivication of the*

Religious Sciences, so we have double assurance of the unimpeachable orthodoxy of this statement of Muslim belief about Allah.

What Muslims believe about the essential nature of the High and Holy One is that He is One God who has no partner. He is from everlasting, having none prior to Him, and He will continue endlessly to exist, having none come after Him. He is eternal, having no ending, continuing without ever being cut off, One who has not ceased and will not cease to be. He is to be described by the attributes of Majesty. For Him there is prescribed no consummation or disjunction by the ceasing of perpetuity or the expiration of fixed terms. Nay, rather (LVII, 3): "He is the First and the Last, the Outward and the Inward, and He knows all things." Yet He is not a body that has been formed, nor does He resemble any created thing, nor any created thing resemble Him. Space does not encompass Him, nor do the earths [1] and the heavens contain Him, although He is seated on the Throne in that manner of which He speaks and in that sense which He means.[2] He is above the Throne and the heavens, above everything, and yet also beneath the lowest reaches of the watery abyss.[3] His being above does not make Him nearer the Throne and the heavens nor further from the earth and the watery abyss. Nay, rather He is many stages higher than the Throne or the heavens, as He is many stages beyond the earth and the watery abyss, yet in spite of this He is near to every existing thing. He is nearer to man than his jugular vein (L, 16/15), though His being near does not resemble bodily nearness, just as His essential being does not resemble the essential being of bodily things. He does not come to rest in anything,

[1] Plural because there are seven earths as there are seven heavens.

[2] This is the famous problem of the *istiwā'* which so exercised Muslim theologians. Some seven times in the Qur'ān it is stated that Allah *istawạ̄* on the Throne, which, if used of some earthly monarch, would mean that he "sat upon the throne."

[3] *Ath-tharā* in the old cosmology is what is below the lowest depths. Sūra XX, 6/5 says: "To Him belongs what is in the heavens, what is on earth, what is between them both, and what is below the *tharā.*"

just as nothing comes to rest in Him. High exalted is He from being included in any space, just as He is far removed from being limited by any time. Nay, indeed, He was before He created time and space, and He is now as He was.

He is known by the intelligence to be existing in His essential being. As such essential being He will be perceived by the sight in the Lasting Abode,[4] as an act of grace on His part and a kindness to the righteous, in some sort a perfecting of His bounties by letting them look upon His noble face. And He—exalted be He—is living, powerful, mighty, overcoming, free from all shortcomings and any inability. "Slumber takes Him not nor sleep" (II, 255/256), and no passing away, no death ever comes upon Him. None but He can create and invent, for He stands uniquely alone in producing and innovating. He knows everything that is knowable, is aware of all that is taking place from the lowest depths of the earths to the highest reaches of the heavens, so that not an atom's weight of anything either on earth or in heaven exists apart from His knowledge. He is aware of the crawling of a black ant upon a hard stone in the darkness of the night, and He perceives the movement of each mote in the atmosphere. "He knows the secret and the most hidden thing" (XX, 7/6). He is acquainted with the promptings of men's consciences, with the movements of their fancies, with their most deeply concealed secrets, [knowing all this] with a knowledge that is from of old and is to eternity, for He will not cease having this attribute for ever and ever.

He—exalted be He—is the One who wills that existing things be, who manages the things that come to pass, so that no affair happens in the world visible or the world invisible[5] except by His determining, His decree, His decision, His will, so that what He wills is, and what He did not will is not, and

[4] *Dār al-Qarār* is one of the names of Paradise, so this is a reference to the Muslim doctrine of the beatific vision.

[5] *Mulk wa malakūt,* words which both mean "kingdom," but refer more particularly to the kingdom of things seen and the kingdom of things unseen.

there is no one who may resist His command or make a change in His decision. He—exalted be He—both hears and sees (XXII, 61/60). There is nothing that may be heard, however faint, that escapes His hearing, and nothing that may be seen, however minute, that is hidden from His vision. Distance does not dim His hearing, nor does darkness hinder His vision, yet His hearing and His seeing have no resemblance to the hearing and seeing of creatures, just as His essential being has no resemblance to that of creatures. He also—exalted be He—speaks, both to bid and to forbid, to promise and to threaten. The Qur'ān, the Torah, the Evangel, and the Psalter are Scriptures of His which He sent down to His messengers—on whom be peace. He also—exalted be He—spoke to Moses with that speech which is an attribute of His essence and not a created thing He created. The Qur'ān is Allah's speech, not a created thing that may perish, nor an attribute of any created thing so that it should be exhausted.

Now He—exalted be He—[is unique in the sense] that there is beside Him no existing thing save that which came into being by His act, proceeding from His equity in the finest and most perfect, in the most complete and equitable way. He is wise in all His actions, just in all His decrees. Everything apart from Him, whether men or jinn or angels, whether heaven or earth, whether animal or plant or mineral, whether perceived by the mind or by the senses, is a new creation which He produced by His power, being brought out from nonexistence and produced as a created thing when it had been no thing. Since He was existing in eternity He was alone, and there was no other with Him. Then He brought forth the creation after that, as a demonstration of His power, a fulfillment of that which He had previously willed, and a verification of the word that He had spoken in eternity. It was not that He had any need for it or was in want of it, for it is of favor that He creates and produces and undertakes things, not out of necessity, and it is as a service that He grants favors and not because He must. So it is He who is the One who grants favors and benefactions, blessings and grace.

A CHAPLET OF ALLAH'S MOST BEAUTIFUL NAMES

From *Tasbīḥ Asmā' Allah al-ḥusnā*, a little manuscript on the ninety-nine "most comely names of Allah," written by Muḥammad al-Madanī (Damascus, 1322 A.H. = 1904 A.D.).

The Muslim rosary (*subḥa*) normally consists of thirty-three beads with a tassel, and is run through the fingers three times to complete the ninety-nine names. The lists of these names as found in the texts varies greatly. Hottinger, in his *Historia Orientalis* (pp. 387, 388 of the edition of 1660), gives a list, as does T. P. Hughes in his *Dictionary of Islam* (London, 1935) under "God," but Redhouse in his article in the *Journal of the Royal Asiatic Society* for 1880 collected from various lists no less than 552 different names for Allah. The fact that the names in this chaplet are arranged roughly in the order of the Arabic alphabet is due merely to the whim of the compiler and has no religious significance. They are mostly epithets derived from the Qur'ān.

1. Allah, the Name that is above every name.
2. al-Awwal, the First, who was before the beginning (LVII, 3).
3. al-Ākhir, the Last, who will still be after all has ended (LVII, 3).
4. al-Badī', the Contriver, who contrived the whole art of creation (II, 117/111).
5. al-Bāri', the Maker, from whose hand we all come (LIX, 24).
6. al-Barr, the Beneficent, whose liberality appears in all His works (LII, 28).
7. al-Baṣīr, the Observant, who sees and hears all things (LVII, 3).
8. al-Bāsiṭ, the Spreader, who extends His mercy to whom He wills (XIII, 26).
9. al-Bāṭin, the Inner, who is immanent within all things (LVII, 3).
10. al-Bā'ith, the Raiser, who will raise up a witness from each community (XVI, 89/91).
11. al-Bāqī, the Enduring, who is better and more enduring (XX, 73/75).

12. at-Tawwāb, the Relenting, who relented toward Adam and relents to all his descendants (II, 37/35).
13. al-Jabbār, the Mighty One, whose might and power are absolute (LIX, 23).
14. al-Jalīl, the Majestic, mighty and majestic is He.
15. al-Jāmi', the Gatherer, who gathers all men to an appointed Day (III, 9/7).
16. al-Ḥasīb, the Accounter, who is sufficient as a reckoner (IV, 6/7).
17. al-Ḥafīẓ, the Guardian, who keeps watch over everything (XI, 57/60).
18. al-Ḥaqq, the Truth (XX, 114/113).
19. al-Ḥākim, the Judge, who gives judgment among His servants (XL, 48/51).
20. al-Ḥakīm, the Wise, who is both wise and well informed (VI, 18).
21. al-Ḥalīm, the Kindly, who is both forgiving and kindly disposed (II, 235).
22. al-Ḥamīd, the Praiseworthy, to whom all praise is due (II, 267/270).
23. al-Ḥayy, the Living, who is the source of all life (XX, 111/110).
24. al-Khabīr, the Well-Informed, who is both wise and well informed (VI, 18).
25. al-Khafīḍ, the Humbler, who humbles some while He exalts others (Cf. LVI, 3).
26. al-Khāliq, the Creator, who has created all things that are (XIII, 16/17).
27. Dhū'l-Jalāl wa'l-Ikrām, Lord of Majesty and Honor (LV, 27).
28. ar-Ra'ūf, the Gentle, who is compassionate toward His people (II, 143/138).
29. ar-Raḥmān, the Merciful, the most merciful of those who show mercy (I, 3/2; XII, 64).
30. ar-Raḥīm, the Compassionate, who is gentle and full of compassion (I, 3/2; II, 143/138).

31. ar-Razzāq, the Provider, who provides but asks no provision (LI, 57, 58).
32. ar-Rashīd, the Guide, who leads believers in the right-minded way (XI, 87/89).
33. ar-Rāfi', the Exalter, who exalts some while He humbles others (VI, 83).
34. ar-Raqīb, the Watcher, who keeps watch over His creation (V, 117).
35. as-Salām, the Peace-Maker, whose name is Peace (LIX, 23).
36. as-Samī', the Hearer, who sees and hears all things (XVII, 1).
37. ash-Shakūr, the Grateful, who graciously accepts the service of His people (LXIV, 17).
38. ash-Shahīd, the Witness, who is witness to all things (V, 117).
39. aṣ-Ṣabūr, the Forbearing, who has great patience with His people.
40. aṣ-Ṣamad, the Eternal, who begets not and is not begotten (CXII, 2).
41. aḍ-Ḍārr, the Afflicter, who sends affliction as well as blessing (XLVIII, 11).
42. aẓ-Ẓāhir, the Outer, who is without as well as within (LVII, 3).
43. al-'Adl, the Just, whose word is perfect in veracity and justice (VI, 115).
44. al-'Azīz, the Sublime, mighty in His sublime sovereignty (LIX, 23).
45. al-'Aẓīm, the Mighty, He who above all is high and mighty (II, 255/256).
46. al-'Afuw, the Pardoner, ever ready to forgive His servants (IV, 99/100).
47. al-'Alīm, the Knowing One, who is well aware of everything (II, 29/27).
48. al-'Alī, the High One, He who is high and mighty (II, 255/256).

49. al-Ghafūr, the Forgiving, who is both forgiving and well disposed (II, 235).
50. al-Ghaffār, the Pardoning, ever ready to pardon and forgive (LXXI, 10/9).
51. al-Ghanī, the Rich, since it is He who possesses all things (II, 267/270).
52. al-Fattāḥ, the Opener, who clears and opens up the Way (XXXIV, 26/25).
53. al-Qābiḍ, the Seizer, who both holds tight and is openhanded (II, 245/246).
54. al-Qādir, the Able, who has the power to do what He pleases (XVII, 99/101).
55. al-Quddūs, the Most Holy One, to Whom all in heaven and on earth ascribe holiness (LXII, 1).
56. al-Qahhār, the All-Victorious, who overcomes all (XIII, 16/17).
57. al-Qawī, the Strong, sublime in His strength and His power (XLII, 19/18).
58. al-Qayyūm, the Self-Subsistent, eternally existing in and for Himself alone (III, 2/1).
59. al-Kabīr, the Great One, who is both high and great (XXII, 62/61).
60. al-Karīm, the Munificent, who is not only rich but generous (XXVII, 40).
61. al-Laṭīf, the Gracious, whose grace extends to all His servants (XLII, 19/18).
62. al-Muta'akhkhir, the Deferrer, who when He wills defers punishment (XIV, 42/43).
63. al-Mu'min, the Faithful, who grants security to all (LIX, 23).
64. al-Muta'ālī, the Self-Exalted, who has set Himself high above all (XIII, 9/10).
65. al-Mutakabbir, the Proud, whose pride is in His works (LIX, 23).
66. al-Matīn, the Firm, firm in His possession of strength (LI, 58).

67. al-Mubdi', the Originator, who both originates and restores (LXXXV, 13).
68. al-Mujīb, the Answerer, who responds when His servants call (XI, 61/64).
69. al-Majīd, the Glorious, praiseworthy and glorious is He (XI, 73/76).
70. al-Muḥṣī, the Computer, who has counted and numbered all things (XIX, 94).
71. al-Muḥyī, the Quickener, who quickens and brings to life the dead (XXX, 50/49).
72. al-Mudhill, the Abaser, who raises to honor or abases whom He will (III, 26/25).
73. al-Muzīl, the Separator, who will separate men from the false gods they vainly worship (X, 28/29).
74. al-Muṣawwir, the Fashioner, who fashions His creatures how He pleases (LIX, 24).
75. al-Mu'īd, the Restorer, who both originates and restores (LXXXV, 13).
76. al-Mu'izz, the Honorer, who honors or abases whom He will (III, 26/25).
77. al-Mu'ṭī, the Giver, from whose hand come all good things (XX, 50/52).
78. al-Mughnī, the Enricher, who enriches men from His bounty (IX, 74/75).
79. al-Muqīt, the Well-Furnished, provided with power over all things (IV, 85/87).
80. al-Muqtadir, He who prevails, having evil men in His powerful grip (LIV, 42).
81. al-Muqaddim, the Bringer-Forward, who sends His promises on ahead (L, 28/27).
82. al-Muqsiṭ, the Observer of Justice, who will set up the balances with justice (XXI, 47/48).
83. al-Malik, the King, who is king of kings (LIX, 23).
84. Mālik al-Mulk, Possessor of the Kingdom, who grants sovereignty to whom He will (III, 26/25).
85. al-Mumīt, He who causes to die, just as He causes to live (XV, 23).

86. al-Muntaqim, the Avenger, who wreaks vengeance on sinners and succors the believers (XXX, 47/46).
87. al-Muhaimin, the Preserver, whose watchful care is over all (LIX, 23).
88. an-Naṣīr, the Helper, and sufficient as a helper is He (IV, 45/47).
89. an-Nūr, the Light, illuminating both earth and heaven (XXIV, 35).
90. al-Hādī, the Guide, who leads believers in the straight path (XXII, 54/53).
91. al-Wāḥid, the One, unique in His Divine sovereignty (XIII, 16/17).
92. al-Waḥīd, the Unique, who alone has created (LXXIV, 11).
93. al-Wadūd, the Loving, compassionate and loving to His servants (XI, 90/92).
94. al-Wārith, the Inheritor, unto whom all things will return (XIX, 40/41).
95. al Wāsi', the Wide-Reaching, whose bounty reaches all (II, 268/271).
96. al-Wakīl, the Administrator, who has charge of everything (VI, 102).
97. al-Waliy, the Patron, and a sufficient patron is He (IV, 45/47).
98. al-Wālī, the Safeguard, other than whom men have no sure guard (XIII, 11/12).
99. al-Wahhāb, the Liberal Giver, who gives freely of His bounty (III, 8/6).

THE VISION OF ALLAH IN THE OTHER WORLD

From Ibn Makhlūf's *Kitāb al-'Ulūm al-fākhira fī'n-naẓr fī Umūr al-Ākhira,* (Cairo, 1317 A.H. = 1899 A.D.), II, 151-153.

Said Ḥammād b. Sulaimān: When the Blessed have entered Paradise and have established themselves there in pleasure and delight, in a magnificent kingdom, a noble residence where they are in security and tranquillity, they quite forget there what they were promised in this world of how they would [one day] see Allah and go to visit Him, so occupied are they with the blessings and the pleasures they are enjoying there. So while they are thus, behold, an angel from before Allah—mighty and majestic is He—looks down upon them from one of the mighty walls of Paradise, from an eminence so high that not a thing in Paradise is hidden from him. [It is a wall] made of glistening pearl whose light shines over against the Throne and shines to the highest point of heaven. This angel will call out at the top of his voice: "O people of Paradise, greeting of peace to you," yet with a voice so full of compassion that, though it is so loud, all ears incline to it and all faces turn toward it, all souls being moved by it, rejoicing at it, and responding eagerly to it. All of them hear the voice and take cognizance that this is a herald from before Allah—mighty and majestic is He. It will evoke no doubt in them, so they will respond: "Labbaika! Labbaika! [1] O summoner from Allah, our Lord. We have heard and we respond." Then he will say: "Welcome to you, O ye saints of Allah! Welcome! most welcome! Allah—mighty and majestic is He—sends you greeting of peace, saying that He is well pleased with you [and asking] are ye well pleased with Him." They will reply: "Praise be to Allah who has guided us to this, for we were not such as would have been guided had not Allah guided us (VII, 43/41). Praise be to Him, since He is well pleased with us and has made us well satisfied. To Him be praise and thanksgiving, since He has been bountiful to us and given us [all this]." Then [the angel] will say: "O saints of Allah, Allah—glory be to Him—sends you greeting of peace and says: 'Have I fulfilled the promises I made to you in the world, or have I come short of them in any way?' " They will answer: "Praise be to Allah, His are the gifts and the favors. He has indeed fulfilled His promises and bestowed on us bounty

[1] This exclamation, whose meaning is little understood, was the ancient cry which used to be raised by those approaching the sacred shrine at Mecca. It is still used by Muslim pilgrims at the present day. The technical word for making devotional use of this exclamation is *talbiya.*

from Himself, this Paradise in which we go about wherever we wish." Then [the angel] will say to them: "Allah—glory be to Him—gives you greeting of peace, and reminds you that in the world He promised you that in Paradise you would visit Him, approach Him, and look upon Him. Now He would fulfill what He promised you, so He gives you here and now permission to prepare yourselves to have your happiness made complete in His presence."

When they hear that, everything they have been enjoying there and all they have so far attained in Paradise will seem to them a little thing compared with that exceeding great happiness. Indeed, all that Paradise contains will seem insignificant over against the fact that Allah is well pleased with them and [is allowing them] to visit Him and look upon Him. So they will get themselves ready for a visit to their Lord in their finest estate and their most beautiful attire. They will clothe themselves with the most precious robes and the choicest ornaments they have, perfume themselves with the most fragrant perfumes, and mount the finest of horses and the most nobly born steeds, the most precious that they have, and putting crowns upon their heads they will come forth, each man from his palace and his garden, till he reaches the farthest end of his property and moves out into the paths of Paradise, his *wildān* [2] preceding him and guiding him on the way to the visitation of the most illustrious King. Meanwhile they raise their voices in expressions of remembrance and encomium and hallelujahs (*tahlīl*), and whenever any man among them comes out into the paths of Paradise he meets his brother [Muslim] who has come out for the same purpose that he has.

Thus they will journey along till they come to a broad open space at the borders of Paradise, where the ground is unencumbered, vacant, white, and camphored, its soil being of camphor mixed with musk and ambergris, and its stones of

[2] Each of the Blessed in Paradise has a provision of male and female attendants of celestial origin. The *wildān* are the celestial youths who wait on them and the *ḥūrīs* are the celestial damsels.

pearl and jacinth. There they will assemble, preceded by the angel who had summoned them and who has traveled on ahead of them till he has brought them to this Garden of Eden. Allah will have given a call to this Garden, [saying]: "Adorn yourself, for I have called My saints to visit Me within you," so the Garden will have adorned itself with the most exquisite and beautiful adornment, and its attendants and *wildān* will likewise have got themselves ready. So when the saints arrive at the gate of the Garden, the angel will precede them, having with him the people of Paradise, and all of them will cry: "Greeting to you, O ye angels of our Lord." Then there will be opened for them a gate between whose leaves is the distance between the East and the West here on earth. This gate is of green emerald and over it are curtains of light of such brightness as almost to destroy the sight. They will enter and pour out into a valley-bed there whose enormous size, both in length and breadth, is known only to Him who created it by His power and fashioned it in His wisdom. Its soil is of finest musk and saffron and ambergris, its stones of jacinths and jewels, its little pebbles and rubble are of gold, while on its banks are trees whose limbs hang down, whose branches are low, whose fruits are within easy reach, whose birds sing sweetly, whose colors shine brightly, whose flowers blossom in splendor, and from which comes a breeze [so delightful] as to reduce to insignificance all other delights, one needle's-eye full of which, were it sent to this world, would cure all the sick.

Beneath these trees are chairs and benches of light that gleam, chairs and benches of jacinth and of jewels, and the like of red gold, of green emerald, of musk and ambergris, set there for the prophets, the messengers, then for the saints and the pious, then for the martyrs and the just, then for the Blessed from among all the rest of the people. Over [these seats] are cloths of brocade and satin and green silk, very precious, the silk woven and hemmed with jacinths and with jewels, and [on them] also are cushions of red brocade. On these they will be given permission to seat themselves in accordance with the honorable rank each has. They will be met by cries of welcome and applause, with ascriptions of honor and merit. So each man of them will take his station according to the measure of honor he has with his Lord, and his position of nearness to Him and in His favor, while the angels and the *wildān* show them great respect in seating them. Then, when every man has taken his place and settled himself according to his rank, orders will be given that they be served with the finest food. So they will eat it and enjoy it with such pleasure that they forget any food they have eaten hitherto, and everything they have ever known before seems insignificant to them. [It will be served to them] on platters the like of which they have never seen before and on tables whose like they have never beheld. Then orders will be given that they be served the finest kinds of fruit such as they never before have seen, and they will eat of these fruits and enjoy thereof as much as they desire. Then orders will be given that they be served the finest varieties of drinks such as they never yet have drunk, [served to them] in vessels of pearl and jacinth which shine brilliantly, giving out lights the like of whose splendor and loveliness they have hitherto never beheld. So they will drink and enjoy it, and then orders will be given for them to be [perfumed] with perfumes such as they have never before enjoyed. Then orders will be given for them to be clothed with garments [of honor] the like of which they have not seen even in Paradise, and of such splendor and beauty as they have never before had for their delight.

This will be their state, so ask not about their happiness and their joy there, for all that they have had before now seems to them of no account. Then Allah—glory be to Him—will say: "O My saints, O My servants, have I fulfilled to you what I promised you in the world? Have I amply fulfilled My promise?" They will answer: "Yea, O our Lord, by Thy might, Thou hast fulfilled to us Thy promise and hast amply fulfilled what Thou didst promise us." Then He—glory be to Him—will say: "Nay, by My might, there still remains for you one thing which you covet yet more and which has a still higher place in your estimation. What is there after you have come to Me but that you should look upon Me, that thereby your blessedness may be complete?" Then He—glory be to Him—will give command to the veils of light so they will be raised, and to the dread awfulness so that it is set aside. Then He—glory be to Him—will reveal Himself to them and they will look upon Him. Thus will they see Him without suffering any injury or any harm, and no joy can equal their joy in that, nor can any happiness or delight stand beside their happiness in that. So they will fall down before their Lord in prostration and deep humility, saying: "Glory be to Thee, O our Lord. In Thy praise Thou art blessed and exalted, and blessed is Thy name."

ALLAH'S SELF-GLORIFICATION

From al-Ghazzālī's *Iḥyā' 'Ulūm ad-Dīn* (Ḥalabī edition; Cairo, 1348 A.H. = 1929 A.D.), I, 286.

'Ali b. Abī Ṭālib—whose face may Allah honor—has related that the Apostle of Allah once said: "Every day Allah—exalted be He—glorifies Himself and says: 'I am Allah, Lord of the worlds. I am Allah, there is no deity save Me, the Living, the Self-subsistent. I am Allah, there is no deity save Me, the High, the Mighty. I am Allah, there is no deity save Me, I do not beget and I was not begotten. I am Allah, there is no deity save Me, the Pardoner, the Forgiver. I am Allah, there is no deity save Me, from Whom everything had its beginning and to Whom everything will return. [I am] the Mighty, the Wise, the Merciful, the Compassionate, Ruler of the Day of Judgment, Creator of both good and evil, Creator of both Paradise and Hell, the One, the Single, the Unique, the Eternal. [I am] He who took for Himself no consort or child, the Unique, the Singular One, He who knows the unseen and the seen, the King, the Holy One, the Peaceful, the Faithful, the Preserver, the Sublime, the Mighty One, the Proud, the

Creator, the Maker, the Controller, the Great One, the Exalted One, the Capable, the Overcomer, the Generous. [I am] He who is worthy of praise and glory. I know the secret and that which is most hidden. I am the Powerful One, the Provider, high above all creatures and created things.' "

HIS ANGELS

This article of the creed is broader than its key word, for it includes all kinds of creatures inhabiting the invisible world. As early as the days of the ancient Sumerians we find nations in the Near East peopling the invisible world with hosts of creatures who lived and acted more or less as human beings do and who exercised a potent influence on both the life of the universe and the life of man. In pre-Islamic Arabia, belief in such spiritual beings, some benevolent, some malevolent, was widespread. Some beliefs about these creatures were of native Arabian origin, but others had come to the Arabs from the higher religions with which they were in contact, in particular from Judaism and Christianity. From the Qur'ān itself we gather that the pagan Arabs knew about angels, whom they were inclined to regard as daughters of Allah, about demons or satans, and about various classes of jinn, though at times the distinction between satans and jinn was not too clearly drawn. From Judaeo-Christian tradition, either directly or indirectly, Muḥammad had learned much about archangels, ministering angels, and fallen angels, and about a certain great Spirit (*Rūḥ*) who seems superior even to the angels. What he had learned in this way he used most effectively in his preaching.

Later Islam systematized and added to this teaching. It maintained belief in:

A. Archangels: Gabriel, the angel of revelation; Michael, the angel of providence; Isrāfīl, the angel of the trump of doom; 'Azrā'īl, the angel of death.

B. Ministering angels: Riḍwān, the Grand Chamberlain of Paradise; Mālik, the Grand Chamberlain of Hell; The recording angels; The questioners of the dead (Munkar and Nakīr); The Thronebearers; The cherubim who surround the Throne; The hosts of ministering angels.

C. Fallen angels: Iblīs or Satan; Hārūt and Mārūt; The hosts of Iblīs.

All angels were sexless, immortal and resplendent, created of light.

D. Jinn, who were created of fire, were male and female, mortal, far from resplendent, and much nearer to human kind. They can possess humans, so that a madman is said to be *majnūn*, i.e., jinn-possessed, and poets, soothsayers, diviners, etc., were to some measure similarly *majnūn*. There are also tales of marriage of jinn with humans; in fact, the famous Queen of Sheba was said to be the daughter of such a mixed marriage.

See articles "Djinn" and "Malā'ika" in *EI*, I, 1045-1046, III, 189-192; T. Nöldeke, "Arabs (Ancient)," in Hastings' *Encyclopedia of Religion and Ethics*, I, 669-670; W. Niekrens, *Die Engel und Geistervorstellungen des Korans* (Rostock, 1906); W. Eickmann, *Die Angelologie und Dämonologie des Korans* (Leipzig, 1908); P. A. Eichler, *Die Dschinn, Teufel und Engel im Koran* (Leipzig, 1928); von Hammer-Purgstall, *Die Geisterlehre der Moslimen* (Wien, 1852); T. Canaan, *Dämonenglaube im Lande der Bibel* (Leipzig, 1929); E. Zbinden, *Die Djinn des Islam* (Bonn, 1953).

ANGELS, JINN AND SATANS IN THE QUR'ĀN

Angels. XXXV, 1.

Praise be to Allah, Creator of the heavens and the earth, He who makes the angels messengers, having wings, some threefold, some fourfold. He adds to creation what He pleases, for Allah has power over everything.

XCVII, 1-5.

We, indeed, sent it down on the Night of Power.
And who shall teach thee what the Night of Power is?
The Night of Power is better than a thousand months,
The angels and the Spirit descend therein, by permission of
their Lord, about every matter.
Peace it is till the breaking of the dawn.

LXXXII, 10-12.

Yet over you, indeed, are Guardians,
Noble ones, those who write.[1]
They know what ye do.

[1] These are the recording angels who keep the record of men's deeds, a record which will have to be faced at Judgment.

XL, 7-9.

Those who bear the Throne, and those who surround it, give glory to their Lord, with praise. They believe in Him and beg forgiveness for those who believe [saying]: "O our Lord, Thy mercy and Thy knowledge extend wide over all things, so grant forgiveness to those who repent and follow Thy way, and protect them from the torment of al-Jaḥīm,[2] O our Lord, and cause them to enter the gardens of delight that Thou hast promised them, also those among their ancestors who have been upright, and their spouses and their progeny. Thou, indeed art the Sublime, the Wise. Protect them from evil deeds, for he whom Thou dost protect from evil deeds on that Day, to him Thou hast indeed shown mercy, and that is the great salvation."

XXXVII, 149-157.

So ask their opinion. Has thy Lord daughters [3] while they have sons? Or did We create the angels as females while they were looking on? Is it not rather that out of their own inventiveness they say: "Allah has begotten"? Yet assuredly they are speaking falsely. Would He choose daughters rather than sons? What is the matter with you? How [wrongly] ye judge. Will ye not then be reminded? Or do ye have clear authority [for your statements]? Then produce your Scripture if ye are speaking the truth.

VII, 206/205.

Verily those who are with thy Lord (i.e., the celestial beings) do not consider themselves too important to serve Him, but they give glory to Him and prostrate themselves to Him in obeisance.

[2] One of the names of Hell, or of a section thereof.

[3] This is said to be a reference to the opinion of the pagan Arabs that the angels, or at least some groups of angels, were daughters of Allah.

Iblīs. XV, 28-43.

And when thy Lord said to the angels: "Behold! I am about to create a man from potter's clay of molded mud; so when I have fashioned him and breathed into him of My spirit, then fall down before him, prostrating yourselves in obeisance." So the angels, all of them together, prostrated themselves in obeisance, save Iblīs (i.e., *diabolos*). He disdainfully refused to be among those prostrating themselves in obeisance. Said [Allah]: "O Iblīs, what is the matter with thee that thou art not among those prostrating themselves in obeisance?" Said he: "I was not one who would prostrate himself in obeisance to a man whom Thou hast created from potter's clay of molded mud." Said [Allah]: "Then get out from it (i.e., from the garden), for thou art stoned and truly on thee shall be the curse till the Day of Judgment." Said he: "O my Lord, give me respite till the Day when they are raised." He answered: "Verily, thou art one of those respited till the day of the appointed time." He said: "O my Lord, inasmuch as Thou hast turned me away, I shall make things look fine to them on earth and turn them away altogether, save Thy servants among them who are single-hearted." Said [Allah]: "This is a straight path for Me. Truly, over My servants thou hast no authority, save over those perverse ones who follow thee, and Gehenna, indeed, is the place appointed for all of them."

Angel of Death. XXXII, 11.

Say: "The angel of death will cause you to die, he who has been given charge of you. Then to your Lord will ye return."

Gabriel and Michael. II, 97/91-98/92.

Say: "Whosoever is an enemy to Gabriel—and he is the one who has brought it (i.e., the revelation) down upon thy heart, by Allah's leave, as a confirmation of what was before it, and as a guidance and a message of good tidings to those who believe. Whosoever [I say] is an enemy to Allah, and to His angels, and to His messengers, and to Gabriel and to Michael, why, the fact is that Allah is an enemy to such unbelievers."

Hārūt and Mārūt. II, 102/96.

And they follow what the satans were reciting during Solomon's reign. Solomon did not disbelieve, but the satans disbelieved. They taught the people magic (*siḥr*) and what had been sent down to the two angels Hārūt and Mārūt at Babylon. Those two, however, do not teach anyone without saying: "We are only a temptation, so do not disbelieve." But from those two they learn that whereby they make separation between a man and his wife, though really they do not do injury to anyone thereby save by Allah's permission. But they learn what injures them and does not profit them, although they know that anyone who purchases that [art] has no place in the hereafter. How bad a bargain they have made for themselves thereby, had they but known.

Jinn. XV, 26-27.

And indeed, We created man from potter's clay of molded mud, but the jinn We created earlier from the fire of the *samūm*.[4]

VI, 128-130.

And on the Day when We gather all together [We shall say]: "O company of jinn, ye have demanded much of men." Then their clients from among men will say: "O our Lord, some of us have derived advantage from others, but now we have reached our term which Thou didst fix for us." He will say: "Hell Fire is your abode in which ye will remain eternally, save such as Allah wills." Thy Lord is indeed wise, knowing. Thus do We make the wrongdoers helpers of one another in what they have been acquiring. [He will say]: "O company of jinn and men, did there not come to you messengers of your

[4] This is the scorching wind that blows in from the parched desert.

own kind relating to you My signs, and giving you warning of encountering this Day of yours?" They will answer: "We bear witness against ourselves." This worldly life deceived them and they bear witness against themselves that they were unbelievers.

LI, 56-57.

I have not created jinn and men save that they might serve Me. I do not desire any provision from them, nor do I desire that they should feed Me.

LXXII, 1-13.

Say: "It has been revealed to me that some folk of the jinn listened and they said: 'Verily, we have heard a marvelous Scripture lesson,[5] which guides to the right direction, so we have believed in it, and we shall never associate anyone with our Lord. [We confess] that He—exalted be our Lord's majesty—has not taken for Himself any female companion nor [does He have] a son; and that the foolish among us used to make extravagant statements against our Lord; and that we have come to the opinion that neither man nor jinn should ever make a false statement against Allah; and that there were individuals among men who used to take refuge with individuals among the jinn so that they increased them in folly; and that they thought as ye think that Allah will never raise up anyone; and that we have touched the heaven and found it full of strong guards and glowing meteors; [6] and that we used to take our seats there in order to hear, but he who listens in now will find a glowing meteor lying in wait; and that we do

[5] Lit., *Qur'ān,* but here it is used in its original sense of any portion of Scripture, a Scripture lesson, not in its later sense of Muḥammad's Book as a whole.

[6] *Shuhub* could mean no more than "flaming fire," but from XXXVII, 8-10 we learn that the jinn who try to listen in to the heavenly Council are driven away by being pelted with "shooting stars," so it would seem to mean meteors.

not know whether evil is intended for those on earth or whether their Lord's intention for them is right direction; and that some of us are righteous and some otherwise, [so that] we are of diverse ways; and that we have come to the opinion that we shall never frustrate Allah on earth, nor shall we frustrate Him by fleeing; and that when we heard the guidance we believed in it. So he who believes in his Lord will fear neither deficiency nor folly.' "

Satans. XXXVII, 6-10.

We have adorned the lower heaven with an adornment of stars, and [set therein] a guard against every insolent satan. They listen not to the High Council [of the celestial powers] but are driven away from every side by being pelted, and for them is torment forever. [They learn nothing] save such as may by stealth catch a chance word, and him there pursues a shining meteor.

XXI, 81-82.

And to Solomon [We made subject] the wind as it blows tempestuously to run at his bidding to the land wherein We have set blessing, and about everything We were knowing. And of the satans there were some who would dive for him and do work other than that, while We were keeping guard over them.

XXVI, 221-226.

Shall I inform you upon whom the satans come down? They come down upon every wicked liar. They impart what they hear, but the majority of them are liars. And the poets—those who are beguiled—follow them. Dost thou not see that in every valley they wander love-distraught, and that they say what they do not do?

ON BELIEF IN ANGELS, JINN, AND SATANS

From Fakhr ad-Dīn ar-Rāzī, *Muḥaṣṣal afkār al-Mutaqaddimīn wa'l-Muta'akhkhirīn* (Cairo, 1323 A.H. = 1905 A.D.), p. 102.

The theologians say that they are subtle bodies capable of taking on various shapes. The philosophers and the early Mu'tazilites denied their existence, because, they said, if their subtlety was as that of the air they would not have power to perform any actions, and the very slightest of causes would [be sufficient to] disorder their constitutive forms. Should they, however, be denser [than air] we would assuredly be able to see them, for otherwise it might well be that there would be mountains in our presence which we do not see. The answer to them is [to ask] why their subtlety might not consist in absence of color rather than in fineness of substance. Let us admit that they have a certain density, yet it is clear that we do not necessarily have to perceive some dense thing when it is present with us. The philosophers claim that they (i.e., angels, jinn, and satans) are not spatially confined nor do they subsist in any special portion of space. Apart from that [the philosophers] differ among themselves. The majority teach that they are quiddities (*māhiyāt*) different in species from human spirits. Others among them teach that they are mortal spirits whose bodies, if they are evil, are strongly drawn to those human souls which resemble them, so that in a way they attach themselves to their bodies and thus aid them in the doing of evil deeds. Such is Satan. If they are good then the matter is the other way around.

To this aṭ-Ṭūsī in his commentary, *Talkhīṣ al-Muḥaṣṣal,* adds on the same page:

It has been handed down about the Mu'tazilites that they taught that angels, jinn, and satans are one in species but different in accordance with their varied ways of acting. Those who do nothing but good are the angels; those who do nothing but evil are the satans; and those who do sometimes the one sometimes the other are the jinn. That is why Iblīs is sometimes among the jinn, at others among angels.[1]

THE ANGELS AND THE PROPHETS

From *Ḥāshiyat al-Baijūrī 'alā Jawharat at-Tawḥīd* (Cairo, 1293 A.H. = 1876 A.D.), pp. 92, 93. The *Jawharat at-Tawḥīd* is a summary exposition in verse form of the essential beliefs of Islam by Ibrāhīm al-Laqqānī (d. 1631 A.D.), the *Ḥāshiya* being a commentary thereon by Ibrāhīm al-Baijūrī (or Bājūrī), who died in 1860 A.D. He quotes the poem half-verse by half-verse and comments thereon.

* *and after them angels of the Lord of grace* *

[The author] means that after the prophets come the angels of Allah, who is Lord of grace, so their rank comes as a whole after that of the prophets. We say "as a whole" because those who really come immediately after the prophets are the angelic chiefs, viz., Gabriel, Michael, Isrāfīl, and 'Azrā'īl, and then come the rest of the angels, for it is commonly agreed that Gabriel and Michael are far superior to the generality of angels. There was some difference of opinion as to which of these two was superior, for some said that Gabriel was the superior, and this is the prevalent opinion, though others hold that Michael is superior. Now this opinion that we have mentioned, namely, that the angelic chiefs and then the other angels come next in rank to the prophets, is the doctrine of the majority of the Ash'arites and is that which has less weight, the preponderant doctrine being that of the Māturīdites.

The Qāḍī and Abū 'Abdallah al-Ḥalīmī,[1] along with some

[1] In Sūra XX, 116/115 Iblīs (our *diabolos*) is among the angels when they were bidden to do obeisance to Adam, but in XVIII, 50/48 he is said to be of the jinn.

[1] By the Qāḍī he means al-Bāqillānī (d. 403 A.H. = 1012 A.D.), one of the most famous members of the second generation of the Ash'arite School. Al-Ḥalīmī, who also died in 403 A.H., was the author of a once-famous work, *Shu'ab al-Īmān*.

others such as the Mu'tazilites, also go so far as to say that the angels are superior to the prophets, save our Prophet—upon whom be Allah's blessing and peace—for, as we have already said, he stands outside these matters about which there is difference of opinion. These base their argument on the fact that they (i.e., the angels) are free from passions, but their opinion is refuted by the consideration that to have passions and yet master them is nearer to perfection. Said he—upon whom be Allah's blessing and peace: "The works dearest to Allah are those hardest to perform," i.e., those that cause most difficulty. As-Sa'd [2] has said: "There is no decisive proof about these rankings," and for this reason Tāj ad-Dīn as-Subkī [3] has said: "The superiority of humans over angels is not a matter it is necessary to believe, nor does ignorance about it do any harm." So the safe thing is to keep silent with regard to this question, for to enter upon a discussion of the relative superiority in the eyes of Allah of these two noble classes, without any decisive proof, is to enter upon dangerous ground indeed and to give decisions in a place where we are unfitted so to do.

Know, then, that angels are delicate bodies of light, able to take to themselves various beautiful forms. Their state is one of obedience [to Allah], their dwelling for the most part in heaven though some of them dwell on earth. They give glory [to Allah] night and day without ever becoming weary, and "they disobey not Allah in what He commands them, but do what they are bidden" (LXVI, 6). They are not to be described as male or female, so one who ascribes masculinity to them transgresses and he who ascribes femininity to them is in unbelief, since against him are the words of the Most High (XLIII, 19/18): "And they make the angels, who are servants of the Merciful, female."

[2] I.e., Sa'd b. 'Abdallah al-Wajahānī, who wrote a commentary on the credal statement of as-Sanūsī (d. 895 A.H. = 1490 A.D.).

[3] The Shāfi'ite Qāḍī in Damascus (d. 771 A.H. = 1370 A.D.), who was the author of the great book of biographies of Shāfi'ite men of learning.

** and some make distinctions when they assign superior rank **

He means some of the Māturīdites, who make a distinction between the chiefs among the angels and the generality of them and the generality of mankind when they assign ranks among the two groups. Thus they say that the prophets are superior to the angel chiefs such as Gabriel and Michael, but the angel chiefs are superior to the generality of mankind and are the patrons of all of them save the prophets, e.g., of Abū Bakr and 'Umar—with whom may Allah be pleased. Now this generality of mankind is not meant to include the transgressors, for the angels are certainly superior to them. The generality of mankind, in the sense mentioned, however, are superior to the generality of angels apart from their chief groups, such as the Throne-bearers. These are four now, but when the Day of Resurrection comes Allah will give them four others to assist them. Allah has said (LXIX, 17): "and above them eight on that Day will bear the Throne of thy Lord," in order to increase His majesty on the Day. [Another chief group is that of] the cherubs who are the angels surrounding the Throne, going constantly around it. They are so called because they obviate supplication by removing anxiety from the community.[4] Others, however, explain [this name] differently.

You have already learned that this is the prevalent view, but should someone say: "But this necessarily means that you are giving those who are not impeccable superiority over those who are impeccable," the answer is that impeccability does not enter into this matter of superiority. It is not what is being considered here, what is being considered being solely the greater amount of reward for service rendered. Now the generality of men will get a greater reward than the generality of angels, since the generality of men suffer much difficulty in

[4] This is folk etymology. The Arabic *Kārūb* represents the Hebrew word for cherub, but the author here suggests that it is derived from the Arabic root *KRB* in the meaning of "grief" or "anxiety."

their service [of Allah] in contradistinction to the generality of angels, whose natural disposition is for obedience, so that they suffer no difficulty in [serving Allah].

ANGELS AND MEN

From the *Ṣaḥīḥ* of al-Bukhārī, ed. L. Krehl (Leiden, 1862), I, 148.

'Abdallah b. Yūsuf has related to us, saying: Mālik has informed us, on the authority of Abū'z-Zinād, from al-A'raj, from Abū Huraira, that the Apostle of Allah—upon whom be Allah's blessing and peace—said: "By night and by day angels come successively to take one another's place by you. They encounter one another at dawn prayers and at the afternoon prayer. Those who have spent the night with you mount up [to heaven] and Allah asks them, though actually He knows better than they do: 'How did you leave My servants?' They answer: 'We left them as they were saying prayers, just as we came to them when they were saying prayers.' "

THE HINDRANCE THAT SATAN IS

From al-Ghazzālī's *Minhaj al-'Ābidīn* (Cairo, 1337 A.H. = 1918 A.D.), pp. 21-22.

It is your duty, O my brother Muslim, to make war on Satan and to overcome him, and that for two very good reasons. The first of them is that he is an enemy who manifestly leads astray, and there is no hope that he will be reformed or will ever spare you. Nay, rather, the fact is that he will be contented with nothing less than your complete destruction. So there is no means of being safe from such an enemy as this or of being neglected by him. Ponder now on two verses from the Book of Allah—exalted be He. One of them is His saying (XXXVI, 60): "Did I not enjoin on you, O ye children of Adam, that ye should not serve Satan, for he is a manifest enemy to you?" The second is His saying (XXXV, 6): "Verily, Satan is to you an enemy, so take him to be an enemy." No warning could possibly go further than that. The second reason is that there was given him an innate disposition to be inimical to you, so he is ever alert to make war with you, and during the watches of the night and at all hours of the day he is shooting his arrows at you while you are heedless of him. So how will the state of things be?

Then there is another point for you [to consider]. You are busied with your service of Allah, Most High, and with summoning creatures to the gate of Allah—glory be to Him—by your actions and your words, and all this is the very antithesis of Satan's work, of his efforts, his desires, his crafty schemes, so that it is as though you have taken your stand and girt your loins to provoke, to stir the rancor, and to oppose Satan. For this very reason he also is girding his loins to treat you as an enemy, to fight you, to circumvent you until he succeeds in doing some mischief. Thus it is up to you to take refuge with Allah with regard to your affair, lest he go so far as to destroy you completely. Never can you consider yourself secure on your side, for he is one who does evil to, and aims at the destruction of, even those who do not rouse his anger or go against him but who are friendly to him and agree with him, such as the unbelievers and the people of error and the people of desire in certain circumstances. [If this is how he treats them] what must be his purpose toward those who take a stand which arouses his rage and who definitely set themselves in opposition to him?

He has leave [from Allah] to indulge in general enmity against folk as a whole, but has a special enmity against you who are diligent in worship and in seeking knowledge. To him your case is one of importance, and against you he has certain helpers, the strongest among whom are your own soul and your passions. He has methods, and a way of access, and openings of which you are heedless. Yaḥyā b. Mu'ādh ar-Rāzī [1] spoke truly when he said: "Satan is unbusied while you

[1] He was a Ṣūfī master contemporary with the famous Bayāzīd al-Bisṭāmī. He died in 258 A.H. (871 A.D.) after having taught the mystical theology of the Ṣūfīs in Cairo. On him see L. Massignon, *Lexique technique* (Paris, 1954), pp. 268 ff.

are very busily engaged. Satan sees you when you do not see him. You may forget all about him but he never forgets you. In your own soul he has helpers against you, so you needs must make war against him and overcome him, otherwise you cannot be safe from corruption and destruction."

Should you ask: "With what shall I make war on Satan, and with what shall I overcome him and ward him off?", then know that for folk of our kind there are in this matter two ways. One of them is that [represented by the words of] some who have said: "The method to be followed in warding off Satan is to take refuge with Allah—glory be to Him. There is no other way, for Satan is a dog whom Allah—glory be to Him—has let loose against you, and when you busily occupy yourself making war on him and stirring yourself up against him, you grow tired and time passes, then he gets the better of you, bites bits from you, and wounds you sorely, so to turn to the Lord of the dog, that He may drive him off from you, is far preferable." The second is what others have said, namely, that the way is to take up the struggle with him, to stand up against him, rejecting him, driving him off, thwarting him.

Now my opinion is that the proper way to deal with him is to combine these two ways. Thus, first of all, you should take refuge with Allah from his evil, as He has bidden us, seeing that He is the unique protector against his evil. Then if we see him getting the upper hand over us we shall know that it is a testing from Allah, Most High, that He may see how genuine our warfare is and our steadfastness in His command—praised and exalted be He—and see how we patiently endure. It is just as when He allows the unbelievers to have authority over us, in spite of His power to deal with them and their evil, in order that we may have the happiness of [going out on] holy war (*jihād*), of showing patient endurance, of gaining forgiveness and martyrdom. It is as the Most High has said (III, 140/134): "That Allah may know those who have believed, and may take from among you martyrs." The Most High has also said (III, 142/136): "Or did ye imagine that ye would enter Paradise while Allah did not yet know those among you who strove mightily, nor know those who patiently endured?" So is it here.

Again, making war on him and overcoming him, according to what has been said by our theologians—with whom may Allah be pleased—depends on three things. The first is that you learn about and become informed of his wiles and his schemes, for then he will not dare to attack you, just as a robber flees when he knows that the master of the house is ready for him. The second is that you should disregard his invitation [to forbidden ways], letting your heart not cleave thereto, nor following him, for he is as a barking dog which you only rouse the more if you approach it but which quiets down if you turn away from it. The third is that you should keep constantly making mention of Allah—glory be to Him—with your tongue and with your heart, for [the Prophet]—upon whom be Allah's blessing and peace—has said: "The mention of Allah is to Satan's side like a canker in the side of a man."

THE JINN

From Muṣṭafā Fahmī, *Asrār al-Jinn* (Cairo, 1354 A.H. = 1935 A.D.), pp. 22-28.

We have ascertained from more than one source which we consider as reliable that the jinn are creatures whom Allah created before He created mankind. They were wandering at will on earth, lusting in their strength, when Allah, Most High, sent against them one of the celestial bands to subdue them. Then when the Most High created Adam [the chief of this band] Iblīs feared that the progeny of Adam would meet the same fate as the jinn who caused corruption, because both men and jinn are swayed by lusts, and everyone possessed of lusts may cause corruption. So the angels said—and there is a report that it was really Iblīs speaking—what is reported in Sūra II, 30/28—34/32: "When thy Lord said to the angels: 'I am going to set a vicegerent on the earth,' they replied: 'Wilt Thou set one thereon who will cause corruption therein and shed blood, whereas we sing Thy praise with glory and hallow Thee?' He said: 'I know what ye do not know.' Now He taught Adam all the names, then He presented them to the angels and said: 'Inform Me of the names of these if ye are those who speak the truth.' They answered: 'Glory be to Thee. We have no knowledge save what Thou dost teach us. Thou art the knowing, the wise!' Said He: 'O Adam, inform them of their names.' When he had informed them of their names, He said: 'Did I not say to you that I know the unseen things of the heavens and the earth, and well know both what ye show openly and what ye have been concealing?' And when He said to the angels: 'Do obeisance to Adam,' they did obeisance, all save Iblīs, who disdainfully refused, thinking himself too important, and was among the unbelievers."

So then the angels accepted guidance and were obedient to the command of their Lord, but Iblīs rebelled and became one of those respited, that is, deferred, till the Day of Judgment. Then his band began to work corruption on the earth, whispering into the breasts of men and keeping them far removed from the remembrance of Allah. It is related from Abū Huraira that Allah, Most High, created angels and jinn and men. Then He arranged them into ten groups, nine of them being angels and one being jinn and men. Then He divided up this last group into ten parts, nine of them jinn and one men. From this it can be understood that the jinn are much more widely distributed than men.

The jinn were created from smokeless fire, so they were created from something quite different from the clay of which men were created. Now if we understand that we who belong to mankind were created from clay, yet today there is not a trace of this clay visible in our bodies because it has been transformed into blood and flesh and bones, we can likewise understand how the jinn, though they were created from fire, have now become such that no trace of it is perceived in their bodies. Nevertheless, after their passing away they return to their origin, which is fire, just as man after his passing away returns to his origin, which is dust.

In any case, the bodies of the jinn resemble vapor particles, so delicate are they, and thus we do not see them. Indeed, no one can see them save those for whom the veil has been drawn, as happened in the days of our master Solomon—on whom be peace. Nevertheless they see us and hear us, and nothing intervenes between us and them save this curtain that has been drawn. These jinn transform themselves into shapes of various kinds and different forms, maybe into the form of a dog, or take wings so as to fly through the atmosphere, or they may be in the form of vipers or other such things. In the days of our master Solomon the jinn appeared in human form. Nevertheless they did not attain to full human stature save in this present age, as we may mention in its place.

It is certain that they hear, for of that we have the evidence of their listening when the Prophet—upon whom be Allah's blessing and peace—recited verses from the noble Book wherein they recognized the words of their Lord, as is told of in Sūra XLVI, 29/28, 30/29: ". . . and when We turned aside unto thee some individuals of the jinn to hearken to the Qur'ān. When they were present at it they said: 'Be ye quiet (to hear),' and when it was finished they returned to their people, giving them warning. They said: 'O our people, we have heard a Book which has been sent down later than Moses, confirming what is before it and guiding to the truth and to a straight path.' "

Now, though we agree that the jinn come in various forms such as those we have mentioned, we do not go so far as to say that they ever come in authentic human form. The way we understand it is that they only seem to transform themselves into this human form which Allah has so distinguished. They have no power of their own to transform themselves, nor is it possible for them to change their nature. Allah—glorified and exalted is He—only allows them to learn certain kinds of activity in which, if any one of them engages and speaks of it, Allah will transform him from one form to another.

When we say that by the word jinn we mean certain vaporous or airy bodies, we do not mean to say that they do not eat or drink. In the *Ṣaḥīḥ* of al-Bukhārī there is a Tradition:

"The jinn asked the Prophet—upon whom be Allah's blessing and peace—for provision, so he made supplication to Allah for them that they might never pass a bone or dung droppings without finding food therefrom." This confirms the statement of certain historians who say that at times the jinn take the form of dogs and suchlike, for dogs find pleasure in eating bones. So the Apostle of Allah—upon whom be Allah's blessing and peace—forbade the use of bones and bits of dung when wiping oneself after natural evacuations, saying: "These are the food of our brethren the jinn."

HIS BOOKS

The Muslim doctrine of scripture is naturally bound up with Muḥammad's conception of his own position as in the succession of the Biblical prophets. Many of these prophets had books of scripture in which were recorded the revelations Allah had given them in connection with their missions. Muḥammad's Qur'ān was his Scripture, but Moses also had a book, named the *Tōrah,* David a book, named the *Zabūr,* and Jesus a book, named the *Injīl.* These are all mentioned in the Qur'ān as earlier books of scripture, as are also the "sheets" (*ṣuḥuf*) of Moses and Abraham, which are "ancient sheets" (LXXXVII, 18, 19), while John the Baptist is bidden "take the book" (XIX, 12/13). Orthodox theory holds that there is in heaven the Preserved Tablet (LXXXV, 21, 22; LXXX, 13, 14; LVI, 78/77) which is called "the Mother of the Book" (XIII, 39; XLIII, 4/3); this is the celestial archetype of scripture from which, as necessity arose, material was revealed through Gabriel to the various prophets in succession. Thus scripture is really one and each successive book confirms those that preceded it, so that Muḥammad can call on the People of the Book to confirm that his message is substantially the same as that of earlier scripture.

The process of revelation is by *waḥy,* which Bell translates as "suggestion," since in XVI, 68/70 Allah *suggests* to the bees where to build their hives, and in XLI, 12/11 *suggests* to each of the seven heavens its special function, just as He *suggests* to Noah how to build the ark (XI, 37/39) and to Moses to strike the sea with his staff (XXVI, 63). This is what we mean by inspiration. Just as all through the Qur'ān it is Allah who is the speaker, so it is believed was the case with all scripture, and one finds in devotional works passages said to be quotations from earlier scriptures and even little booklets of selections from the *Tōrah,* the *Zabūr,* and the *Injīl* which closely resemble the style of the Qur'ān. With the appearance of the Qur'ān these previous scriptures, it is believed, were abrogated, and what the Jews and the Christians now have are not the original Torah of Moses and Evangel of Jesus but later productions by the hands of men. The Qur'ān itself, however, seems to assume that the real Torah and the real Evangel were in the hands of contemporary Jews and Christians.

On this doctrine of Scripture see: O. Pautz, *Muhammad's Lehre von der Offenbarung* (Leipzig, 1898); W. Goldsack, *The Qur'ān in Islam* (Madras, 1912); W. St. Clair Tisdall, *The Original Sources of the Qur'ān* (London, 1911); W. Rudolph, *Die Abhängigkeit des Korans von Judentum und Christentum* (Stuttgart, 1922); J. Henninger, *Spuren christlicher Glaubenswahrheiten im Koran* (1951); A. Jeffery, *The Qur'ān as Scripture* (New York, 1952); also Wensinck's article "Waḥy" in *EI,* IV, 1091-1093, and the articles "Indjīl," "Koran," "Tawrat," and "Zabūr" in that work.

THE SCRIPTURES IN THE QUR'ĀN

IV, 163/161-165/163.

We have given revelation to thee [O Muḥammad] just as We gave revelation to Noah and to the prophets after him. We also gave revelation to Abraham, and to Ishmael, and to Isaac, and to Jacob, and to the Tribes,[1] and to Jesus, and to Job, and to Jonah, and to Aaron, and to Solomon, while to David we gave a Psalter (*zabūr*).[2] [There were] also messengers whose stories We have told thee before, and messengers whose stories We have not told thee. And Allah spoke with Moses face to face. [They were] messengers who brought good tidings and who brought warnings that the people might have no argument against Allah after the messengers [had delivered their message]. Allah is sublime, wise.

V, 44/48-48/52.

Truly, We sent down the Torah in which is guidance and a light. By it the prophets who had submitted themselves [to

1 *Al-asbāṭ* probably means the twelve patriarchs descended from Jacob.
2 This word seems to be a corruption from the Hebrew *mizmōr,* a psalm.

Allah] gave judgment for those who became Jews, as did the rabbis and the learned by such portion as they were put in charge of from the Book of Allah and they were witnesses for it. So fear ye not the people, but fear Me, and sell not My signs at a little price. Whoso does not judge according to what Allah has sent down, such are the unbelievers. Now We ordained for them therein (i.e., in the Torah): "A life for a life, an eye for an eye, a nose for a nose, an ear for an ear, a tooth for a tooth, and for wounds retaliation," though should anyone charitably remit it, for him it is an expiation, but whoso does not judge according to what Allah has sent down, such are the wrongdoers.

And We made Jesus, son of Mary, follow in their traces, confirming what of the Torah was before him, and We gave him the Gospel, in which is guidance and a light, confirming what of the Torah was before him, and a guidance and an admonition to those who show piety. So let the people of the Gospel judge by what Allah sent down therein, for whoso does not judge according to what Allah has sent down, such are wicked transgressors. And We have sent down to thee [O Muḥammad] the Book with truth, confirming what of scripture was before it, and being a protector for it. So give judgment between them by what Allah has sent down to thee, and do not follow their desires as against the truth that has come to thee.

LIII, 35/36-42/43.

Does he have knowledge of the unseen, so that he sees?
Or has he not been told of what is in the scrolls (*ṣuḥuf*) of Moses?
And of Abraham who carried out [what he was bidden]?
How no burdened [soul] may bear the burden of another,
And that there is nothing for man save that for which he has striven,
And that what he has been striving for will one day be seen?
Then he will be recompensed with the fullest recompense.
And [has he not been told] that to thy Lord is the final coming?

VI, 154/155-157/158.

Then We gave Moses the Book, perfect for him who does well and a clear exposition of everything, and a guidance and a mercy. Perhaps they will believe in the meeting with their Lord. And this is a Book which We have sent down. [It is] a blessed thing, so follow ye it and show piety, perhaps ye may have mercy shown you, lest ye should say: "Scripture has been sent down to only two groups before us even though we were careless about studying them"; or lest ye should say: "Had we had Scripture sent down to us we should have been better guided than they are," though, indeed, clear evidence has come to you from your Lord, and a guidance and a mercy. So who does greater wrong than he who treats Allah's signs as false and turns away from them? We shall recompense those who turn from Our signs with an evil punishment because they have been turning away.

XVI, 43/45-44/46.

Before thee [O Muḥammad] We have sent none but men to whom We gave revelation—so question the People of the Reminder (i.e., those who have Scriptures) if ye do not know—with evidential signs and Scriptures. And We have sent down to thee the Reminder, that thou mayest make clear to the people what has been sent down to them, that perchance they may ponder.

VI, 91-93.

And they have not truly measured Allah's power when they say: "Allah has not sent down anything to any human." Say: "Who sent down the Book that Moses brought as a light and a guidance to the people? Ye make it parchment sheets which ye show though ye conceal much. And [by it] ye were taught what ye did not know, neither ye nor your fathers." Say: "Allah," then let them alone playing in their vain discussions.

This is a Book which We have sent down. [It is] a blessed

thing, confirming what is before it, and [sent to thee] that thou mayest warn the Mother of Cities (i.e., Mecca) and those round about it, and those who believe in the hereafter will believe in it, for they keep watch over their prayers. And who does greater wrong than one who lays a falsehood to the charge of Allah or says: "A revelation has been given to me," when nothing has been revealed to him at all, or who says: "I shall send down the like of what Allah has sent down"? Would that thou couldst see when the wrongdoers are in the pangs (lit., floods) of death, while the angels stretch out their hands [saying]: "Out with your souls! Today ye shall be recompensed with the torment of humiliation for what ye were saying untruthfully about Allah, while ye were arrogantly rejecting His signs."

III, 81/75-84/78.

And when Allah took the covenant of the prophets [saying]: "Whatever I have given you in the way of scripture or of wisdom, and then there comes to you a messenger confirming what is with you, ye are to believe in him and ye are to assist him." He said: "Do ye agree, and do ye take up My burden[3] on that condition?" They said: "We agree." Said He: "Then bear ye witness, and I am with you among those who bear witness." So whoever after that turns away, they indeed are the evildoers. Is it that they desire something other than Allah's religion? Yet to Him everyone in the heavens and on earth makes submission, willingly or unwillingly, and to Him are they made to return.

Say: "We believe in Allah and in what He has sent down to us, also in what He sent down to Abraham, and Ishmael, and Isaac, and Jacob, and the Tribes (i.e., the Patriarchs), and in what has been given to Moses and to Jesus and to the prophets from their Lord. We make no distinction between any of them, and we are submissive to Him."

[3] *Aṣrī*, which calls to mind the "burden" of the Old Testament prophets, e.g., Isa. 13:1, 15:1, 17:1, 19:1, etc.

II, 174/169-176/171.

Verily those who conceal what Allah has sent down of the Book, and thereby purchase a little gain—such take naught but fire into their bellies as food. Then on the Day of Resurrection Allah will not speak to them, nor will He clear them, but for them there shall be a painful punishment. Those are the ones who purchase error at the price of guidance, and punishment at the price of forgiveness. How patiently enduring will they be at the Fire? That is because Allah sent down the Book with the truth, so those who differ among themselves about the Book are indeed far gone in schism.

ON WHAT IS OF FAITH AS TO ALLAH'S BOOKS

From Ṭāhir al-Jazā'irī, *al-Jawāhir al-kalāmiyya* (Cairo, n.d.), pp. 17-21. This is a modern statement of belief; the author died in 1920.

It is to be believed that Allah—exalted be He—has books which He sends down to His prophets, and in which He makes clear His commands, His prohibitions, His promises, and His threats, and that they are truly the speech of Allah, having their origin from Him, though we do not know just how He spoke. These books He sent down by way of inspiration (*waḥy*), and among them are the Tōrah, the Injīl, the Zabūr, and the Qur'ān.

It is to be believed that the Tōrah is one of the books of Allah—glorious and exalted is He—which He sent down to his *kalīm* [1] Moses—upon whom be peace—doing this to make clear the religious ordinances, the genuine articles of belief which are well pleasing [to Allah], and to give the good news of the coming appearance of a prophet from among the children of Ishmael,[2] namely our Prophet—on whom be blessings and

[1] This is the special title of Moses among the prophets, meaning the one who spoke with Allah face to face.

[2] In Mingana's translation of 'Alī Ṭabarī's *Book of Religion and Empire* (Manchester, 1922), pp. 85-133, can be seen a selection of the passages of the Old Testament which Muslims claim are predictions of the coming of Muḥammad. The favorite passage is Deut. 18:18.

peace—indicating that he would bring a new divine code which would guide to the Dwelling of Peace (*Dār as-Salām*).[3]

According to the most eminent theologians, it is to be believed that the Tōrah which exists at the present time has been tampered with. One of the things which indicate this is the fact that in it is to be found no mention of Paradise or Hell, nor anything about the resurrection, the assembling [for Judgment, and the assessment of] the recompense [for good and evil], which are among the most important matters dealt with in divine Scriptures. Another indication that it has been tampered with is the fact that it mentions in its final section the death of Moses—on whom be peace—whereas the fact is that he was the one to whom it was sent down.

It is to be believed that the Zabūr is one of the books of Allah—glorious and exalted is He—which He sent down to our master David—on whom be peace—and which is a setting forth of exhortations, reminders, admonitions, and wise sayings, but has in it no religious ordinances, for David—on whom be peace—was bidden to follow the Mosaic ordinances. It is also to be believed that the Injīl is one of the books of Allah—glorious and exalted is He—which He sent down to the messiah Jesus—on whom be peace—and that was done in order to make clear what things are really true, to summon all creatures to [believe in] the unity of the Creator, to abrogate some of the ordinances of the Tōrah which had become unessential, and to give the good news of the coming appearance of the Seal of the Prophets.[4]

According to the most eminent theologians, it is to be believed that the Injīl which is at present in circulation consists of four transcripts composed by four individuals, some of whom had not even seen the Messiah—on whom be peace. These were Matthew, Mark, Luke, and John, the Gospel of

[3] This is one of the names of Paradise, derived from Sūra VI, 127.

[4] Muḥammad, according to Sūra XXXIII, 40, is the Seal of the Prophets. The favorite passage in the New Testament quoted as a prediction of the coming of Muḥammad is the Paraclete passage in John 14-16. See 'Alī Ṭabarī, *op. cit.*, p. 140.

each of whom in many points contradicts the others. The Christians also have many other gospels besides these four, but more than two hundred years after our master Jesus—on whom be peace—had been taken up to heaven they determined to suppress all save these four, in order to be rid of the numerous contradictions and to be relieved of the many opposing and conflicting statements.

It is to be believed that the Qur'ān is the noblest of the books, and that Allah—glorious and exalted is He—sent it down on the noblest of the prophets, Muḥammad—upon whom be Allah's blessing and peace. It is the last of the God-given scriptures to come down, it abrogates all the books which preceded it, and its ordinances are to remain in force till the Day of Resurrection. It is impossible for it to suffer any change or alteration, and it is the greatest sign sent to support the prophetic office of our Prophet Muḥammad—upon whom be Allah's blessing and peace—since it is the greatest of all miracles.

THE PRESERVED TABLET AT JUDGMENT

From 'Abd al-Wahhāb ash-Sha'rānī, *Mukhtaṣar at-Tadhkirah* (Cairo, 1320 A.H. = 1902 A.D.), p. 51. As Allah's chosen people, with their revelation contained in the Qur'ān, the Muslims are to be the arbiters of the fate of other communities at Judgment. In the following selection, Judgment has already commenced and the animal creation has just been disposed of.

Then there will come a call from before Allah, Most High: "Where is the Preserved Tablet?" Thereupon it will be brought in to Him in great distress, and Allah, Most High, will ask: "Where is what I wrote on you of the Tōrah, the Injīl, the Zabūr, and the Furqān?" It will answer: "O Lord, the Faithful Spirit transmitted it from me." Then Gabriel will be brought in terror-stricken and his knees all trembling, and Allah will say to him: "O Gabriel, this Tablet claims that you transmitted from it My word and My revelation (*kalāmī wa waḥyī*); is that true?" Gabriel will answer: "Yea, O Lord." Then He will say: "And what did you do with it?" He will reply: "I passed on the Tōrah to Moses, I passed on the Zabūr to David, I passed on the Injīl to Jesus, and I passed on the Furqān to Muḥammad—upon whom be Allah's blessing and peace. To each messenger I gave his message, and to those of the *ṣuḥuf*[1] I gave their sheets." Then a call will go out for Noah, and he will be brought in terror-stricken, with his knees and flanks trembling. Allah will say: "O Noah, Gabriel claims that you were one of the messengers." He will answer: "He but speaks the truth, O Lord." Then He will say: "And what did you do with regard to your people?" He will reply: "Night and day did I summon them, but my summoning increased them only in flight [therefrom]." Then a call will go out for Noah's community and they will be brought in in a single party. He will say to them: "This brother of yours, Noah, claims that he transmitted to you the message [from the Preserved Tablet]," but they will answer: "He lies, O our Lord, not a thing did he transmit to us," and they will deny the message. So Allah, Most High, will say: "O Noah, do you have any evidence?" He will answer: "Yea, O my Lord, My evidence against them is Muḥammad—upon whom be blessings and peace—and his community." They will say: "How is this, seeing that we are the first community and they are the last community?" Then the Prophet—upon whom be Allah's blessing and peace—will be called. Allah will say: "O Muḥammad, Noah here calls you as witness. Do you bear witness that he delivered his message?" Thereupon he—upon whom be Allah's blessing and peace—will recite Sūra LXXI, 1 ff.: "Verily We did send Noah to his people," etc. So Allah—mighty and majestic is He—will say to them: "You should have told the truth. 'Just is the sentence of punishment on the unbelievers'" (XXXIX, 71), and in one single group they will be ordered to the Fire. Then a herald will summon each prophet with his

[1] Cf. Sūra LXXXVII, 18, 19. Here it seems to mean the revelations earlier than the four specifically mentioned.

community in the same manner, and they will not cease coming forward community after community, while Muḥammad—upon whom be Allah's blessing and peace—and his community will give witness for them or against them [on the basis of the Qur'ān].

HIS PROPHETS

Allah's mind and will and purpose are revealed to mankind that they may know how to worship Him and how to guide their lives aright. This revelation has been set down in a formal way in the various scriptures that have been sent to mankind, each book by the hand of a messenger; but there have also been many messengers sent from Allah with oral messages. Three words are used by Muḥammad in the Qur'ān for the messengers from Allah, viz., *mursal* (envoy), *rasūl* (apostle), *nabī* (prophet), and they seem to be used interchangeably: Moses, e.g., is sometimes called a *mursal,* sometimes a *rasūl,* and sometimes a *nabī.* Muslim theology later made a distinction between the more general messengers, of whom as many as two hundred thousand are said to have been sent from Allah, and a special prophetic succession which stretches from Adam to Muḥammad, who was the last, the seal of the prophetic order. Some twenty-five of this series are mentioned in the Qur'ān by name, viz., Adam, Idrīs (Enoch), Noah, Hūd, Ṣāliḥ, Abraham, Lot, Ishmael, Isaac, Jacob, Joseph, Job, Shu'aib, Moses, Aaron, Dhū'l-Kifl, David, Solomon, Elijah, Elisha, Jonah, Zachariah, John, Jesus, Muḥammad. Whether Ezra, Luqmān, and Dhū'l-Qarnain, who are also mentioned in the Qur'ān, belong to the series is disputed. Since in such passages as LVII, 26, XXIX, 27/26, and XLV, 16/15 the gift of prophecy is expressly said to be in the family of Noah and Abraham and associated with the Israelites, attempts have been made to find Biblical correspondences for Hūd, Ṣāliḥ, Shu'aib, and Dhū'l-Kifl, but the probability is that they are ancient Arabian worthies whose legends suggested an association with the prophetic order. Each prophet, in confirmation of his mission, was given the gift of miracles; those worked by Moses and by Jesus, for example, are expressly mentioned. Muḥammad's miracle was the Qur'ān itself.

See: J. Horovitz, *Koranische Untersuchungen* (Leipzig, 1926); M. Lidzbarski, *De Propheticis quae dicuntur legendis arabicis* (Leipzig, 1893); G. Weil, *Biblische Legenden der Muselmänner* (Frankfurt, 1845); A. Geiger, *Judaism and Islam* (London, 1898); D. Sidersky, *Les Origines des légendes musulmanes dans le Coran* (Paris, 1933).

PROPHETS AND PROPHECY IN THE QUR'ĀN

X, 47/48.

Every community has [its] messenger, and when their messenger comes to them a judgment among them is given with justice, and they are not being wronged.

XVII, 15/16.

Whosoever submits to guidance submits only his own soul to the guidance, and he who goes astray leads only it astray. No burdened [soul] will bear another's burden. It has not been Our wont to punish till We have sent a messenger.

XVI, 36/38.

In every community We have raised up a messenger [to proclaim]: "Worship ye Allah and shun idolatry." Now among them were some whom Allah has guided, and among them were some for whom error was the right thing. So journey in the land and see how the final outcome was for those who counted [the message] false.

LVII, 26-27.

And, indeed, We sent Noah and Abraham, and We appointed both prophecy and scripture [to be] in their posterity. So among them [you will find] the rightly guided, though many of them are evildoers. Then We made Our messengers follow in their traces, and made Jesus son of Mary follow, to whom We gave the Evangel, and in the hearts of those who follow him We set both kindliness and mercy.

VI, 83-90.

Now that argument of Ours We gave to Abraham [to use] against his people. We raise the rank of whom We will. Verily, thy Lord is wise, knowing. And We granted to him Isaac and

Jacob, both of whom We guided; and Noah We had previously guided. And from his (i.e., Abraham's) progeny are David and Solomon and Job and Joseph and Moses and Aaron. Thus do We reward those who do well. And [later came] Zachariah and John and Jesus and Elijah, each [of whom was] of the righteous, and Ishmael and Elisha and Jonah and Lot, to each of whom We gave preference over [the rest of] mankind, and of their fathers, and their progeny, and their brethren, choosing them and guiding them to a straight path. That is Allah's guidance. He guides thereby whom He will among His servants, but should they associate [other deities with Him] of no avail to them will be what they have been doing. These are they to whom We gave scripture and judgment and prophecy, so if these disbelieve in it We have assuredly entrusted with it a people who are not such as disbelieve in it. These [above-mentioned] are those whom Allah has guided, so do thou [O Muḥammad] take their guidance as a pattern. Say: "I ask no reward from you for it; it is naught but a reminder to mankind."

WHAT IS TO BE BELIEVED ABOUT THE PROPHETS

From al-Jazā'irī's *al-Jawāhir al-kalāmiyya* (Cairo, n.d.), p. 24.

It is to be believed that Allah, Most High, has messengers whom He sent as a mercy from Himself and a grace. They were [sent in order] to give good tidings of reward to such as do good, and to warn those who do ill of coming punishment. They were to make clear to people all they had need to know of what was befitting in religion and in secular life, and to make specific to them those things whereby they would attain the highest ranks [in the hereafter]. He aided them by clearly apparent signs and by splendid miracles. The first of [the prophet series] was Adam, and the last of them was our Prophet, Muḥammad—upon whom be Allah's blessing and peace.

THE IMPECCABILITY OF THE PROPHETS

From al-Juwainī, *Kitāb al-Irshād,* ed. J. D. Luciani (Paris, 1938), pp. 204-205. The word translated "impeccability," *'iṣma,* is derived from a root meaning "to preserve, to keep safe." In the case of the prophets it means their being kept safe from sin.

Should anyone say: "Demonstrate to us the impeccability of the prophets and what must necessarily [be ascribed] to them," we answer [as follows]. That they should be impeccable is necessary to prevent there being anything to contradict what is indicated by the miracle. This is something we know by our own reason. Now what is indicated by the miracle is their trustworthiness in what they transmit [to men from Allah]. Should someone ask: "Is it necessary [to believe that] they were preserved from acts of disobedience?", we reply: [If you are thinking of] acts of turpitude such as would lead to a fall, or [show that they had but] little religion, then necessarily [we must believe] that the prophets were preserved from such acts, as is unanimously agreed on [by Muslims]. This is not something shown by reason, reason only testifying that they must necessarily be preserved from anything that would contradict what is indicated by the miracle. As for those sins which are counted as venial, and which we shall later explain in detail, reason does not deny [that prophets may have committed] them, and in my opinion there is no decisive proof that has come down either to deny such or to affirm them. Decisive proofs would have to be either such as are textually reported or have the unanimous consent [of Muslims]. Now there is no unanimous consent (*ijmā'*), since the theologians differ from one another as to whether or not venial sins may be ascribed to the prophets, and there just do not exist any textual reports whose origins may be determined decisively and whose meaning admits of no alternative interpretation. Should someone ask: "If the question then is one of opinion, what in your judgment is the most probable opinion?", we reply: In our judgment the most probable opinion is that [venial sins] are possible [in their case], since stories of the prophets recounted in verses in the Book of Allah—exalted be He—testify to that. But Allah knows best what [the real truth of the matter is].

IBN KHALDŪN ON PROPHECY

From the *Muqaddima* of Ibn Khaldūn (el-Mahdī edition; Cairo, 1930), pp. 77-79.

Be it known to you that Allah—glory be to Him—has [at various times] chosen individuals from among mankind whom He has honored by Himself speaking to them to mold them according to His understanding, and to make them the mediators between Himself and His servants. As a result, they teach men what things are for their betterment, urging them to take the right path and laboring to hold them back from Hell Fire by pointing out to them the way of escape. Now part of the knowledge He gives them of wondrous things, and the extraordinary information He reveals by way of their tongues, is that which has to do with matters hidden from mankind and to knowledge of which there is no way save [as that is given] by Allah through the mediation of these men, for they cannot know about them unless Allah instructs them. Said he —upon whom be Allah's blessing and peace: "Is it not the truth that I know nothing save what Allah has taught me?"

Be it also known to you that the information they bring in this way is characteristically and necessarily veracious, as will be made clear to you when you clearly understand the real nature of prophecy. One of the characteristic marks of men of this class is that when receiving revelation (*waḥy*) they are rapt away from those present with them and groan [in physical distress] as if to the outward eye this were a fainting fit or a swoon. It is, however, not in the least either of these things, but in reality only their being overcome by meeting with the angel from the spiritual world, perceiving what is befitting them but which is entirely beyond the perception of men. Then [what they are experiencing] resolves itself into what is [within the range of] human perception, either the hearing of speech sounds which they understand, or seeing the form of some individual appearing and addressing to them a message brought from Allah. Then they come out of that state [of rapture], keeping in mind, however, what Allah has given them. Said he—upon whom be Allah's blessing and peace—when he was asked about revelation: "Sometimes he comes to me like the tinkling of a bell, which is the most distressful for me, but then he departs from me and I remember what he said. Sometimes the angel takes for me the form of a man who speaks with me, and I keep in mind what he says." While this is happening [the prophet] may be subject to distress and to such groaning as cannot be described. In the Traditions there is much that treats of this distress during the reception of a revelation. 'Ā'isha has said: "Revelation would come down upon him on a very cold day, yet when it departed from him his forehead would be dripping with perspiration." The Most High said (LXXIII, 5): "We are going to cast on thee a weighty discourse." It was because of this state [into which they were thrown] at the coming of revelation that the polytheists used to charge the prophets with being possessed by jinn,[1] and say: "He has a familiar or a follower from among the jinn," but that only shows that they were deceived by what they saw of the external manifestations of the state, and [as Allah has said] (XIII, 33): "Whom Allah sends astray, for him there is no guidance."

Another of their characteristic marks is that before the coming of revelation to them they were all found to be naturally good and sagacious, such men as shun blameworthy actions and all things unclean. This is the meaning of their impeccability (*'iṣma*). Thus they seem to have an instinctive inclination to rise above things that are blameworthy, and even

[1] Ibn Khaldūn is thinking here of the accounts of the prophets in the Qur'ān, where both Noah and Moses are specifically said to have been called "jinn-possessed" by their contemporaries as Muḥammad was by his, and Sūra LI, 52 says that no messenger ever came to a people but they said he was jinn-possessed.

shrink from them as though such things were repugnant to their inborn disposition. . . . Also among their characteristic marks is the fact that wondrous signs (*khawāriq*) are wrought by their hands as testimony to their truthfulness. These are deeds the like of which are beyond human capacity, for which reason they are called miracles (*mu'jizāt*),[2] since they are not in the class of things of which men are capable but fall outside their abilities.

Folk differ as to how they happen and how they bear testimony to the truthfulness of the prophet. The scholastic theologians (*mutakallimūn*), relying on belief in a free agent, teach that they happen by the power of Allah, not by the act of the prophet, and even if, as the Mu'tazilites hold, they are human actions emanating from them (i.e., from the prophets), yet the miracle does not belong to the class of things they perform. The other scholastic theologians teach that all the prophet has to do with them is to make the challenge[3] by Allah's permission. That is, the prophet, before their happening, asks that by them testimony be given to the truth of the claims he makes, then when they happen they are just the same as an explicit statement from Allah that the prophet is speaking veraciously. In such a case their testimony to his veracity is completely convincing, so the miracle bears testimony both to the wonder (*khāriq*) and to the challenge, and the challenge is thus part of it. This challenging is, according to the theologians, what distinguishes miracles from both thaumaturgy (*karāma*) and magic (*siḥr*).[4]

[2] *'ajz* is "inability," so a *mu'jiza* is something outside man's normal abilities. The other word *Khawāriq* is related to a root meaning "to make a hole in," so they are wonders which violate the normal course of things.

[3] I.e., he challenges his audience to perform the like, as in the Qur'ān (LII, 34; XI, 13/16; X, 38/39) Muḥammad challenges the Meccans to produce any revelation like his.

[4] *Karāmāt* are also properly miracles, but they are the miracles associated not with prophets but with saints. Magic is mentioned here because in the Qur'ān we read how the miracles performed by the messengers who came with Allah's message to their peoples were commonly discounted as works of *siḥr*.

THE PROPHET STORIES

Since Muḥammad, in the belief of his followers, is the Seal of the Prophets, i.e., the last member of a prophetic order, there has quite naturally been a considerable interest among Muslims in the labors of his predecessors in this task of making known to mankind the will and purpose of Allah. In the Qur'ān (XL, 78) we find Allah saying to Muḥammad: "The stories of some of them We have recounted to thee, but of some We have not." Generally the commentators, in explaining passages in which earlier prophets are mentioned, will give some account of their lives and labors, and the historians, such as aṭ-Ṭabarī (d. 311 A.H. = 923 A.D.), who tell of world history from the creation up to the coming of Muḥammad, naturally include accounts of the prophets who have been successively sent by Allah to the various communities. There grew up, however, a special genre of devotional literature which concerned itself with the pious elaboration of these prophetic histories (*qiṣaṣ al-anbiyā'*), in much the same way as the hagiographical literature dealt with the lives of the saints and Ṣūfī masters. The most famous works of this kind are the *'Arā'is al-Majālis* of ath-Tha'labī (b. 427 A.H. = 1035 A.D.), of which there are numerous Arabic editions and adaptations in Persian, Turkish, Urdu, and Malay, and the *Qiṣaṣ al-Anbiyā'* of al-Kisā'ī, another writer of the fifth century A.H. which has been edited by I. Eisenberg, *Vita (sic) Prophetarum auctore Muḥammad ben 'Abdallah al-Kisā'ī* (Lugduni Batavorum [Leiden], 1922-23).

THE LAST DAY

Under this article is included the whole eschatology of Islam, for just as Islam has its own account of the beginning of all things in its creation story, so it has its own peculiar account of the consummation of all things, its doctrine of the Last Things. This includes its account of Death and the Grave, the events leading up to the Last Day, the Resurrection of the Dead, the Grand Assizes for a Final Judgment, and the passing on from Judgment to one's final destiny either in Paradise or Hell. Two things make the eschatology of Islam of unusual interest. The first is the way in which material of varied provenance has been worked into a system in Islam, partly by the Prophet himself, but to a large extent by the theologians of later times. The second is the fact that in its final form this Muslim eschatology from the ninth century on began to exercise in its turn a quite extraordinary influence on eschatological thought both in Europe, as is evident in Dante's *Divina Commedia,* and in Asia even as far as China.

The roots of this eschatological teaching are of course in the Qur'ān, but the doctrine was expanded in the Traditions and then worked out in detail in very numerous little popular eschatological tractates.

All the standard treatises on Islamic theology have a section on eschatology, but there is more particular discussion in the relevant articles in *EI,* and in: F. A. Klein, *Religion of Islam* (London, 1906), pp. 80-96; M. Wolff, *Muhammedanische Eschatologie* (Leipzig, 1872); L. Gauthier, *Ad-Dourra al-fakhira: traité d'eschatologie musulmane* (Geneva, 1878). For the influence on East and West see: Miguel Asin, *La escatologia musulmana en la Divina Commedia* (Madrid, 1943); E. Cerulli, *Il Libro della Scala* (Roma, 1949); J. J. L. Duyvendak, *A Chinese Divina Commedia* (Leiden, 1952).

THE DAY OF JUDGMENT IN THE QUR'ĀN

CI, 1-11/8.

The Striker!
What is the Striker?
And what will teach thee what the Striker [1] is?
On a Day when people will be like scattered moths,
And the mountains will be like carded wool.
As for him whose balances weigh heavy,
He shall be in a life well pleasing.
But as for him whose balances weigh light,
Hāwiya [2] will be his mother.
And what will teach thee what it is?
[It is] a scorching fire.

LXXXII, 1-19.

When the heavens shall be rent asunder,
And when the stars shall be dispersed,
And when the seas shall be commingled,
And when the graves shall be upturned,

[1] *al-Qāri'a* is the fem. of the active participle of the verb "to strike." It is sometimes translated "adversity" and is one of the names of the Last Day.

[2] A word about whose meaning there has been much dispute. It is a name for Hell, or perhaps for a particular section thereof.

A soul will know what it has sent forward and kept back.
O man, what has led thee away from thy generous Lord?
Who created thee and formed thee and shaped thee rightly,
Building thee up in such form as He willed?
Nay, indeed, but ye count the judgment as something false,
Yet over you, indeed, are guardians,
Noble ones, those who write.
They know what ye do.
Verily, the righteous [shall be] in delight,
While the wicked assuredly [will be] in Jaḥīm,[3]
Where they will roast on the Judgment Day,
And they may not be absent therefrom.
What will teach thee what the Day of Judgment is?
Again, what will teach thee what the Day of Judgment is?
It is a Day when no soul will avail aught for another soul, but the matter on that Day will be with Allah.

LXIX, 13-37.

So when one single blast will be blown on the Trump,
And the earth and the mountains will be borne away, and both of them crushed [to dust] at a single crushing,
On that Day will come that which must inevitably come.
The heaven will be cleft asunder, for on that Day it will be fragile,
And the angels will be at its edges, and above them eight on that Day will bear the Throne of thy Lord.
On that Day ye will be presented [before Him], not one of your hidden deeds being concealed.
As for him who is given his book (i.e., his record) in his right hand, he will say: "Take ye, read my book.
I, indeed, always thought I should meet with my reckoning."
He shall be in a pleasing life,
In a lofty garden
Whose fruit clusters are near at hand [while the angels say]:
"Eat and drink with relish [as recompense] for what ye paid for in advance in days that are past."
But as for him who is given his book in his left hand, he will say: "Oh, would that I had not been given my book,
And had never known what my reckoning was.
Oh, would that [death] had been my finishing.
My wealth has not profited me,
My authority has perished from me."

[3] One of the names of Hell, or of a section thereof.

[The angels will say]: "Seize him and fetter him,
Then into a chain whose length is seventy cubits thrust him."
For he used not to believe in Allah, the Mighty One,
Nor stir up [folk] to feed the unfortunate,
So he has not here today any friend,
And no food save *Ghislīn*,[4]
Which none but the sinners eat.

LVI, 1-56.

When that which must inevitably come has come,
[And] as to its coming there is no falsity,
[A coming which will cause] abasing [for some and for others] exalting.
When the earth will be shaken a shaking,
And the mountains will be pounded a pounding,
So that they become as scattered dust,
Then ye will be three groups.
The Companions of the Right Hand, what are the Companions of the Right Hand?
And the Companions of the Left Hand, what are the Companions of the Left Hand?
And those who have precedence, those who have precedence,
They are those who are brought near
In gardens of delight,
Quite a number from the former generations,
And a few from the latter,
On couches inlaid [with jewels]
On which they will recline facing one another,
While around them circle immortal celestial youths (*wildān*)
With goblets and ewers and a cup from a flowing spring,
From which they will suffer no headache nor will they become intoxicated,
Also with such fruits as they may choose,
And such flesh of fowl as they may desire.
And large-eyed celestial damsels (*ḥūrīs*)
Like unto hidden pearls,
A reward for what they have been doing.

[4] A word of unknown origin, perhaps a made-up word, like *Ghassāq* in XXXVIII, 57 and LXXVIII, 25. Both are described as the food of the Damned, and 'Abdallah b. 'Umar reported a Tradition that, were a bucket of it dropped on this world, the stench would make life unbearable all the way from the East to the West.

Therein they will hear neither inconsiderate language nor accusation,
But only the saying: "Peace! Peace!"
The Companions of the Right Hand, what are the Companions of the Right Hand?
Among thornless *sidra* trees
And *ṭalḥ* [5] trees heavy with fruit,
And extended shade,
And flowing waters,
And abundant fruit,
Never cut off (i.e., never failing) and never forbidden,
And high-raised mattresses.[6]
We, indeed, have produced them (i.e., the damsels) a special creation,
For We have made them ever virgin,
Beloved ones, of equal age,
For the Companions of the Right Hand,
Quite a number from the former generations,
And quite a number from the latter.
But the Companions of the Left Hand, what are the Companions of the Left Hand?
[They] are amid scorching winds (*samūm*) and boiling water (*ḥamīm*),
And shadow from black smoke,
Neither cool nor agreeable.
They were, indeed, before that living bountifully,
But they were persisting in great wickedness.
They were saying:
"Can it be that when we are dead and have become dust and bones, we are then to be raised?
And our fathers also, [those of] the former generations?"
Say: "Both the former and the latter generations
Will be gathered together to the meeting place of a well-known Day.
Then ye, O ye erring ones, who treat [the message] as false,
Ye will assuredly eat from a tree, even from *Zaqqūm*,[7]

[5] The *sidra* is said to be the lote tree and the *ṭalḥ* a species of acacia.

[6] *Furush* is the pl. of *firāsh*, a sleeping mat or mattress, but it is used metaphorically for a wife, so some translate here "and damsels on lofty couches."

[7] This tree of the infernal regions is mentioned also in XXXVII, 62/60 and XLIV, 43 as providing food for the Damned which is as hot in their insides as molten lead.

Filling [your] bellies therefrom,
And then drink upon it the hot water (*ḥamīm*),
Drinking [as avidly] as drinks a thirst-crazed camel.
This will be their banquet on the Day of Judgment."

ON JUDGMENT DAY

From the Arabic text in Hottinger's *Historia Orientalis* (1660), pp. 418-421, a statement which is largely made up of phrases from the Qur'ān.

[It is to be believed] that the Hour is coming, a thing about which there can be no doubt, and that Allah will assuredly raise the dead from their tombs. Just as He created them will they be brought back. Also Allah—glory be to Him—will double the good deeds [recorded to the merit] of His believing servants, will condone their mortal sins if they repent, and will forgive their venial sins if they abstain from mortal sins. Yet Allah will not forgive the associating of anyone with Him (*shirk*), though He will forgive anything short of that to whom He wills. Likewise [it is to be believed] that those He punishes in His Fire He will withdraw therefrom because of their faith and will make them enter Paradise, that whosoever has wrought an atom's weight of good will see it, as also whosoever has wrought an atom's weight of evil. It is by the intercession of His Prophet Muḥammad that there will be withdrawn from it those of his community for whom he intercedes who may have committed mortal sins.

[It is to be believed] that Allah—glory be to Him—has created Paradise and has prepared it as an eternal dwelling for His saints whom He will honor there by a vision of His face. This is the same Paradise from which His Prophet and vicegerent Adam fell to the earth, in accordance with what He had foreknown. He has also created Hell for those who disbelieve in Him. [It is to be believed] that Allah—exalted be He—will bring on the Resurrection Day and set the angels in ranks for the confrontation of the peoples, holding a reckoning with them and assigning rewards and penalties, that the balances will be set up for weighing the works of men and those whose balance weighs heavy will be those who prosper. All will be given their record sheets, and he who receives his book in his right hand will be given an easy reckoning, but those who are given their book behind their backs will roast in as-Sa'īr. [It is to be believed] that the Bridge is real, and men will have to cross according to their works, those who are saved differing in the speed of their safe crossing over the fires of Gehenna, but some will perish thereon because of their works.

THE SIGNS WHICH PRECEDE THE HOUR

In Judaism, Zoroastrianism, and Christianity, as is well known, there are accounts of various signs which will appear visibly before men whereby they may know that the Last Day is drawing very near. In Islamic eschatology also, though no one save Allah knows just when the Hour will be, there are accounts of the signs which will indicate that it is approaching. Various lists of these are given, that which we translate here being a famous set of Traditions from the *Sunan* of Abū Dāwūd (Tāzī edition; Cairo, 1348 A.H. = 1929 A.D.), II, 212.

Mu'ammil b. Hishām has related to us, on the authority of Ismā'īl, from Abū Ḥayyān at-Taimī, from Abū Zur'a, who said: Some folk came to Marwān in Madīna and listened to him relating Traditions about these signs, how that the first of them would be [the appearance of] ad-Dajjāl.[1] [When I heard about this] I went to 'Abdallah b. 'Amr and told him. 'Abdallah said: He knows nothing about it. I heard the Apostle of Allah—upon whom be Allah's blessing and peace—say that the first sign to appear would be the rising of the sun from the place of its setting, or the Beast coming upon the people in the forenoon, and whichever of them it was that came first the other would follow right after it. 'Abdallah was one of those who read scripture, and he said: My opinion is that the first of them to show itself will be the rising of the sun from its place of setting.

[1] The False Messiah, who will work miracles and perform wonders and deceive many, pretending that he is the Lord. Jesus will be sent down to earth again from heaven to put an end to him.

Musaddad and Hannād have related to us much the same thing. Musaddad said: Abū'l-Aḥwaṣ has related to us on the authority of Furat al-Qazzāz, from 'Āmir b. Wāthila, and Hannād related from Abū'l-Fuḍail, from Ḥudhaifa b. Asyad al-Ghifārī, who said: We were sitting talking in the shade of the chamber of the Apostle of Allah—upon whom be Allah's blessing and peace—and when we made mention of the Hour our voices rose, so the Apostle of Allah—upon whom be Allah's blessing and peace—said: "The Hour will not come till ten preliminary signs have been fulfilled, viz., the rising of the sun from its place of setting, the appearance of the Beast,[2] the coming of Gog and Magog,[3] of ad-Dajjāl, of Jesus son of Mary, and the smoke,[4] and three eclipses,[5] an eclipse in the West, an eclipse in the East, and an eclipse in the Arabian peninsula. After that a fire will break out in the Yemen, from the hollow of Aden, and will drive all men to the place of assembling [where they wait for Judgment]."

Aḥmad b. Abī Shu'aib al-Ḥarrānī has related to us, on the authority of Muḥammad al-Fuḍail, from 'Ammāra, from Abū Zur'a, from Abū Huraira, that the Apostle of Allah—upon whom be Allah's blessing and peace—said: "The Hour will not come till the sun arises from the place of its setting, so when it does arise there and folk see it, whoever is present will believe, but that is a time when believing will not profit any soul that has not believed before or earned some good by its belief."

2 This is said to be an enormous beast, made up of parts of many beasts, which will come forth from a cleft on Mt. Ṣafā near Mecca and will brand all men on their faces so that it will be visibly apparent who are believers and who not.

3 These barbarian hosts will break through the barrier Alexander the Great set up against them (Sūra XVIII, 93/92-99) and cause great destruction and distress until Allah, at the intercession of Jesus, sends destruction on them. The Descent of Jesus is thus to end the troubles caused by both the False Messiah and the hosts of Gog and Magog.

4 This dense smoke will cover the earth for a period of days.

5 *Khusūf,* which some say means not "eclipses" but "earthquakes."

THE MAHDĪ

From the *Sunan* of Abū Dāwūd (Tāzī edition; Cairo, 1348 A.H. = 1929 A.D.) II, 207-208.

Though the Mahdī of the Sudan is the figure most familiar to the English-speaking world, there have been many impostors during the course of Muslim history who have announced themselves as the expected Mahdī and gained a following in various Muslim countries. In many ways the expectation of the coming of the Mahdī is the Islamic equivalent of the expectation of a coming messiah or deliverer. There is no reference to any such person in the Qur'ān, nor is there in the earliest strata of Tradition, nor in the earliest creeds. Some famous Muslims, such as Ibn Khaldūn, have rejected with scorn the Mahdī-expectation. Among Shī'ites the twelfth Imām, who "went into occultation" in 265 A.H. (878 A.D.), is expected to appear again some day as the Mahdī. Among Sunnī Muslims his appearance is invariably associated with the signs which announce the near approach of the Hour.

On the Mahdī see, besides the articles by Macdonald in *EI,* III, 111-115, and Margoliouth in Hastings' *Encyclopedia of Religion and Ethics,* VIII, 336-340, the older studies of James Darmesteter, *Le Mahdi, depuis les origines de l'Islam jusqu'à nos jours* (Paris, 1887), and C. Snouck Hurgronje, *Der Mahdi,* reprinted in his *Verspreide Geschriften* (Bonn, 1923), I, 147-181.

'Ubaidallah has related to us from Faṭar, from 'Āṣim, from Zirr, from 'Abdallah that the Apostle of Allah—upon whom be Allah's blessing and peace—said: "Were only one day of this duration remaining, Allah would lengthen that day till He could send therein a man from me or from the people of my house, whose name will correspond to my name, and his father's name to that of my father,[1] who will fill the earth with justice and equity as it has been filled with injustice and oppression." In Sufyān's version of this Tradition he said: "This world will not pass away, or will not come to an end, till there rule over the Arabs a man from the people of my house whose name will correspond to my name." Saith Abū Dāwūd: Abū Bakr and 'Umar used the same wording as Sufyān.

[1] I.e., his name will be Muḥammad and his father's name 'Abdallah.

'Uthmān b. Abī Shaiba has related to us, on the authority of al-Faḍl b. Dukain, from Faṭar, from al-Qāsim b. Abī Bazza, from Abū'ṭ-Ṭufail, from 'Ali—with whom may Allah be pleased—that the Prophet—upon whom be Allah's blessing and peace—said: "Were there remaining but one day of the duration of all time, Allah would send forth a man from the people of my house, who will fill the earth with equity as it has been filled with oppression." Aḥmad b. Ibrāhīm has related to us, on the authority of 'Abdallah b. Ja'far ar-Raqqī, from Abū'l-Malīḥ al-Ḥasan b. 'Umar, from Ziyād b. Bayyān, from 'Ali b. Nufail, from Sa'īd b. al-Musayyib, from Umm Salama, who said that she had heard the Apostle of Allah—upon whom be Allah's blessing and peace—say: "The Mahdī will be of my kinsfolk from the sons of Fāṭima." . . . Sahl b. Tamām b. Bazī' has related to us, on the authority of 'Imrān al-Qiṭṭān, from Qatāda, from Abū Naḍra, from Abū Sa'īd al-Khudrī, that the Apostle of Allah—upon whom be Allah's blessing and peace—said: "The Mahdī [will be descended] from me, bald on the forehead, hook-nosed, who will fill the earth with justice and equity as it has been filled with injustice and oppression. He will reign seven years."

Muḥammad b. al-Muthannā has related to us, on the authority of Mu'ādh b. Hishām, who said: My father related to me from Qatāda, from Ṣāliḥ Abū'l-Khalīl, from a friend of his, from Umm Salama the Prophet's wife, that he—upon whom be Allah's blessing and peace—said: "There will be disagreement after the death of a certain caliph. Then a man of the people of Madina will go forth, fleeing to Mecca, and some of the people of Mecca will come to him and against his will they will lead him forth and swear fealty to him between the *rukn* and the *maqām*.[2] A troop will be sent toward him from Syria, but the earth will swallow them up at al-Baiḍā' between Mecca and Madina. When the people see that, then there will come

2 The *rukn* is the corner on the quadrangular Ka'ba at Mecca in which the Black Stone is set, and the *Maqām* is the separate structure somewhat to the north of it named the *Maqām Ibrāhīm*.

from Syria the *abdāl*[3] and the chief men from the people of Iraq, and they too will swear fealty to him between the *rukn* and the *maqām*. Then there will rise up a man from the Quraish whose maternal uncles are of the tribe of Kalb, who will send a band against them, but they will overcome them. Now that expedition of Kalb and the failure will be for one who has never seen booty from Kalb so he will divide up the wealth and will act among the people according to the custom (*sunna*) of their Prophet—upon whom be Allah's blessing and peace. By his course he will spread Islam in the earth, and he will remain seven years, after which he will die and the Muslims will pray over him." Saith Abū Dāwūd: Some report from Hishām [that his stay will be] nine years, but others say seven years.

PREDESTINATION

Orthodox Islam teaches the absolute predestination of both good and evil, that all our thoughts, words and deeds, whether good or evil, were foreseen, foreordained, determined and decreed from all eternity, and that everything that happens takes place according to what has been written for it. There was great discussion among the early Muslim theologians as to free will and predestination, but the free-will parties (*al-qadariyya*) were ultimately defeated, and a Tradition has even been put in the mouth of the Prophet: "The Qadariyya have been cursed by the tongues of seventy prophets" (as-Suyūṭī, *al-Jāmi' aṣ-ṣaghīr*, No. 7258). Since such a doctrine seems to inpugn both the justice and the mercy of Allah, the orthodox theologians have been much exercised to explain how absolute predestination is consonant with the Divine justice and mercy, and how under such circumstances a man's acts can be termed sinful so as to call for repentance and need forgiveness. The favorite solution is a doctrine of *iktisāb*, according to which, though each individual action is foreordained, the individual "acquires" it by identifying him-

[3] Lit., "the proxies" and so here may merely mean the representatives from Syria, but the word occurs in Traditions about Muḥammad telling of forty saintly Muslims who dwell in Syria, Traditions made much of by the Ṣūfī writers. See the article "Abdāl" in *EI*, I, 67.

self with it in action and so becomes responsible. (See the articles *Ḳaḍā', Ḳadar,* and *Kasb* in *EI,* II, 603-605, 785-786.) The Prophet himself seems to have expressed himself more and more definitely on this issue of predetermination as his mission proceeded, and there are no real grounds for supposing that such utterances on his part represent merely a "hang-over" from a certain strain of fatalism in the thought of pagan Arabia.

See A. de Vlieger, *Matériaux pour servir à l'étude de la doctrine de la Prédestination dans la théologie musulmane* (Leyde, 1903); F. L. Bakker, *De Verhouding tusschen de almacht Gods en de zedelijke verantwoordelijkheid van den Mensch in den Islam* (Amsterdam, 1922); A. J. Wensinck, *The Muslim Creed* (Cambridge, 1932), Index, s.v. "Predestination"; F. Ulrich, *Die Vorherbestimmungslehre im Islam und Christentum* (Gütersloh, 1912); H. Ringgren, *Studies in Arabian Fatalism* (Upsala, 1955).

PREDESTINATION IN THE QUR'ĀN

IX, 51.

Say, Nothing will ever befall us save what Allah has written for us. He is our Patron, so let the believers put their trust in Allah.

VII, 178/177-179/178.

He whom Allah guides is he who is rightly guided, but whom He leads astray, those are the losers. Indeed, We have assuredly created for Gehenna many of both jinn and men. They have hearts with which they do not comprehend, they have eyes with which they do not see, they have ears with which they do not hear. Such are like cattle; nay, they are even further astray. Such are the heedless ones.

XXXVI, 7/6-10/9.

Verily the sentence comes true on most of them, so they will not believe. We, indeed, have set shackles on their necks which reach to the chins so that they perforce hold up [their heads]. And We have set a barrier in front of them, and a barrier behind them, and We have covered them over so that they do not see. Thus it is alike to them whether thou warn them or dost not warn them; they will not believe.

XXXII, 13.

Had We so willed We should have brought every soul its guidance, but true is that saying of Mine: "I shall assuredly fill up Gehenna with jinn and men together."

XVII, 13/14.

And We have fastened every man's bird [of fate] on his neck, and on the Day of Resurrection We shall produce for him a book which he will meet spread wide open.

ON PREDESTINATION AND THE DECREE

From As-Suyūṭī, *Al-La'ālī al-maṣnū'a* (Cairo, 1317 A.H. = 1899 A.D.), I, 131-132.

'Abd ar-Raḥmān b. Aḥmad al-Anṣārī has related to us on the authority of 'Abdallah b. Muḥammad b. 'Abd al-'Azīz, from Dāwūd b. Rushd, from Yaḥyā b. Zakariyā', from Mūsā b. 'Uqba, from Abū'z-Zubair, from Ja'far b. Muḥammad, from his father, from his grandfather, who said: While we were sitting in company with the Apostle of Allah—upon whom be Allah's blessing and peace—and a group of his Companions, Abū Bakr and 'Umar entered through one of the gates of the mosque. With them was quite a large body of people disputing with loud voices, the one contradicting the other, till they came to the Apostle of Allah—upon whom be Allah's blessing and peace. Said he: "What is it you are disputing about that causes you to raise your voices so and make such a clamor?" "It is about the decree," they answered. "Abū Bakr asserts that Allah decrees good but does not decree evil, but 'Umar says that He decrees both alike." Said the Apostle of Allah—upon whom be Allah's blessing and peace: "Shall I not decide among you over this with the decision Isrāfīl [the archangel] gave between [his fellow archangels] Gabriel and

Michael?" "Did Gabriel and Michael discuss such a thing?" someone asked. He replied: "By Him who sent me with the truth, they were the very first creatures to discuss it. Gabriel took the position of 'Umar, but Michael took that of Abū Bakr. Said Gabriel: 'If we two differ about it, will not the inhabitants of heaven also come to differ? Is there not some judge who will give a decision between us?' So they requested Isrāfīl to be the judge, and he gave a decision between them which is my decision between you." "O Apostle of Allah," they said, "what was his decision?" "It was," he replied, "that the decree necessarily determines all that is good and all that is evil, all that is harmful and all that is beneficial, all that is sweet and all that is bitter, and that is my decision between you." Then he slapped Abū Bakr on the shoulder, and said: "O Abū Bakr, if Allah Most High had not willed that there be disobedience, He would not have created the Devil." Said Abū Bakr: "I seek pardon from Allah. I slipped and stumbled, O Apostle of Allah, but never again will I fall into error about this matter," nor did he till he was called to meet Allah.

From Muslim, *Ṣaḥīḥ* ('Alī Ṣubeiḥ edition; Cairo, n.d.), VIII, 44.

It may be that one of you will be performing the works of the people of Paradise, so that between him and Paradise there is the distance of only an arm's length, but then what is written (i.e., decreed) for him overtakes him, and he begins to perform the works of the people of Hell, into which he will go. Or maybe one of you will be performing the works of the people of Hell, so that between him and Hell there is the distance of only an arm's length, but then what is written for him will overtake him, and he will begin to perform the works of the people of Paradise, into which he will go.

From Abū Ḥanīfa, *Musnad* (Cairo, 1328 A.H. = 1910 A.D.), p. 5.

Said the Apostle of Allah—upon whom be Allah's blessing and peace: "There is no soul but Allah has written its entrance and its exit and what it will meet." He was asked:

"Then what is the point in acting, O Apostle of Allah?" He answered: "Go on acting, for everyone is inclined to that for which he was created. If he is for Paradise, he will be inclined to the works of the people of Paradise, and if he is for the Fire he will be inclined to the works of the people of the Fire."

From al-Malaṭī, *Kitāb at-Tanbīh,* ed. Sven Dedering (Istanbul, 1946), pp. 104-106.

Said Ibn 'Abbās: Allah extracted the progeny of Adam from his loins [at the time He was creating him] in the form of tiny particles, and said to each: "O So-and-So, act thus and thus. O So-and-So, take this and that." Then He took up one portion in His right hand and another portion in His left hand, and said to those in His right hand: "Enter Paradise in security," and to those in His other hand He said: "Enter Hell, and it is no care of Mine." Ibn 'Umar has related that the Prophet said: "The first thing Allah—majestic be His name—created was the Pen, which He took in His right hand, though both His hands are right hands, and wrote [concerning] this present world and all that there is to be in it." Rāfi' b. Khadīj tells how he asked the Apostle of Allah—upon whom be Allah's blessing and peace—what he should believe about predestination, and the Prophet answered: "You are to believe in Allah alone, that He has no partner, and that no one shares control with Him over what is harmful and what is beneficial. You are also to believe in Heaven and Hell, knowing that Allah created them before He created any creatures, and that when He did create creatures He appointed whom of them He willed for Heaven and whom He willed for Hell, that being pure equity on His part."

From the *Ṣaḥīḥ* of al-Bukhārī, ed. L. Krehl (Leiden, 1862), I, 342-343.

'Alī said: We were one day at a funeral in the Baqī' al-Gharqad, when the Prophet—upon whom be Allah's blessing and peace—came and sat, and we sat around him. He had with him a staff and he bowed his head and began to make marks with his staff on the ground. Then he said: "There is no one of you, no soul that has been born, but has his place in Paradise or in Hell already decreed (lit., written) for him, or, to put it otherwise, his unhappy or his happy fate has been decreed for him." A man spoke up: "O Apostle of Allah, shall we not then just entrust ourselves to what is written for us, and renounce works, since he amongst us who belongs to the Blessed will inevitably be led to the works of the Blessed, and he amongst us who belongs to the Damned will inevitably be led to the works of the Damned?" He answered: "As for those [who are to be among the] Blessed, the works of the Blessed will be made easy for them, and as for those [who are to be among the] Damned, the works of the Damned will be made easy for them." Then he recited (XCII, 5-13): "So as for him who gives [generously] and shows piety, and gives credence to what is best, We shall ease the way for him to that which is easy, but as for him who is miserly and takes pride in [his] wealth, and treats what is best as false, for him We shall ease the way to that which is hard, nor will his wealth avail him when he is perishing. It is Ours to give guidance, and to Us belong both the First and the Last."

THAT A MAN'S REWARD IS NOT A CONSEQUENCE OF HIS WORKS

From Fakhr ad-Dīn ar-Rāzī, *Maʿālim Uṣūl ad-Dīn* (Cairo, 1325 A.H. = 1907 A.D.), p. 135.

Good works are not the reason one is deserving of reward. Against the teaching of the Muʿtazilites of Baṣra [that it is incumbent on Allah to reward duly the good works of men], we urge three considerations.

Firstly, were it incumbent on Allah, Most High, to give rewards, then either He could possibly refrain from so giving, or could not possibly refrain. If He could possibly refrain then He might become deserving of blame or be considered as having some defect, neither of which is to be thought of in the case of Allah. [On the other hand] if He could not possibly refrain, that would impugn His being able to do whatever He chooses.

Secondly, Allah, Most High, has conferred very great favors on man, for which favors he needs must be thankful and obedient. Now since these acts of obedience were performed in recognition of having received an abundance of favors, that prevents their being, beyond that, a necessary reason for reward, since the fulfillment of an incumbent duty does not necessarily involve anything further [as recompense].

Thirdly, we have shown elsewhere that what any man does happens only because the coming together of the power [to do it] with the incitation [to do it] makes it necessary, and this [bringing together] is the act of Allah, Most High. Now the one who brings about the cause is also the one who brings about the effect (lit., "that which was caused"), so a man's deed is really a deed of Allah, Most High, and a deed of Allah, Most High, makes nothing further incumbent on Him —exalted be He.[1]

ON REFRAINING FROM DISCUSSING THE MATTER OF PREDESTINATION

From the Shī'ite tractate *Risālat al-I'tiqādāt,* by Ibn Bābawaih (Najaf, 1343 A.H. = 1924 A.D.), pp. 100-102.

Saith the Shaikh Abū Ja'far (b. Bābawaih): Our belief concerning this is what [the Imām Ja'far] aṣ-Ṣādiq replied to Zarāra, when he asked: "What do you say, O my Imām, about *al-qaḍā'* and *al-qadar?*" He answered: "I say that when Allah —exalted be He—gathers together mankind on the Day of Resurrection He will question them with regard to what He has enjoined on them, but will not ask them about those things He has decreed for them." Now discussion about [this matter of Allah's] decree is forbidden. When the Commander

1 Ar-Rāzī is not consistent, for in other passages in this same work he speaks of the measure of a man's reward in the hereafter as being in accordance with his deeds, and likewise the measure of his punishment.

of the Faithful was asked about the decree he replied: "It is a deep sea, venture not into it." The man asked him a second time, and he replied: "It is an obscure path, walk not along it." He asked him a third time, whereat he said: "It is one of Allah's secrets, do not talk about it." The Commander of the Faithful also said with regard to the decree: "Most assuredly *qadar* is a secret among Allah's secrets, a veil among Allah's veils, a thing carefully guarded among Allah's carefully guarded things, something raised up within Allah's veil, kept hidden from Allah's creatures, and sealed by Allah's own seal. It has prior place among all the things within Allah's knowledge, but Allah has excused His servants from [having to have any] knowledge of it, raising it up beyond the range of their perception and their reason. Thus they are unable to attain to [any understanding of] its real nature, or its continuing power, or its magnitude, or its glorious oneness, for this is a billowing ocean known only to Allah. Deep is it as the distance between the heavens and the earth, wide as the distance between the east and the west, dark as a starless night. [It is an ocean] full of sea monsters and fish, which now come to the surface, now dive down to the bottom of the sea, at which bottom there is what has been determined, of which it befits no one to seek knowledge save the One, the Peerless, the Eternal. He who attempts to seek knowledge of it goes contrary to Allah's command, disputes His sovereignty, and is probing into His secret and His veil, [whereby] he has assuredly incurred the wrath of Allah, so his abode will be Gehenna. What an evil destination" (VIII, 16).

V. THE DUTIES OF ISLAM

CONFESSION

The technical term for the Muslim confession is *tashahhud,* "giving one's testimony," i.e., confessing and professing that one is a Muslim and a follower of Muḥammad. The normal formula of confession is that called the *kalima* ("word"), viz., *lā ilāha ill' Allāh; Muḥammad rasūl Allāh,* "There is no deity save Allah; Muḥammad is the messenger (or Apostle) of Allah." This "word" is constantly on the lips of Muslims, as constantly as the *Honover* on the lips of Parsis, often on what strike the Western observer as singularly inappropriate occasions. To the Muslim, however, the mere pronouncement of it is an act of piety. It is commonly asserted that merely to pronounce it is sufficient to make one a convert to Islam. The orthodox divines, however, say that six conditions must be observed before it can effectively make one a Muslim. These are: (1) it must be repeated aloud; (2) it must be perfectly understood; (3) it must be believed in the heart; (4) it must be professed till death; (5) it must be recited correctly; (6) it must be professed and declared without hesitation.

ON THE VIRTUE OF RECITING THE KALIMA

From the *Khazīnat al-Asrār* of Muḥammad Ḥaqqī an-Nāzilī, ed. Aḥmad Maḥmūd Khalīl (Cairo, 1343 A.H. = 1924 A.D.), pp. 186-87.

Muslim has reported from 'Ubāda b. aṣ-Ṣāmit—with whom may Allah be pleased—that the Apostle of Allah—upon whom be Allah's blessing and peace—said: "Allah will forbid the Fire [from touching] anyone who has testified: 'There is no deity save Allah and Muḥammad is the Apostle of Allah.'" Aṭ-Ṭabarānī and Abū Nu'aim have quoted from 'Ubāda b. aṣ-Ṣāmit how he told that the Apostle of Allah—upon whom be Allah's blessing and peace—said: "The faith that has most virtue is that you should recognize that Allah is with you wherever you may be." Aṭ-Ṭabarānī has reported from Abū'd-Dardā'—with whom may Allah be pleased—that the

Apostle of Allah—upon whom be Allah's blessing and peace—said: "There is no person who says a hundred times: 'There is no deity save Allah, and Muḥammad is the Apostle of Allah,' but will be raised up by Allah on the Day of Resurrection with a face shining like the moon on the night of its fullness. No one on that Day will hand up [for assessment] works superior to his works save those who have said the like of what he has said or have increased [the number of times]." Muslim has reported from al-Muṭṭalib b. Ḥinṭab—with whom may Allah be pleased—that the Prophet—upon whom be Allah's blessing and peace—said: "The finest thing I have ever said, and that the Prophets who were before me have ever said, is to bear witness that there is no deity save Allah."

Muslim has reported from 'Uthmān—with whom may Allah be pleased—that the Prophet—upon whom be Allah's blessing and peace—said: "He who dies while acknowledging that there is no deity save Allah, and holds fast to his belief in it, will enter Paradise." That he should have said "Allah will forbid the Fire [from touching] him" is seen by the divines to be in contradiction with other texts which indicate that some disobedient believers will be tormented therein. Some seek to reconcile them by saying that this promise can be claimed only by him who repents of his wickedness before dying, others by saying that the promise was made before the incumbent duties had been ordained. Al-Ḥasan al-Baṣrī said that the meaning was: "Whosoever says this *kalima* and fulfills all that it connotes and all the incumbent duties." The preferred explanation is that it means that confession of the Divine Unity (*tawḥīd*) will prevent one from being kept eternally in the Fire.

'Abdallah b. 'Amr b. al-'Āṣ—with whom may Allah be pleased—has told how the Apostle of Allah—upon whom be Allah's blessing and peace—said: "A man will be brought along to the Balances on the Day, and there will be brought out for him ninety-nine scrolls, every scroll of them stretching [when unrolled] as far as eye can reach, in which are written his sins and his guilty acts, and they will be put in one pan of the Balances. Then a fragment of papyrus will be brought out about the size of an ant, on which is written the confession: 'There is no deity save Allah, and Muḥammad is His servant and His Apostle,' which will be put in the other pan, and it will outweigh all his wrongdoings."

Now in the Tradition that he who dies while still acknowledging that there is no deity save Allah will assuredly enter Paradise, there is a reply to those extravagant Murji'ites [1] who say that merely to pronounce aloud the confession in its two parts is sufficient to assure one of entering Paradise even though one does not have any real belief therein. There is also in it an argument against those who say that merely to pin one's faith on Allah and His Apostle is effective without speaking the confession aloud.

ON THE MERITS OF FAITH

From the *Inṣāf* of al-Bāqillānī, ed. Mḥd al-Kawtharī (Cairo, 1950), pp. 48-50.

It should be recognized that faith (*al-īmān*) is of two kinds, an eternal faith and a temporal faith. The eternal faith is that of the True One—glorious and exalted is He—for He has called Himself one who has faith (*mu'min*), in His words (LIX, 23): "the Peacemaker, the Faithful, the Guardian." Now faith on His part—glorious and exalted is He—is His putting trust in Himself, as He has said (III, 18/16): "Allah bears witness that there is no deity save Himself." It is likewise His putting trust in His prophets by [granting them] His word, for His word is from eternity (*qadīm*), one of the attributes of His essence.

Temporal faith [on the other hand] is the faith of creatures, because Allah—exalted be He—has created it in their hearts, as is proved by His words (LVIII, 22): "These are they on

[1] They were an early sect in Islam who refused to pronounce a man an unbeliever on the ground of external appearances, arguing that Allah alone knew the truth of the matter and judgment must be left to Him. See Macdonald's *Muslim Theology*, p. 123 and Index *sub voc.*

whose hearts He has inscribed faith," and by His words (XLIX, 7): "But Allah has made the faith dear to you, has beautified it in your hearts." Now the faith of a human is a human attribute, and the attribute of one who has been created is a created thing, just as an attribute of the Creator is from eternity, i.e., is an attribute of His essence. Also, since the definition of eternal is that which has no limits to its existence and no end to its continuance, and the definition of temporal is that once it was not and then it was, then just as an attribute of the eternal cannot be temporal, so an attribute of the temporal cannot be eternal. Indeed, how should an attribute of the temporal be eternal when it is an accidental thing which cannot maintain itself save by something that bears it, and which is unable to subsist by itself? For example, movement cannot exist without something that is moved, nor stillness without something that stands still, nor knowledge without someone who knows, nor blackness without something that is black, and so on with other temporal attributes.

It should be recognized that true faith means putting one's trust [in some one] (*taṣdīq*). The proof of this is the word of the Most High (XII, 17), telling about Joseph's brethren [who said]: "Thou art not one who believes (*mu'min*) in us," i.e., thou art not putting trust in us.[1] We also have the case of the Apostle of Allah, who, when he was told how the cow and the wolf had spoken,[2] said: "I believe in it, as do Abū Bakr

1 There is a point here difficult to bring out in a translation. *Īmān*, the word for "faith," is the verbal noun of the verb *āmana*, which means both "to have faith in" and "to believe in." *Mu'min* is the active participle of the same verb, and so can mean either "he who puts his trust" or "he who believes." So *taṣdīq* is the verbal noun of *ṣaddaqa* which may mean either "to put trust in," or "to consider as true." He is using both meanings of both these verbs in this passage.

2 The reference is to popular stories of the miracles that accompanied the mission of Muḥammad. Not only did holy men of the other religions recognize in him the Prophet who was to come, but representatives of the animal, vegetable, and mineral worlds did also. Thus we have tales of stones talking, trees bowing, and animals informing men that this was the expected Prophet. The speaking cow and the speaking wolf are two well-known stories of this kind.

and 'Umar." That is, he meant to say: "I consider it as true." Similarly people who use our (Arabic) language say: "So-and-So believes in (or puts faith in) the resurrection, Paradise and Hell," i.e., he considers them to be true; or they say: "So-and-So does not believe in torment in the hereafter," i.e., he puts no faith in it.

It should also be recognized that the seat of this putting of trust (*taṣdīq*) is the heart. That is, the heart puts its trust in the fact that Allah is a God who is one, and that the Apostle is true, that all that the Apostle brought is true. What the tongue does is to confess it, and what the members do is to act in accordance with it, but that is only an indication of what is in the heart and a proof thereof. Now it is possible that it may be called true faith from one point of view and yet from another point of view only seeming. The meaning of this is that if a man in his heart puts his trust in what we have said, confesses it with his tongue and with his members acts in accordance with it, then he is a true believer in the sight of Allah and in ours. But as for him who in his heart gives it the lie, yet confesses the Divine Unity with his tongue and with his members performs acts of obedience, such a man is not a true believer, but only a seeming believer. Yet that preserves his blood and his property[3] with regard to judgments of this world, for he is outwardly a believer though before Allah he is no believer.

Proof of the soundness of all this is in the words of the Most High (LXIII, 1): "When the hypocrites come to thee they say: 'We bear witness that thou art assuredly the messenger of Allah.' Allah well knows that thou art His messenger, and Allah bears witness that the hypocrites are liars." Here He —glory be to Him—gives information about their falsity, but we know, and every intelligent person knows, that He did not give the lie to what they confessed with their tongues, but

[3] Were he to profess unbelief openly he would be a *kāfir,* whose blood may be shed with impunity, and whose property may be plundered to the benefit of the Muslim community. See the article "Kāfir" in *EI,* II, 618-620.

was giving the lie only to [what was in] their hearts, for what they held inwardly was different from what they showed outwardly. The faith of a dumb man who believes in his heart is genuine, even though he is unable to speak and confess it with his tongue. The opposite of this is likewise true, so that a believer who really believes in his heart is a believer in the sight of Allah, Most High, even though what he utters is unbelief. A proof of the soundness of this is to be found in the words of the Most High (XVI, 106/108): "Whosoever disbelieves in Allah after belief [in Him]—save one who is under compulsion, though his heart is tranquil in the faith—but whoso relieves his breast by unbelief, on such is anger from Allah, and for them is punishment severe." Here He informs us that mere utterance of the faith by the tongue where the heart is persisting in unbelief is of no avail, and that to confess unbelief by the tongue does no harm so long as the heart truly believes.

Now it should be recognized that we do not deny that our statement to the effect that faith is held in the heart, confessed by the tongue and put into practice by the members, is dependent on what has come [down to us] in Tradition. He—upon whom be Allah's blessing and peace—meant only by that that thus is information given about the true quality of the faith that is beneficial in this world and the next, for when a man confesses with his tongue, and believes in his heart, and acts with his members [in accordance therewith], we judge that he belongs to the faith and comes under its regulations in this world, without any hesitation or qualification. We also judge that he will have reward in the next life and an excellent future existence, because this is what the circumstances indicate. We are assured that that is how he will fare in the hereafter provided that what is known to Allah, Most High, is that he is one whom He will cause to live and then cause to die in this condition. Were he to confess with his tongue and perform good works with his members, but not believe in his heart, that would be beneficial to him as regards the regulations in this world, but it would be of no benefit to him in the hereafter. He—upon whom be Allah's blessing and peace—made that quite clear when he said: "O company of those who profess belief with the tongue but into whose hearts faith has not yet entered." If you consider deeply this inquiry [we have been conducting] and exert yourself therein, you will find—and the praise is to Allah and from Him—that the Qur'ān and the Sunna have in them nothing to cause confusion, have no contradiction, but that the confusions, the disorders, the contradictions, are solely in the understanding of him who has heard about these things but has not understood them properly nor pictured them aright. From this we take refuge in Allah.

Likewise we do not deny that we say expressly that faith is subject to increase and decrease. This teaching appears both in the Qur'ān and the Sunna, but the decreasing and the increasing in the case of faith have to do with one of two matters. It may be that it is concerned with matters of speaking and acting quite apart from believing, for in both these cases it can be imagined as occurring while faith still remains. Or it may concern believing, and when that is tainted even in the slightest measure faith is ruined. The explanation is this. Should one who has put his trust in all that the Apostle—upon whom be peace—brought, give up praying or fasting, or paying the legal alms, or reciting the Qur'ān where it ought to be recited, or give up any of the other incumbent duties of religion, he is not characterized as in unbelief because of what he has given up, since he still believes completely in it and holds fast therein. On the other hand, were he to perform all the acts of obedience, and confess all the things that are incumbent, and believe in all that the Prophet brought except the prohibition of wine, or of marriage relations with one's mother, even though he actually indulged in neither of these things, he would be characterized as in unbelief, would have stripped himself of the faith, and all that [he had done] would not profit him at all so long as his beliefs were tainted in this one matter of judgment. Thus increase and decrease of faith are possible in the way of saying or doing, but not possible in the way of believing. He—upon whom be Allah's blessing and peace—has made that quite clear by his saying: "A man's faith is not made perfect till he craves good for his brother Muslim," or in another saying: "until his neighbor is safe from any injustice at his hands." He meant by that his desisting from doing harm, and this would not negate true belief because did he consider it lawful to harm him he would not possess the faith at all, whether to increase or decrease. So understand that.

PRAYER

The two technical terms for prayer are *du'ā* and *ṣalāt*. The former means "supplication," and is used for all kinds of extempore prayer, intercession, and spontaneous outpouring of the soul to the Divine. The latter, which is a word borrowed from Aramaic, is used for liturgical prayer with its ritual of stated prayers and genuflections. In India this latter is commonly called *namāz*. In the earliest days of Islam prayers were said twice a day, at morning and at evening (XVII, 78/80; XVIII, 28/27; XI, 114/116; XXX, 17/16), to which a noon prayer was added later (XXX, 18/17; II, 238/239; cf. XXIV, 58/57). The traditional five daily prayer services are nowhere expressly mentioned in the Qur'ān, but Tradition holds that they were prescribed for the Prophet at his interview with Allah during his Ascension (*Mi'rāj*). These five prayer times are at dawn, midday, afternoon, evening, and night. They may be said either in private or in congregation, but if in congregation there is a prayer-leader (*imām*) who directs the ritual. At these five times each day there is a prayer call (*adhān*) to bring the faithful to prayers made by the *muezzin* from the court or from the minaret of the mosque. Liturgical prayer must be preceded by ritual purification both of the person and the place. Ablutions (*wuḍu'* or *ghusl*) secure bodily purity and the common use of prayer rugs is an attempt to secure purity of the place. In a state of purity the worshipers must take up a position facing the *qibla,* the sacred shrine at Mecca, a direction which is indicated in a mosque by the *miḥrāb* in one of the mosque walls. After the worshipers have put themselves in a state of sanctity for the purpose of prayer, a standard ritual is followed consisting of ascriptions of praise and glory to Allah, recitation of passages of the Qur'ān, formulas of prayer, bowings (*rukū'*) and prostrations (*sujūd*). A certain number of these make up a *rak'a* and are gone through again and again till the requisite number of *rak'as* for any particular prayer service are complete, then a place is left for the *du'ā,* or spontaneous petitions of the individual worshiper, and, after a number of further ritual formulas and actions, that particular prayer service is completed and the state of sanctity ended.

Besides the five prescribed daily prayers, many pious Muslims observe extra prayer services, particularly at three points: between the dawn and the midday prayer, between evening and night prayer, and after the night prayer. There are also certain special congregational prayers that are in common observance. The most important of them is the Friday prayer service in the mosque, which takes somewhat the place for Muslims that the Sabbath has for Jews and Sunday for the Christians, though it has never been a "day of rest" in Islamic countries. There are also special prayers for time of eclipse of sun or moon, for time of drought, for funeral services, for time of special danger, and for the annual festivals of Islam. The saying of prayers is a prime method of storing up merit, but to be meritorious liturgical prayer must observe the proper forms. The *arkān,* or fundamentals of proper prayer, are commonly said to be eight: (1) *niyya* (intention), i.e., stating what prayer service one proposes to perform; (2) *iḥrām* (sanctification), i.e., pronouncing a *takbīr* whereby the worshiper cuts himself off from profane things for the period of the prayer; (3) *qiyām* (standing), i.e., taking up one's position standing, with head and pudenda covered, facing the *qibla* and ready for prayer; (4) *qirā'a* (recitation), i.e., the recitation of the *Fātiha* (Sūra I) and some other portion from the Qur'ān; (5) *rukū'* (bowing), i.e., bending the body so that the palms touch the knees; (6) *sujūd* (prostration of obeisance), i.e., going on hands and knees so that the forehead touches the praying place; (7) *salām* (peace greeting), which ends the formal liturgy; (8) *tartīb* (arrangement), i.e., performing all the above in proper sequence.

On prayer see: M. T. Houtsma, "Iets over den dagelijkschen Çalat der Mohammedanen," in *Theol. Tijdschrift,* XXIV (1890), 127 ff.; E. Mittwoch, *Zur Entstehungsgeschichte des islamischen Gebets und Kultus* (Berlin, 1913); the article "Ṣalāt" in *EI,* IV, 96-105; E. E. Calverley, *Worship in Islam* (Madras, 1925).

PRAYER IN THE QUR'ĀN

CVII, 1-7.

Hast thou seen him who considers the religion false?
That fellow is the one who repulses the orphan
And does not stir [folk] up to feed the unfortunate.

So woe to those who pray
But who are careless about their praying,
Who are all for making a show,
But withhold assistance [from the needy].

LXXVI, 24-26.

So [O Muḥammad] wait in patience for the decision of thy Lord, and do not obey any guilty or unbelieving person among them, but remember the name of thy Lord morning and evening, and during the night. So prostrate thyself in obeisance to Him, and give glory to Him through the long night.

LII, 48-49.

And wait in patience [O Muḥammad] for the decision of thy Lord, for thou art in Our eyes, and give glory with praise of thy Lord when thou risest, and during the night give glory to Him while the stars are withdrawing.

XI, 114/116.

And do thou [O Muḥammad] observe prayer at the two ends of the day and when night draws nigh. Verily, good deeds drive away evil deeds; that is a reminder for those who remember.

II, 238/239, 239/240.

Observe strictly the prayers and the middle prayer, and stand up to [worship] Allah devoutly. But should ye fear anything, then on foot or mounted; but when ye are secure then remember Allah, as He has taught you what ye used not to know.

III, 190/187-194/192.

Verily, in the creation of the heavens and the earth, and in the interchange of night and day, are signs for those who possess intelligence, who remember Allah standing, sitting, reclining, and who meditate on the creation of the heavens and the earth [saying]: "O our Lord, Thou didst not create this in vain. Glory be to Thee! Guard us from the torment of Hell Fire. O our Lord, the fact about Thee is that whomsoever Thou dost make enter the Fire, him Thou hast assuredly put to shame, and for the wrongdoers there are no helpers. O our Lord, the fact about us is that we have heard a Caller calling to the faith [saying]: 'Believe ye in your Lord,' and we have believed. O our Lord, forgive us our sins, and make expiation for us for our evil deeds, and have us die along with the righteous. O our Lord, grant us what Thou hast promised us by [the word of] Thy messengers, and put us not to shame on the Day of Resurrection. Thou, indeed, wilt not fail the appointment."

XXIX, 45/44.

Recite [O Muḥammad] what has been revealed to thee of the Book, and observe prayer, for prayer restrains from conduct that is abominable and unlawful, whereas remembrance of Allah is something greater, and Allah knows what ye are doing.

XVII, 78/80-81/83.

Do thou [O Muḥammad] observe prayer from the declining of the sun till the darkening of the night, and [observe also] the recitation at dawn. Verily, the dawn recitation is witnessed. And [observe somewhat] of the night, so keep vigil (*tahajjud*) therein as something in addition (*nāfila*) for thyself; it may be that thy Lord will raise thee up to a highly praised position. And say: "O my Lord, make me enter with a right entrance and come forth with a right exit, and appoint for me from Thyself a helpful authority." Say also: "The truth has come and the false has vanished." Verily, the false has become a vanishing thing.

XVII, 110-111.

Say: "Invoke Allah, or invoke the Merciful: Whichever of them it is ye invoke, He has the most beautiful names." So do not [O Muḥammad] utter [the words] loudly in thy praying, nor yet utter them in too low a voice, but seek out a way between these, and say: "Praise be to Allah, who has not taken for Himself a son, who has no partner in the Kingdom, and has no [need of] anyone to protect Him from abasement." So magnify Him with a magnificat (*takbīr,* i.e., by saying "Allah is very great").

XX, 132.

[O Muḥammad] enjoin prayer on thy household, and continue thyself steadfastly therein. [Unlike the pagan deities] We ask thee for no provision, rather do We provide for thee, and the final outcome depends on piety.

IV, 43/46.

O ye who believe, come not to prayers when ye are drunken until ye know what ye are saying, nor [when ye are] polluted —unless ye are travelers along the way—until ye have washed yourselves. Should ye be sick, or on a journey, or if one of you has come from the privy, or if ye have touched women, and ye find no water, then purify yourselves [1] with good surface sand, rubbing your faces and hands. Allah is indeed One who is good at forgiving and pardon.

IV, 101/102-103/104.

When ye are moving about in the land it is no sin on your part that ye shorten the prayers, [or] if ye are afraid that those who do not believe may afflict you. Verily, the unbelievers are

[1] Purification before cult practices is normally by means of water, but this is the verse legalizing *tayammum,* or purification by fine sand, which is said to be permissible when water is unprocurable, either because of distance therefrom or because of intervening danger, or when the use of water might be injurious to health.

manifestly hostile to you. And when thou[2] [O Muḥammad] art with them and hast started the prayers for them, let a party from among them stand [praying] with thee, and let them take their weapons, and when they prostrate in obeisance let them be behind you. Then let another party come who have not yet prayed, and let them pray with thee, and let them take their precautions and [keep hold of] their weapons. . . . Then when ye have finished the prayer service remember Allah standing, or sitting, or reclining, and when ye are in tranquillity observe prayer [in the normal fashion]. Prayer, indeed, is for the believers something prescribed for certain fixed times.

Friday prayers. LXII, 9-10.

O ye who believe, when the call to prayer comes on the day of assembly,[3] then hasten to the remembrance of Allah, and leave [your] bargaining. That is better for you did ye know it. And when the prayer service is finished then disperse yourselves in the land seeking Allah's bounty, but remember Allah oft and maybe ye will prosper.

THE CALL TO PRAYERS

Five times a day the *muezzin,* either from the court of the mosque or more commonly from the minaret, calls the faithful to prayer. Tradition has tales of how the Prophet rejected the various mechanical means of sounding the call to prayers used by Jews and Christians in favor of the human voice. Orthodoxy demands that in all countries the call (*adhān*) be in Arabic.

Allah is very great (repeated four times).
I testify that there is no deity save Allah.
I testify that there is no deity save Allah.
I testify that Muḥammad is the messenger of Allah.
I testify that Muḥammad is the messenger of Allah.

[2] This transition to the singular marks a late insertion having reference to prayer services when in danger of the enemy.

[3] *Yaum al-Jum'a,* i.e., Friday, which apparently was the weekly day of assembly in pre-Islamic days.

Come to prayers. Come to prayers.
Come to salvation. Come to salvation.
(Shi'ites here add: Come to good works.)
There is no deity save Allah.
(At the dawn prayers there is added the phrase:
Prayer is better than sleep.)

THE PRAYER LEADER

From the *Ṣaḥīḥ* of al-Bukhārī, ed. L. Krehl (Leiden, 1862), I, 180.

Mālik has informed us on the authority of Hishām b. 'Urwa, from his father, from 'Ā'isha, mother of the Believers, who said: The Apostle of Allah—upon whom be Allah's blessing and peace—said prayers in my house in distress during his [last] illness, so he prayed in a sitting posture, while a group behind him prayed standing up. He signed to them to sit, and when he had finished, he said: "The only reason a prayer leader (*imām*) is appointed is that he may be imitated. So when he bows, do ye bow; and when he rises up, rise up. When he says: 'May Allah hear those who praise Him,' say ye: 'O our Lord, to Thee be praise.' Should he pray sitting, then do ye pray sitting."

'Abdallah b. Yūsuf has related to us, saying: Mālik has informed us, on the authority of Ibn Shihāb, from Anas b. Mālik, that the Apostle of Allah—upon whom be Allah's blessing and peace—once rode a horse, but was thrown and hurt his right side. Consequently he prayed one of the prayers seated, so we prayed behind him seated. When he had finished he said: "The only reason a prayer leader is appointed is that he be imitated. So when he prays standing, do ye pray standing; when he bows, do ye bow; when he rises, rise. When he says: 'May Allah hear those who praise him,' say ye: 'O our Lord, to Thee be praise.' Should he pray sitting, then do all of you pray sitting."

Saith Abū 'Abdallah (i.e., al-Bukhārī himself): Al-Ḥumaidī declares that this has been abrogated. The statement: "Should he pray sitting, then do ye pray sitting," refers only to his former illness. After that the Prophet—upon whom be Allah's blessing and peace—prayed sitting while the people behind him [prayed] standing, and he did not bid them sit. Only the final is to be taken [as authoritative], and the final [pattern] of the Prophet—upon whom be Allah's blessing and peace—is that during that illness of which he died he himself prayed sitting, but the people behind him standing.

TAWADDUD THE SLAVE GIRL ON PRAYER

From *The Thousand and One Nights,* nights 439 and 440 (Ḥalabī edition; Cairo, 1328 A.H. = 1910 A.D.), II, 331-332. The story is about a slave girl named Tawaddud who was offered at a very high figure to the Caliph Hārūn ar-Rashīd. When the Caliph learns that the figure is high because this is a highly educated slave, he calls in his learned men to examine her. The passage here is part of her examination on the subject of prayer, and as these stories are popular reading this is an excellent illustration of the popular understanding of prayer.

Q. With what do you take up your stand for a prayer service?

A. With intention of devotion, acknowledging the Divine Lordship.

Q. How many things has Allah bidden you observe before you take up your stand for a prayer service?

A. Ritual purification, covering the pudenda, avoiding garments that are ritually impure, taking one's stand on a place that is ritually pure, facing toward the *qibla,* standing erect, making the intention (*niyya*), and uttering the *takbīra* of consecration.

Q. With what do you come forth from your house for prayers?

A. With intention of worshiping.

Q. And with what intention do you enter the mosque?

A. With intention of service.

Q. With what do you confront the *qibla?*

A. With three incumbent and one traditional (*sunna*) ordinance.

Q. What is the beginning act of prayer? What its desacralizing and its sacralizing acts?

A. The beginning of prayer is the ceremonial purification, its sacralizing act is the *takbīra* of consecration, and its desacralizing act is the salutation of peace which ends the prayer service.

Q. What is the necessary consequence for one who neglects prayers?

A. It is related in the authentic Traditions that one who willfully and of purpose neglects prayers, having no excuse, has no share in Islam.

Q. What is prayer?

A. Prayer is a means of communion between man and his Lord. It has ten virtues, viz., it illumines the heart, it brightens the countenance, it makes the Merciful well pleased, it makes Satan wroth, it wards off trial, it spares one from the evil wrought by enemies, it increases mercy, it defends against vengeance, it brings the servant near to his Master, it restrains from lewdness and what is disapproved. Thus it is one of the obligatory, incumbent, ordained duties, and is among the pillars of religion.

Q. What is the key to prayer?

A. Ablution (*wuḍu'*).

Q. And what is the key to ablution?

A. The *tasmiya* (i.e., pronouncing the phrase "In the Name of Allah, the Merciful, the Compassionate").

Q. What is the key to the *tasmiya?*

A. Assurance.

Q. What is the key to assurance?

A. Putting one's trust [in Allah].

Q. What is the key to putting one's trust?

A. Hope.

Q. What is the key to hope?

A. Obedience.

Q. What is the key to obedience?

A. Confessing the Divine Unity and acknowledging His Lordship.

Q. What are the ordinances for ablutions (*wuḍu'*)?

A. According to the Shāfi'ite rite they are six things, viz., expressing intention at the washing of the face, washing the face, washing the two hands along with the forearms, rubbing part of the head, washing the two feet along with the ankles, and [doing all the above in] proper sequence. Besides these ten things are held to be customary (*sunna*), viz., [to begin with] the *tasmiya,* to wash the two palms before putting them into the water container, to rinse the mouth, to snuff water up the nostrils, to rub the whole head, to rub the ears both outside and inside with fresh water, to finger-comb the thick beard, to finger-comb the fingers of the hands and the toes of the feet, to do the right before the left, to purify each part thrice and without break in the sequence. Then when one has finished the *wuḍu'* he should say: "I bear witness that there is no deity save Allah alone, who has no partner. I bear witness that Muḥammad is His servant and His Apostle. Allahumma! make me one of those who repent, make me one of those who have purified themselves. Glory be to Thee, Allahumma, and by Thy praise I bear witness that there is no deity save Thyself. Thy pardon I seek and to Thee do I repent." It has been handed down in the noble Traditions from the Prophet—upon whom be Allah's blessing and peace—that he said: "Whosoever will say this at the conclusion of each ablution will have opened for him the eight gates of Paradise, through whichever he pleases he may enter."

Q. When a man desires to perform ablutions, how will he be with regard to the angels and the satans?

A. When a man prepares for ablution the angels come to his right and the satans to his left. If he makes mention of Allah at the commencement of the ablutions the satans flee from him and the angels spread over him a pavilion of light, having four ropes, at each rope of which there is an angel glorifying Allah, Most High, and begging forgiveness for him for so long as he is silent or is making mention [of Allah]. But if he does not make mention of Allah—mighty and majestic is He—at the commencement of the ablutions, and does not keep silent, the satans take charge of him and the angels depart from him. So Satan keeps whispering to him till doubts enter him and he has nullified his ablution.

THE QIBLA

Orientation for prayer, i.e., the custom of facing in some particular direction during prayers, was common from early times in the Near East. Al-Bīrūnī, in his *Chronology of Ancient Nations*, p. 331, records having heard how the Ḥarranians always turned to the south in prayer, while the Ṣābians, like the Manichaeans, always turned toward the north. He also knows how the Christians always turn toward the east (p. 249), and quotes with approval a writer who reproaches those who think that a particular orientation is necessary for prayer, since, if God is everywhere, a truly religious person does not need any *qibla*. In the earliest years of Islam Muḥammad and his followers faced toward Jerusalem as they prayed, but in the second year of the Hijra, after Muḥammad had broken with the Jews, he changed the *qibla* to the Ka'ba at Mecca.

II, 143/138-150/145.

We appointed the qibla thou hast been wont to make use of (i.e., Jerusalem) only that We might know who would follow the Apostle from him who would turn on his heels. If it be a great matter it is not so to those whom Allah has guided. Allah was not One who would let your faith come to naught. Allah, indeed, is gentle and compassionate with the people.

We, indeed, see thee turning thy face toward the skies, so We shall assuredly make thee [O Muḥammad] turn around to a *qibla* that will please thee. Turn, therefore, thy face toward the Sacred Shrine (in Mecca), and wherever ye [Muslims] may be, turn your faces toward it. Verily, those to whom the scripture has been given know that it is the truth from their Lord, and Allah is not heedless of what they are doing.

Even shouldst thou bring to those to whom scripture has been given every sign they would not follow thy *qibla*. Thou art not now a follower of their *qibla*, even as some of them are not followers of the *qibla* of others. Shouldst thou follow their desires, after the knowledge that has come to thee, thou wouldst in that case be among the wrongdoers.

Those to whom We have given the scripture recognize it as they recognize their own sons, but a party among them conceals the truth, and they know [that they are doing so].

The truth is from thy Lord, so on no account be thou among those who doubt.

To each [has been given] a direction to which he turns [in prayer], so strive for pre-eminence in the good things. Wheresoever ye may be, Allah will bring you all together. Allah, indeed, is powerful over everything.

So from wherever thou hast gone forth turn thy face to the Sacred Shrine, for it, indeed, is the truth from thy Lord, and Allah is not heedless of what ye are doing.

So from wherever thou hast gone forth turn thy face toward the Sacred Shrine, and wheresoever ye [Muslims] may be, turn your faces toward it, that the people may have no argument against you, save those among them who do wrong. Do not fear them, fear Me. [Do this] that I may perfect My favor upon you, and maybe ye will be guided.

From the *Ṣaḥīḥ* of al-Bukhārī, ed. L. Krehl (Leiden, 1862), I, 18.

'Amr b. Khālid has related to us, on the authority of Zuhair, who said: Abū Isḥāq has related to us from al-Barā', that the Prophet—upon whom be Allah's blessing and peace—when he first arrived at Madina lodged with his grandparents or, some say, with his maternal uncles among the Ansār. For some sixteen or seventeen months he was praying with the Jerusalem shrine as *qibla,* though he would have liked to have the [Meccan] shrine as his *qibla.* The first prayer that he prayed [facing the Ka'ba], however, was a certain afternoon prayer (*'aṣr*). Some folk were praying with him and a man from among those who were praying with him went out to the people in a mosque, who were at [the stage of] bowing down, and said: "I testify by Allah. I was praying with the

Apostle of Allah—upon whom be Allah's blessing and peace—and he was turned facing Mecca." So they changed around, just as they were, and faced the [Meccan] Shrine. Now the Jews and Christians had been delighted that [the Prophet] used to pray facing the Jerusalem shrine, so when he turned his face around to face the [Meccan] shrine, the [People of the Book] disapproved of that. Said Zuhair: Abū Ishāq related to us from al-Barā', in this Tradition, that some men had died while using the old *qibla* before it had been changed. They had been killed [in the fighting] and we did not know what to say about them, but Allah—mighty and majestic is He—sent down the verse: "Allah is not one who would let you lose [the fruits of] your faith." [1]

ON GOING OUT TO THE MOSQUE

From al-Ghazzālī's *Bidāyat al-Hidāya* (Cairo, 1337 A.H. = 1918 A.D.), pp. 17-18.

When you have finished your ceremonial purifications pray in your house two *rak'as* of the dawn prayer service, if the dawn has already broken. This is what the Apostle of Allah—upon whom be Allah's blessing and peace—used to do. Then make your way to the mosque, and do not neglect to pray in congregation, especially in the morning, for a congregational prayer is twenty-seven degrees superior to a prayer said alone. If you treat lightly such a profit as that, what benefit is it to you to seek for knowledge, for the fruitage of knowledge is to act in accord therewith. Then when you go out to the mosque walk quietly and calmly and do not hurry. As you go along the way, say: "Allahumma! by the claim on Thee each petitioner has, by the claim on Thee each one who yearns for Thee has, by the claim of this my walking toward Thee, for I have not come forth lightheartedly nor saucily nor hypo-

[1] That is, he takes this verse to mean that those who had been using the old *qibla* would not lose the merit gained by their prayers offered while facing the Jerusalem shrine.

critically nor for display, but I have come forth to avoid Thy wrath and in desire to be well pleasing to Thee, I beg of Thee that Thou save me from Hell Fire and forgive me my sins, for there is none to forgive sins save Thee."

PRAYERS MUST BE PERFORMED CORRECTLY

From Al-Bukhārī, *Ṣaḥīḥ,* ed. L. Krehl (Leiden, 1862), I, 195-196.

Muḥammad b. Bashshār has related to us on the authority of Yaḥyā, from 'Ubaidallah, on the authority of Sa'īd b. Abī Sa'īd, from his father, from Abū Huraira, that the Apostle of Allah—upon whom be Allah's blessing and peace—once entered the mosque, when a man also entered, said his prayers, and then came and saluted the Prophet—upon whom be Allah's blessing and peace—who returned the salutation but said: "Go back and pray, for you did not say the prayers [properly]." He went back and said the prayers as he had said them before. Then he came and saluted the Prophet—upon whom be Allah's blessing and peace—who said: "Go back and pray, for you did not say the prayers [properly]." This happened three times, whereat [the man] said: "By Him who sent thee with the truth, I do not know how to do it better than that, so pray teach me." Said [the Prophet]: "When you stand up to pray, give the *takbīr,* then recite from the Qur'ān whatever you find you can do easily. Then bow till you are properly stooped in the bowing, then rise up till you are standing erect. Then prostrate yourself till you are properly prostrated, then rise [from the prostrate position] till you are sitting properly. Do it like that in all your saying of prayers."

ON THE PAUSE AFTER THE TAKBĪR IN DAILY PRAYER

The *takbīr* is the ejaculation "Allah is very great" which occurs at the very beginning of the prayer service, and which, after a pause, is followed by the recitation of a passage from the Qur'ān.

From al-Bukhārī, *Ṣaḥīḥ,* ed. L. Krehl (Leiden, 1862), I, 192.

As to What is to be Recited after the Takbīr.

Ḥafṣ b. 'Umar has related to us on the authority of Shu'ba, from Qatāda, from Anas, that the Prophet—upon whom be Allah's blessing and peace—and Abū Bakr and 'Umar used to open the prayers with: "Praise be to Allah, Lord of the worlds."

Mūsā b. Ismā'īl has related to us on the authority of 'Abd al-Wāhid b. Ziyād, who said: 'Umara b. al-Qa'qā' has related to us on the authority of Abū Zur'a, that Abū Huraira said: The Apostle of Allah—upon whom be Allah's blessing and peace—used to maintain a silence between the *takbīr* and the recitation. I think he (i.e., Abū Huraira) said it was but a short silence. I said [continued Abū Huraira]: "By my father and my mother, O Apostle of Allah, what do you say during that silence of yours between the *takbīr* and the recitation?" He answered: I say: "Allahumma! put between me and my sins the distance Thou hast put between the East and the West. Allahumma! cleanse me from my sins as a white garment is cleansed from defilements. Allahumma! wash out my sins with water, with snow and with the hail."

HOW THE PROPHET USED TO PRAY DURING THE NIGHT

From the *Musnad* of Abū 'Uwāna (Hyderabad, 1944), II, 312-313.

Yūsuf b. Muslim and Abū Humaid have both related to us, on the authority of Hajjāj b. Muḥammad, who said: Shu'ba related to me from Salama b. Kuhail, from Karīb, from Ibn 'Abbās, who said: I spent the night in the house of my maternal aunt Maimūna,[1] and I watched the Apostle of Allah—upon whom be Allah's blessing and peace—or maybe he said "I observed" or "I sought to see"—how he would say his prayers. Now he slept, and then he arose and washed his face and hands, but went to sleep [again]. Then he arose, went to the water skin, lifted the strap, and poured into the bowl—or the wooden vessel—and then poured it over his hand and per-

1 Maimūna bint al-Hārith was one of the Prophet's wives.

formed an excellent ablution between the two lustrations. Then he stood up and said his prayers. So I came and stood at his left, but he took me and set me at his right. Now the prayers of the Apostle of Allah—upon whom be Allah's blessing and peace—were completed in thirteen *rak'as,* after which he slept till he snored. We used to recognize him when he slept by his snoring. Then he went out to [morning] prayers and said his prayers.

He used to say during his prayer, or during his prostration: "Allahumma! set a light in my heart, a light in my hearing, a light at my right and a light at my left, a light before me, a light below me, a light above me, and make me a light." Said Shu'ba: Or he would say: "Make a light for me."

TAHAJJUD

From the *Ṣaḥīḥ* of al-Bukhārī, ed. L. Krehl (Leiden, 1862), I, 283-284.

> On *Tahajjud* at night, and on His saying (XVII, 79/81): "And keep vigil therein, as something in addition (*nāfila*) for thyself," meaning "keep wakeful therein."

'Alī b. 'Abdallah has related to us on the authority of Sufyān, who said: Sulaimān b. Abī Muslim has related to us from Ṭāwūs, who heard Ibn 'Abbās say: The Prophet—upon whom be Allah's blessing and peace—if he rose up at night used to perform vigil (*tahajjud*). He would say: "Allahumma! to Thee be praise. Thou art the guardian of the heavens and the earth and of whoever is in them. To Thee be praise. Thou art the light of the heavens and the earth and of whoever is in them. To Thee be praise. Thou art the sovereign of the heavens and the earth, and of whoever is in them. To Thee be praise. Thou art the truth. Thy promise is the truth. The meeting with Thee is something true. Thy word is something true. Paradise is something true. Hell is something true. The prophets are something true. Muḥammad is something true. The Hour is something true. Allahumma! to Thee do I submit myself; in Thee do I believe; on Thee do I rely for help; to Thee do I repent; by Thee do I contend; to Thee do I come for judgment. Forgive me my former and my latter sins, both the secret ones and the open ones. Thou art the One who hurries things up or delays them. There is no deity save Thee—or no deity other than Thee."

Said Sufyān: 'Abd al-Karīm Abū Umayya added to the above [that he also said]: "There is no might and no power unless with Allah."

PRAYER DURING AN ECLIPSE

From the *Ṣaḥīḥ* of al-Bukhārī, ed. L. Krehl (Leiden, 1862), I. 271-272.

On Making Mention of Allah During an Eclipse: a Tradition from Ibn 'Abbās

Muḥammad b. al-'Alā' has related to us, on the authority of Abū Usāma, from Buraid b. 'Abdallah, from Abū Burda, from Abū Mūsā, who said: [One day] there was an eclipse of the sun, and the Prophet—upon whom be Allah's blessing and peace—rose up terrified, thinking that it might be the Hour. So he went to the mosque and prayed with the longest standings, bowings, and prostrations I had ever seen him perform. He said: "These are signs which Allah—mighty and majestic is He—sends. They are not sent to indicate the death of anyone, nor anyone's birth, but by them Allah would terrify His servants. So when you see anything of this nature, seek refuge in making mention of Him, in supplication to Him, in seeking forgiveness from Him."

On Supplication During an Eclipse, as Related by Abū Mūsā and 'Ā'isha from the Prophet

Abū'l-Walīd has related to us, on the authority of Zā'ida, who said: Ziyād b. 'Ilāqa related to us, saying: I heard al-Mughīra b. Shu'ba say that the sun was eclipsed on the day [the Prophet's little son] Ibrāhīm died. Folk said: "It is eclipsed because of Ibrāhīm's death." The Apostle of Allah—

See I. Goldziher, "Die Sabbathinstitution im Islam," in *Gedenkbuch zur Erinnerung an David Kaufmann* (Breslau, 1900), pp. 86-103; T. W. Junyboll, art. "Djum'a" in *EI,* I, 1061-1062; C. H. Becker, "Zur Geschichte der islamischen Kultus," in *Der Islam* (1911), III, 374-399.

From the *Sunan* of Abū 'Abd ar-Raḥmān Aḥmad an-Nasā'ī (d. 303 A.H. = 915 A.D.) (Cairo, 1312 A.H. = 1894 A.D.), I, 201-211.

That the Assembling [on Friday] is a Duty

Sa'īd b. 'Abd ar-Raḥmān al-Makhzūmī has informed us on the authority of Sufyān, from Abū'z-Zinād, from al-A'raj, from Abū Huraira, as also Abū Ṭā'ūs, from his father, from Abū Huraira, that the Apostle of Allah—upon whom be Allah's blessing and peace—said: "We are the last and yet the first. [We Muslims are] last since they (i.e., the Jews and Christians) were given scripture before us, we being given it later than they were, and [they were given] also this day which Allah—mighty and majestic is He—ordained for them, but they differed about it, i.e., about Friday, so Allah guided us to it so that other communities follow us (i.e., come after us) in this, the Jews tomorrow and the Christians the day after tomorrow." [1]

Wāṣil b. 'Abd al-A'lā has informed us on the authority of Ibn Fuḍail, from Abū Mālik al-Ashja'ī, from Abū Ḥāzim, from Abū Huraira, and from Rab'ī b. Ḥirāsh from Ḥudhaifa, both of whom reported that the Apostle of Allah—upon whom be Allah's blessing and peace—said: "Allah—mighty and majestic is He—led astray from Friday those who came before us, so that the Jews have Saturday and the Christians Sunday; then Allah brought us along and guided us to Friday. [The order of days as] He has appointed them is Friday, Saturday, Sunday, so on the Last Day [when peoples are called in their

[1] The point is that the original day for weekly worship was Friday, the day appointed for both Jews and Christians, but they came to differ about what day should be the weekly holy day, and with Islam Allah has guided the Muslims back to the original day He had appointed, so now the Muslims, who are a later community, yet precede the others in the day on which they meet for community worship.

communities] they will be following after us. Thus in this world we are the last people [to be formed into a religious community] but on the Day we shall be the first, those who receive their judgment before [other] creatures."

On How Serious it Is to Neglect Friday

Ya'qūb b. Ibrāhīm has informed us, on the authority of Yaḥyā b. Sa'īd, from Muḥammad b. 'Amr, from 'Ubaida b. Sufyān al-Ḥaḍramī, from Abū'l-Ja'd aḍ-Ḍamrī, who was on friendly relations with the Prophet—upon whom be Allah's blessing and peace—that Allah will put a brand on the heart of anyone who passes three Fridays in neglect.[2]

Muḥammad b. Ma'mar has informed us, on the authority of Ḥibbān, from Ābān, from Yaḥyā b. Abī Kathīr, from al-Ḥaḍramī b. Lāḥiq, from Zaid, from Abū Sallām, from Ḥakam b. Mīnā', that he heard Ibn 'Abbās and Ibn 'Umar relating how the Apostle of Allah—upon whom be Allah's blessing and peace—said while in the pulpit: "There will be those who neglect that with which they were entrusted in regard to Friday, on whose hearts Allah will put a seal so that they become of those who neglect."

Muḥmūd b. Ghailān informed me, on the authority of al-Walīd b. Muslim, from al Mufaḍḍal b. Fuḍāla, from 'Ayyāsh b. 'Abbās, from Bukair b. al-Ashajj, from Nāfi', from Ibn 'Umar, from Ḥafṣa the wife of the Prophet, that the Prophet—upon whom be Allah's blessing and peace—said: "Going out on Friday [to perform one's religious duties] is incumbent on every male who has attained puberty." [3]

On Expiation for Inexcusable Neglect of Friday

Aḥmad b. Sulaimān has informed us, on the authority of Yazīd b. Hārūn, from Humām, from Qatāda, from Qudāma

[2] The commentary says that this means that if a man neglects the Friday service for three Fridays in succession Allah will put a veil on his heart and will withdraw from him His favors.

[3] *Muḥtalim* means a youth who has reached the age of having nocturnal emissions.

b. Wabara, from Samūra b. Jundub, that the Apostle of Allah —upon whom be Allah's blessing and peace—said: "He who neglects Friday without excuse must give a *dīnār* in charitable alms, but if he finds he has not sufficient, then half a *dīnār*."

On the Excellence of Friday

Suwaid b. Naṣr has informed us, on the authority of 'Abdallah, from Yūnus, from az-Zuhrī, who said that 'Abd ar-Raḥmān al-A'raj related how he had heard Abū Huraira say that the Apostle of Allah—upon whom be Allah's blessing and peace—once said: "The sun rises on no better day than Friday, for on it Adam—on whom be peace—was created, on it he was put in the Garden, and on it he was expelled therefrom."

On Being Diligent in Calling Down Blessings on the Prophet on Fridays

Isḥāq b. Manṣūr has informed us, on the authority of Ḥusain al-Ju'fī, from 'Abd ar-Raḥmān b. Yazīd b. Jābir, from Abū'l-Ash'ath aṣ-Ṣan'ānī, from Aus b. Aus, that the Prophet—upon whom be Allah's blessing and peace—said: "Most excellent among your days is Friday, for on it Adam was created and on it he died, and on it will be both the *nafkha* and the *ṣa'qa*,[4] so be diligent in calling down blessings on me [on that day], for your prayers will be presented to me." They said: "O Apostle of Allah, how will our prayers be presented to you when you are no more?" They meant: "when you have crumbled to dust." He answered: "Allah—mighty and majestic is He—has forbidden the earth to devour the bodies of the prophets—upon whom be peace."

[4] Both these words are used in connection with the Last Trump at the end of time, the former meaning a "blast" and the latter the sound of a thunderbolt. Those who say that Isrāfīl blows only two blasts on the Trump hold that the first is the "blast of destruction" which kills off all life on earth, and the second the "blast of resurrection" which raises them all to life to face Judgment. Both blasts will be on a Friday.

On Using the Toothpick on Friday

Muḥammad b. Salama has informed us, on the authority of Ibn Wahb, from 'Amr b. al-Ḥārith, that Sa'īd b. Abī Hilāl and Bukair b. al-Ashajj reported from Abū Bakr b. al-Munkadir, from 'Amr b. Salīm, from 'Abd ar-Raḥmān b. Abī Sa'īd, from his father, that the Apostle of Allah—upon whom be Allah's blessing and peace—said: "To take a bath on Friday is incumbent on everyone who has reached puberty, as also to use the toothpick and let him make use of perfume as he is able." Bukair, however, does not mention 'Abd ar-Raḥmān, and as to the perfuming he says: "even if it is such perfume as women use."

On the Incumbent Duty of Bathing on Friday

Qutaiba has informed us, on the authority of Mālik, from Nāfi', from Ibn 'Imrān, that the Apostle of Allah—upon whom be Allah's blessing and peace—said: "Let each one of you when Friday comes take a bath." Qutaiba also informed us on the authority of Mālik, from Safwān b. Salīm, from 'Aṭā' b. Yasār, from Abū Sa'īd al-Khudrī, that the Apostle of Allah—upon whom be Allah's blessing and peace—said: "To bathe on Friday is incumbent on everyone who has reached puberty." Ḥumaid b. Mas'ada has informed us, on the authority of Bishr, from Dāwūd b. Abī Hind, from Abū'z-Zubair, from Jābir, that the Apostle of Allah—upon whom be Allah's blessing and peace—said: "It is incumbent on every man who is a Muslim to take a bath one day in seven, and that day is Friday."

ALMSGIVING

The two technical terms for almsgiving are *zakāt* and *ṣadaqa,* both being words borrowed from the Aramaic. In the Qur'ān they seem to be used interchangeably for that practical sharing with others less fortunate the bounty one receives from Allah, a sharing which was to be one of the marks of a true Muslim. In the later orthodox teaching of Islam a distinction is generally drawn between the terms, *zakāt* being used for the obligatory tithing every practicing Muslim must observe and *ṣadaqa* used to mean any charitable almsgiving over and above the legal alms. Almsgiving was a pre-Islamic practice, as is evident from the story in the *Ṣaḥīḥ* of al-Bukhārī (ed. L. Krehl [Leiden, 1862], I, 363) which tells of how Ḥakīm b. Ḥizām came to Muhammad and asked whether the religious practices he had been wont to observe in his heathen days, such as *ṣadaqa,* the freeing of slaves, and being attentive to one's kinsfolk, would still count to his credit now that he had accepted Islam, and the Prophet assured him that they would.

On the question of almsgiving, see the articles "Ṣadaka" and "Zakāt" in *EI,* IV, 33-35 and 1202-1205; N. P. Aghnides, *Muhammadan Theories of Finance* (New York, 1916), pp. 203-347 and 439-464; C. Snouck Hurgronje, *Nieuwe Bijdragen tot de Kennis van den Islam* (Haag, 1882).

ALMSGIVING IN THE QUR'ĀN

LXXVI, 7-10.

They (i.e., the virtuous) fulfill vows, and are fearful of a Day whose evil is about to fly forth. They give food, out of love for Him, to the unfortunate, the orphan, the prisoner [saying]: "We feed you only for Allah's sake; we wish from you no recompense and no thanks, for we fear from our Lord a grim, calamitous Day."

XXXV, 29/26-30/27.

Verily, those who read Allah's Book, and observe prayer, and contribute both publicly and privately out of that which We have given them as provision, may hope for a gain that will never perish. He, indeed, will pay them their rewards, and of His bounty give them something extra. He, indeed, is forgiving, grateful.

XIII, 22.

And those who patiently endure, desiring the face of their Lord, and observe prayer, and out of that which We have given them as provision contribute both publicly and privately, and who drive out evil by good, these are they for whom is the reward of the [celestial] Dwelling.

II, 43/40-44/41.

Now observe prayer and pay the *zakāt* and bow down along with those who bow down. Do ye bid people to be upright and then yourselves forget, though ye read the Book? Do ye have no intelligence?

II, 177/172.

Being upright does not consist in turning your faces to the East or to the West, but being upright is to believe in Allah, and the Last Day, and the angels, and the Books, and the Prophets, and in bestowing one's wealth, in spite of love for it, upon relatives, on the orphans, the unfortunate, the son of the way, beggars, and for [ransoming] those enslaved, to observe prayer, and pay the *zakāt*. Those [are upright] who fulfill their covenants when they have entered into such, who patiently endure under adversities and hardships and when under attack. Those are they who are sincere, and those are the ones who are pious.

II, 215/211.

They will ask thee [O Muḥammad] about what they contribute. Say: "What good ye contribute is for parents and kinsfolk, for the orphans and the unfortunate and for the son of the way. Whatsoever good ye do, Allah, indeed, knows all about it."

II, 261/263-277.

The similitude of those who contribute of their wealth in the way of Allah is that they are like a seed which produces seven ears, in every ear of which are a hundred seeds, seeing that Allah gives double to whom He wills, and Allah is wide-reaching, knowing. Those who contribute of their wealth in the way of Allah and do not follow up what they have contributed with reminders or annoyance, they have their reward with their Lord, no fear will be upon them nor will they grieve. Polite language and forgiveness are better than charitable alms followed by annoyance. Allah is rich, forbearing. O ye who believe, do not spoil your charitable almsgiving by reminders and annoyance, like one who contributes of his wealth to be seen of men, and has no belief in Allah and the Last Day. His similitude is that he is like a hard rock on which is earth, and which, when rain falls on it, is left bare. Such have no power over anything of what they have gained, and Allah does not guide the unbelieving people. But the similitude of those who contribute of their wealth out of a desire that Allah be well-pleased, and that they themselves be strengthened, is that they are like a garden on a hill on which rain falls and it yields double produce, and even if no rain falls on it there is dew. And Allah is observant of what ye are doing. Would any one of you like it if he had a garden of date palms and grapevines beneath which streams flow, in which he has all kinds of fruits, yet old age comes on him and the progeny he had are weaklings, when a fiery whirlwind comes upon it so that it is burned up? Thus does Allah make clear to you the signs that maybe ye will ponder.

O ye who believe, contribute of the good things ye have gained and out of that which We have produced from the earth for you, and do not choose the filthy parts thereof to contribute, such as ye yourselves would not accept unless ye were conniving therein.[1] Be it known to you that Allah is rich, praiseworthy. Satan promises you poverty while bidding you commit crimes, whereas Allah promises you forgiveness from Himself and bounty, and Allah is wide-reaching, knowing. He gives wisdom to whom He wills and whosoever has been given wisdom has indeed been given much good. Yet none are admonished save those possessed of intelligence. Whatsoever contribution ye make, or whatsoever vow ye vow, Allah as-

[1] The verb *aghmada* refers to a type of commercial trickery whereby there is connivance to pay less than full value for merchandise.

suredly knows about it, and for the wrongdoers there are no helpers. If ye give charitable alms publicly it is good, but if ye do it privately (lit., conceal it), and give it to the poor, that is better for you, and it will atone for some of your evil deeds, for Allah is well-informed about what ye do. Guiding them is no responsibility of thine [O Muḥammad]. Allah will guide whom He wills. Whatever good ye [Muslims] contribute is for your own souls, seeing that ye contribute with no desire for anything save the face of Allah, and whatever good ye contribute will be fully repaid you, and ye will not be wronged. [It is] for the poor who have been restricted in the way of Allah, being unable to move around in the land. The ignorant man considers them rich because of their modest demeanor. By their marks thou mayest know them. They do not beg importunately from folk. Whatsoever good ye contribute Allah knows about it.

Those who contribute of their wealth by night and by day, privately or publicly, such have their reward with their Lord, no fear will be upon them nor will they grieve. Those who devour usury will not arise [on the Day] save as he will arise whom Satan has affected by his touch. That is because they said: "Usury is only like bargaining," though Allah has made bargaining licit but usury illicit. So whoever has a warning from his Lord come to him, and stops, he may have what is past, and his affair is with Allah, but he who returns [to it], such are the companions of the Fire, in which they will eternally abide. Allah is wiping out usury but is making charitable alms bear interest, and Allah does not love any guilty infidel. Verily, those who believe and perform works of righteousness, who observe prayer and pay the *zakāt*, they have their reward with their Lord, no fear will be upon them, nor will they grieve.

IX, 58-60.

There are some of them who defame thee in the matter of the charitable contributions. If they are given a share thereof they are pleased, but if they are not given a share thereof, behold, they are angered. Would that they had been pleased with what Allah and His messenger gave them, and had said: "Allah is our sufficiency. Allah will give us of His bounty, and so will His messenger. Verily, toward Allah is our desire." The charitable contributions are for the poor, for the unfortunate, for those who labor therein,[2] for those whose hearts are to be changed, for those enslaved, for [expending] in the way of Allah, and for the son of the way. [This is] an ordinance from Allah, and Allah is knowing, wise.

ABŪ BAKR'S INSTRUCTIONS ABOUT ZAKĀT

From the *Ṣaḥīḥ* of al-Bukhārī, ed. L. Krehl (Leiden, 1862), I, 368.

On the Zakāt to be Paid on Cattle

Muḥammad b. 'Abdallah b. al-Muthannā has related to us, on the authority of his father, who said: Thumāma b. 'Abdallah b. Anas has related to me that Anas told him that Abū Bakr wrote for him this document when he sent him to al-Baḥrain:

In the name of Allah, the Merciful, the Compassionate.

This is the ordinance concerning alms which the Apostle of Allah—upon whom be Allah's blessing and peace—laid down for the Muslims, and about which Allah had given command to His Apostle, so let whosoever of the Muslims is asked for it according to its measure pay it, but if anyone is asked for more than that let him not pay it. For twenty-four camels or less cattle [the assessment is] a ewe for each five. If they reach from twenty-five to thirty-five it is a yearling she-camel, but if no yearling she-camel is available then a yearling male. If they reach from thirty-six to forty-five, it is a two-year-old she-camel. If they reach from forty-six to sixty, it is a three-year-old she-camel ready for the stallion. If they reach from sixty-one to seventy-five it is a four-year-old she-camel. If

[2] This is said to mean the tax collectors who busied themselves collecting alms from the community for various charitable works. The changing of hearts refers to those who received money from the community in order to become converts to Islam.

they reach from seventy-six to ninety it is two two-year-old she-camels. If they reach from ninety-one to a hundred and twenty it is two three-year-old she-camels ready for the stallion. If they reach more than a hundred and twenty, then for every forty it is a two-year-old she-camel, and for every fifty a three-year-old she-camel. He who does not have with him more than four camels does not have to pay the alms save if His Lord wills, but if he reaches five camels then it is a ewe. The alms on small cattle if they are pasturing, if they are between forty and a hundred and twenty it is a ewe. If they are more, from a hundred and twenty up to two hundred it is two ewes, if they are between two hundred and three hundred it is three ewes, and if they are more than three hundred it is a ewe for every hundred. If those a man has pasturing are less than forty single sheep then there is no alms due unless his Lord wills. On coinage it is the fourth of a tenth, but if the amount is not more than a hundred and ninety [*dirhams*] then he pays nothing at all, unless his Lord wills.

ON THE SINFULNESS OF WITHHOLDING ZAKĀT

From the *Ṣaḥīḥ* of Muslim ('Alī Ṣubeih edition; Cairo, n.d.), III, 70-71.

Suwaid b. Sa'īd has related to us, on the authority of Ḥafṣ, i.e., Ibn Maisara aṣ-Ṣan'ānī, from Zaid b. Aslam, that Abū Ṣāliḥ Dhakwān informed him that he had heard Abū Huraira say that the Apostle of Allah—upon whom be Allah's blessing and peace—said: "There is no one in possession of gold or silver who does not pay what is due thereon but will find himself on the Day of Resurrection plated with plates of fire and roasted upon them in the fire of Gehenna, so that his sides, his forehead, his back are scorched, and as soon as they have cooled off they are returned to him, during 'a Day whose length is fifty thousand years' (LXX, 4), until the judgment among men is finished and he is shown his path, either to Paradise or to Hell." Someone said: "O Apostle of Allah, what about camels?" He answered: "There is no owner of camels who does not pay what is due thereon, and what is due on their milk on the day they come down to water, but on the Day will be cast down before them on a level spot, and however numerous they may be not a single young weaned camel will be missing, and they will trample him under their feet and bite him with their mouths, and whenever the last has finished with him the first will begin again, during a Day whose length is fifty thousand years, till the judgment among men is finished, and he is shown his path either to Paradise or to Hell." Someone asked: "O Apostle of Allah, what about cattle and sheep?" He replied: "There is no owner of cattle or sheep who does not pay what is due thereon, but on the Day he will be cast down before them on a level spot, and not one of them will be missing, whether horned, or hornless, or broken-horned, and they will gore him with their horns and trample him with their hooves, and whenever the last have finished with him the first will begin again, during a Day whose length is fifty thousand years, until the judgment among men is finished, and he is shown his path either to Paradise or to Hell."

ON THE MERIT OF ALMSGIVING

From the *Ṣaḥīḥ* of al-Bukhārī, ed. L. Krehl (Leiden, 1862), I, 359.

On the merit of the alms given in charity by a niggardly person in sound health, on the grounds of the words of the Most High (II, 254/255): "O ye who believe, contribute from that which We have given you as provision before there comes a Day on which there will be no bargaining, no amity, no intercession. The unbelievers they are the wrongdoers" [and LXIII, 10]: "and contribute from that which We have given you as provision before death come to one of you, and he says: 'O Lord, wilt Thou not defer me a little that I may give alms and become one of the upright?'"

Mūsā b. Ismā'īl has related to us, on the authority of 'Abd al-Wāhid, on the authority of 'Umāra b. al-Qa'qā', on the authority of Abū Zur'a, on the authority of Abū Huraira, who said that a man came to the Prophet—upon whom be Allah's blessing and peace—and asked: "O Apostle of Allah, what charitable alms gets the greatest reward?" He answered: "It is that you should give charitable alms when you are a niggardly person in good health, who is afraid of poverty and puts his hopes in riches. So do not put it off till [your departing soul] reaches your throat, for then you will say: 'This is for So-and-So, this is for So-and-So,' when it already belongs to somebody else."

Mūsā b. Ismā'īl has related to us, on the authority of Abū 'Uwāna, from Firās, from ash-Shā'bī, from Masrūq, from 'Ā'isha—with whom may Allah be pleased—that some of the wives of the Prophet—upon whom be Allah's blessing and peace—once asked him: "Which of us will be the quickest to rejoin you [after your death]?" He answered: "She who has the longest hand." Thereupon they got a rod and began to measure themselves, and Sawda had the longest hand. Afterwards we learned that the length of hand had reference to almsgiving. Sawda was the one of us who went most quickly to meet him, and she used to love to give charitable alms.

FASTING

The annual fast of the month of Ramaḍān, the ninth month of the Muslim year, is, with the annual pilgrimage to Mecca in the twelfth month, one of the two prominent external manifestations of the religious life of Islam. Since the Muslim calendar is a lunar one, this month of Ramaḍān moves progressively through all the seasons of the solar year. In all Muslim countries it is announced by the appearance of the new moon of the month of Ramaḍān, and ends with the appearance of the new moon of Shawwāl. During that whole month all practicing Muslims in normal health abstain from food, drink, and sex enjoyment from the time a white thread can be distinguished from a black one in the morning till they can be no longer distinguished in the evening. At night, however, there is general rejoicing, the mosques are specially lit up for services, and there is great feasting and merriment in the houses. At various times other than Ramadān meritorious fasts may be practiced by the pious, and fasting for so many days is one of the ways of expiating various breaches in the observance of the religious law.

On fasting see the articles "Ṣawm" and "Ramaḍān" *EI,* IV, 192-199, III, 1111; F. Goitein, "Zur Entstehung des Ramaḍān," *Der Islam,* XVIII (1929), pp. 189 ff.; G. Vajda, "Jeune musulman et jeune juif," *Hebrew Union College Annual,* XII (1937-38), 367-385; Georg Jacob, *Der Muslimische Fastenmonat Ramaḍān* (Greifswald, 1894); Karmaly Hiridjee, *Le Ramadan, ses rites, ses bienfaits* (Cachan [Seine], 1950).

FASTING IN THE QUR'ĀN

II, 183/179-187/183.

O ye who believe, fasting is prescribed for you as it was prescribed for those who preceded you. Maybe ye will show piety. [It is for] a calculated number of days, but should anyone of you be sick, or on a journey, then a number of other days. For those who are able [yet do not perform] it, a redemption [is provided, viz.,] the feeding of an unfortunate, though it is better for one to do good voluntarily, and that ye should fast is better for you did ye know it. [It is for] the month of Ramaḍān, in which the Qur'ān was sent down as a guidance for men, and as evidential signs of the guidance, and the Furqān. So whoever of you sees the month let him fast [during] it, but should anyone be sick or on a journey, then a number of other days. Allah desires it to be easy for you, with no desire that it be difficult, and that ye may complete the number [of days], and that ye may magnify Allah for the way He has guided you, and maybe ye will be thankful.

Now if My servants ask thee [O Muḥammad] about Me, why, I am near at hand. I answer the call of him who calls when he calls upon Me, so let them respond to Me, and let them believe in Me; perchance they will be rightly guided.

Going in to your wives on the night of the fast is lawful for you. They are a clothing for you, and ye are a clothing for them. Allah knows that ye have been defrauding yourselves, so He has relented toward you and has pardoned you. So now lie with them and seek what Allah has prescribed for you, and eat and drink till at the dawning a white thread is distinguishable by you from a black thread. Then fulfill the fast till night, and do not be lying with them when ye should be occupying your place in the houses of worship. These are the limits [set by] Allah, so draw not near to them. Thus does Allah make clear His signs to men; maybe they will show piety.

ON THE EXCELLENCE OF FASTING

From the *Ṣaḥīḥ* of Muslim ('Alī Ṣubeiḥ edition; Cairo, n.d.), III, 157-158.

Muḥammad b. Rāfi' has related to me, on the authority of 'Abd ar-Razzāq, on the authority of Ibn Juraij, from 'Aṭā', from Abū Ṣāliḥ az-Zayyāt, that he heard Abū Huraira—with whom may Allah be pleased—say: Said the Apostle of Allah—on whom be Allah's blessing and peace: "Allah—mighty and majestic is He—has declared: 'Every good work a man does is done for himself save fasting, which [is done] for Me, wherefore I Myself shall reward him for it.' Fasting is a protection, so when it is a fast day for any one of you let him use no unseemly language on that day, nor raise any clamor. Should anyone abuse him or pick a fight with him, let him say: 'I am a man who is fasting.' By Him in whose hand is Muḥammad's soul, the bad breath from the mouth of one who is fasting will smell sweeter to Allah on the Day of Resurrection than the perfume of musk. He who fasts has two occasions for rejoicing. When he finishes his fast he rejoices at its finishing, and when he meets his Lord he will have joy because of his fasting."

Abū Bakr b. Abī Shaiba has related to us, on the authority of Abū Mu'āwiya and of Wakī', from al-A'mash; and Zuhair b. Ḥarb has related to us, on the authority of Jarīr, from al-A'mash; and Abū Sa'īd al-Ashajj, whose wording we give, has related to us, on the authority of Wakī', from al-A'mash, from Abū Ṣāliḥ, from Abū Huraira—with whom may Allah be pleased—that the Apostle of Allah—upon whom be Allah's blessing and peace—said: "Allah—mighty and majestic is He—has declared: 'For every good work a man does, merit tenfold to seven hundredfold will be reckoned, save [in the case of] fasting, for it [is done] for Me, and I Myself will reward it, since it is for My sake that he gives up his sex indulgence and his food.' He who fasts has two occasions for rejoicing. There is a rejoicing when he has finished his fast, and there is a rejoicing when he meets His Lord, for the bad breath of his mouth will smell sweeter to Allah than the perfume of musk."

THE INSTITUTION OF THE FAST OF RAMAḌĀN

From al-Khuḍarī, *Nūr al-Yaqīn* (3rd ed.; Cairo, 1326 A.H. = 1908 A.D.), pp. 111-112.

In [the month of] Sha'bān of this year (i.e., end of year 2 A.H.), Allah enjoined on the Islamic community fasting during the month of Ramaḍān. He—upon whom be Allah's blessing and peace—had before this been accustomed to fast for three days each month. Fasting is thus one of the pillars of this religion, and one of the practices by which its rule of life (*niẓām*) is made perfect. Man has a natural inclination to love of himself, and to endeavor to turn whatever comes to him to his own particular advantage, leaving what is beyond that, [such as consideration for] the necessities of the weak and the unfortunate. Thus there must be some incentive to urge him on to [consideration of] the needs of those people whose strength is insufficient for the securing of their necessities. Now there is nothing more powerful [in this connection] than to taste the pangs of hunger and thirst, since by them his ego is softened up and his character is educated, so that it becomes easy for him to bestow [of his wealth] in charity.

THE FAST OF 'ĀSHŪRĀ'

From Muslim *Ṣaḥīḥ* ('Alī Ṣubeiḥ edition; Cairo, n.d.), III, 146, 149.

This is a fast observed on the tenth day of Muḥarram, the first month of the Muslim calendar. It was taken over by the Prophet from the Jewish *'āsōr* fast of the Day of Atonement, which fell on the tenth of Tishri. After his break with the Jews, the fast of Ramaḍān was instituted as the proper Muslim fast, but the custom of fasting on 'Āshūrā' has persisted, being now said to commemorate the day Noah left the ark. It is the day when the doors of the Ka'ba in Mecca are opened for visitors.

See Wensinck's article 'Āshūrā' in *EI*, I, 486 and his *Mohammed en de Joden te Medina* (Leiden, 1908), pp. 121-125; Bīrūnī, *Chronology of Ancient Nations*, tr. Sachau (London, 1879), p. 327; Snouck Hurgronje, *Mekka* (Haag, 1889), II, 51; Gaudefroy-Desmombynes, *Pèlerinage* (Paris, 1923), p. 60.

Zuhair b. Ḥarb has related to us on the authority of Jarīr, from Hishām b. 'Urwa, from his father, from 'Ā'isha—with whom may Allah be pleased—who said: "The Quraish used to fast on 'Āshūrā' in pre-Islamic days, and the Apostle of Allah—upon whom be Allah's blessing and peace—also used to fast on it, so when he migrated to Madina he continued to fast on it and commanded it to be kept as a fast, but when the fast of Ramaḍān was made obligatory, he said: 'Let anyone who so wishes fast on it and let anyone who so wishes abandon it.'" Abū Bakr b. Abī Shaiba and Abū Kuraib have related to us, saying: Ibn Numair related it to us from Hishām with the same *isnād*, but he did not include at the beginning the words: "and the Apostle of Allah used to fast on it," and toward the end he had: "and he abandoned 'Āshūrā', so whoever so wished fasted on it and whoever so wished abandoned it," not making [this ending] part of the words of the Apostle of Allah—upon whom be Allah's blessing and peace—as Jarīr does.

Ḥarmala b. Yaḥyā has related to us, on the authority of Ibn Wahb, on the authority of Yūnus, from Ibn Shihāb, who was informed by Ḥumaid b. 'Abd ar-Raḥmān that he heard Mu'āwiya b. Abī Sufyān [1] preaching in Madina, i.e., on an occasion when he visited Madina and preached there on the Day of 'Āshūrā', when he said: "Where are your theologians, O people of Madina? I heard the Apostle of Allah—upon whom be Allah's blessing and peace—say of this day: 'This is

[1] He was the first Umayyad caliph, who reigned at Damascus 40-60 A.H. (= 661-680 A.D.).

the Day of 'Āshūrā'. Allah has not decreed it as a day of fasting for you, but I am fasting, so whoever of you would care to fast let him fast, but whoever would care to break it let him break it.' "

Yaḥyā b. Yaḥyā has related to us on the authority of Hushaim, from Abū Bishr, from Sa'īd b. Jubair, from Ibn 'Abbās —with whom may Allah be pleased—who said: "When the Apostle of Allah—upon whom be Allah's blessing and peace—came to Madina he found the Jews fasting on the Day of 'Āshūrā'. When they were asked about it they said: 'This is the day on which Allah gave victory to Moses and the Children of Israel over Pharaoh, so we keep it as a fast to honor it.' Said the Prophet—upon whom be Allah's blessing and peace: 'We are more worthy of Moses than you are,' so he commanded that it be kept a fast."

FASTS OF EXPIATION

Fasting may be used as a means of expiation. From the amount of attention given in the books to these fasts of expiation (*ṣaum al-kaffāra*) one suspects that, though other means are prescribed, that of fasting is the easiest and most commonly employed. The four commonly recognized cases are:

1. For homicide, i.e., where the life of a fellow Muslim has been taken, but accidentally taken, so that it is not murder but manslaughter. This is based on Sūra IV, 92/94-93/95.

It is not for any believer to kill a believer except by mistake. Whosoever kills a believer by mistake must free a believing slave, and blood-wit (*diya*) is to be handed over to his family, unless they choose that it be spent in charitable alms. Should he belong to a people with whom ye are at enmity, yet is a believer, then [the expiation is merely] the freeing of a believing slave. Should he belong to a people between whom and you there is a covenant, then the blood-wit is to be handed over to his family, and [the expiation is] the freeing of a believing slave. Should one not find [the wherewithal to do that, then the expiation is] fasting for two months consecutively as a penitence prescribed by Allah, for Allah, indeed, is knowing, wise. But should one kill a believer intentionally, his recompense is Gehenna, therein to abide eternally, for Allah will be wroth with him, will curse him, and prepare for him a mighty torment.

2. For a mistaken or a broken oath. This is based on Sūra V, 89/91.

Allah will not take you to task for foolishness in your oaths, but He will take you to task for pacts ye have made by oath [should ye break them]. The expiation for such is the feeding of ten unfortunates with the average amount ye feed to your own families, or the clothing them (i.e., the aforesaid ten unfortunates), or the freeing of a slave. However, should one not find [the wherewithal to do that, then the expiation is] fasting for three days. That is the expiation for oaths when ye have sworn, so watch your oaths.

3. For killing game while on pilgrimage. This is based on Sūra V, 95/96.

O ye who believe, do not kill game while ye are in sacral state (*ḥurum*). Should anyone of you kill such intentionally, then he must from [his own] flocks pay as compensation the like of what he has killed, according as two just persons from among you decide, to be an offering delivered at the Ka'ba, or as an expiation [in place of a compensation, either] the feeding of unfortunates, or the equivalent thereof in fasting, that he may taste the heinousness of his affair.

4. For illegitimate divorce. This is based on Sūra LVIII, 3/4-4/5.

For those who by formula [1] divorce their wives and then retract what they have said, the [expiation is the] freeing of a slave before they touch one another again. Thereby Allah admonishes you, and Allah is well informed of what ye are doing. But should one not find [the wherewithal to do that,

[1] The word is *taẓāhara,* which is said to mean divorcing a woman by using the formula: "May you be to me as my mother's back."

then the expiation is] fasting for two months consecutively before they touch one another again. And should anyone not be able [to do that, then the expiation is] the feeding of sixty unfortunates. That is in order that ye may believe in Allah and in His messenger, and those are the limits set by Allah, whereas for the unbelievers there is a painful torment.

PILGRIMAGE

Pilgrimage to holy places has been a religious custom from very ancient times in the Near East, and Mecca was the center of an annual pilgrimage in Arabia long before Muhammad was born. Apparently there were several sacred sites in the Meccan area, each with its own special rites and ceremonies, and when Muhammad in the year II of the Hijra changed the *qibla* from Jerusalem to Mecca and made its shrine, the Ka'ba, the point to which Muslims were to turn in prayer, it was inevitable that the pilgrimage to the Meccan shrine should be Islamized. This Muhammad did by severing it from its pagan connections, associating it with Abraham and Ishmael of Biblical story, and endeavoring to combine the rites at the various sites into a single complex of ceremonies which could be accomplished during the pilgrimage days at the beginning of the twelfth month, Dhū'l-Ḥijja. Had he lived longer and himself led more pilgrimages, the welding of this combination might have been more complete. As it has come down in Islam, however, the pilgrimage consists of two things, viz., the *'umra*, or visitation, which is concerned more particularly with the central shrine at Mecca itself, and the *ḥajj*, or "going round" the various holy places within and without Mecca, including the visits to Mina, Muzdalifa and 'Arafāt, with rites of prayer, lapidation and sacrifice, with a final rite of circumambulation and desacralization at Mecca itself. Since the sanctity of a holy place extends for some distance around it, no unbeliever may come within a certain distance of the city, and even believers making pilgrimage to it must at that distance put themselves into a sacral state (*iḥrām*) and wear a special pilgrim garb. Since few, if any, of the pilgrims arriving would be familiar with the minutiae of the rites and ceremonies for the days of pilgrimage, numbers of the local inhabitants have found a lucrative profession in being a pilgrim guide (*muṭawwif*). Though it is one of the five "pillars" of Islam, the difficulties of making a pilgrimage prevent all but a small fraction of Muslims from accomplishing it, the majority being excusable since they cannot meet the fourth of the four requirements of being free, Muslim, of age, and able. The visit to Madina is an act of piety but is not part of the *ḥajj.*

On pilgrimage see: C. Snouck Hurgronje, *Het mekkaansche Feest* (Leiden, 1880) and *Mekka mit Bilderatlas* (Haag, 1889); Sir Richard Burton, *Pilgrimage to al-Medinah and Meccah* (London, 1913); A. Rhalli, *Christians at Mecca* (London, 1909); S. Spiro Bey, *The Moslem Pilgrimage* (Alexandria, 1932); M. Gaudefroy-Desmombynes, *Le pèlerinage à la Mecque* (Paris, 1923); C. Rathjens, *Die Pilgerfahrt nach Mekka* (Hamburg, 1948); J. Roman, *Le pèlerinage aux lieux saints de l'Islam* (Paris, 1954).

PILGRIMAGE IN THE QUR'ĀN

XXII, 26/27-37/38.

And [make mention of] when We prepared as a habitation for Abraham the site of the House [1] [saying to him]: Do not associate anything with Me, but make pure My House for those who circumambulate, those who stand, those who bow and those who make prostration. And announce among the people the pilgrimage (*ḥajj*). Let them come to thee on foot, on every kind of worn-out beast, coming in from every deep ravine, to witness things beneficial to them, and on days that have been specified to make mention of Allah's name over such beasts of the flocks as He has given them for provision. So eat ye of them and feed the misfortunate, the poor. Then let them finish with their uncleanness,[2] let them fulfill their

[1] I.e., the Ka'ba at Mecca, where it is the central shrine. *Bait,* "house," is the Arabic equivalent of the Hebrew *beth,* which we find in Beth-el, Beth-dagon, Beth-peor, Beth-shemesh, and such names in the Old Testament.

[2] *Tafath* here means the state of neglect into which they have been forced to let their persons get because of the ritual restrictions of their sacral state as pilgrims. The rites being now over, they are to cut their nails, trim their beards, etc., in a kind of desacralization which allows them to resume normal life again.

vows, and let them circumambulate the ancient House. So! and if anyone makes much of [showing respect to] the things Allah has forbidden, that will be good for him with his Lord. Allowable for you are the cattle save what is recited to you,[3] so avoid the pollution of idols, and avoid any false speaking, being Ḥanīfs to Allah, not such as associate [others] with Him. Should anyone associate [any other] with Allah it is like something that has fallen from heaven which the birds snatched away or the wind blew away to some distant place. So! and if anyone makes much of [showing respect to] Allah's rites,[4] that is [a sign] of purity of heart. Yours are the benefits from them (i.e., the cattle) until a set term, then their place is at the ancient House. For each community We have appointed some sacrificial rites (*mansak*) that they should mention the name of Allah over some of the beasts of the flocks which He has given them as provision. Your God is One God, so to Him surrender ye yourselves, and do thou [O Muḥammad] give good tidings to those who humble themselves, whose hearts are moved with awe when Allah is mentioned, also to those who steadfastly endure what befalls them, and to those who observe prayer and from what We have given them as provision give freely [in charity]. The sacrificial victims (*budn*) We have appointed for you as among Allah's rites in which there is good for you, so make mention over them of the name of Allah as they stand in line, and when they have fallen on their sides eat of them and feed both the contented and the clamorous. Thus have We subjected them (i.e., the cattle) to you. Mayhap ye will give thanks. Their flesh reaches not to Allah, nor does their blood, but piety on your part will reach Him.

[3] I.e., the Qur'ānic passages concerning foods forbidden to a Muslim, such as swine, the flesh of an animal that has died of itself, or of any animal offered in sacrifice to other than Allah. Such forbidden foods are listed in XVI, 115/116; II, 173/168; V, 1-3/4.

[4] *Sha'ā'ir* here probably means the rites and ceremonies at the holy sites other than the Ka'ba.

II, 196/192-199/195.

Now fulfill ye the *ḥajj* and the *'umra* to Allah, but if ye are hindered[5] then [send along] such sacrificial gift as may be easy for you, and shave not your heads till the sacrificial gift has reached its place. Should anyone of you be sick, or have an injury to his head, then [he must pay] compensation by fasting, or by distributing charitable alms, or [performing some sacrificial] rite. But when ye are safe, should anyone use for himself [the period from] the *'umra* to the *ḥajj*, then such sacrificial gift as may be easy, and should anyone not find [a gift possible] then a fast for three days during the pilgrimage and seven when ye have returned [home], that will be ten full days. This is for anyone whose family is not present at the Sacred Shrine, so show piety toward Allah, and know that Allah punishes severely.

The pilgrimage (*ḥajj*) is during specified months, so if anyone undertakes the duty of pilgrimage therein let there be no sex indulgence, no transgression, and no disputing during the pilgrimage. Whatever good ye do Allah knows it. Take provision for the journey, but the best provision is piety, so show piety toward Me, O ye who possess intelligence. It is no crime on your part that ye seek bounty from your Lord, so when ye pour forth from 'Arafāt remember Allah at the sacred monument,[6] and remember Him as He gave you guidance, even though ye formerly were of those astray. Then pour forth from where the people have poured forth, and seek Allah's forgiveness. Allah, indeed, is forgiving, compassionate.

[5] This hindrance is said to mean being prevented by the presence of enemies or some danger, so the being safe, a little further on, means when there are no enemies or danger preventing.

[6] This place, *al-mash'ar al-ḥaram,* is a spot near Muzdalifa where a stop is made and appointed prayers recited on the way back from 'Arafāt to Mecca.

ON THE DUTY OF PILGRIMAGE

From Ibn Māja, *Sunan* (Cairo, 1349 A.H. = 1930 A.D.), II, 207-208, 224.

'Alī b. Muḥammad and Muḥammad b. 'Abdallah have related to us, on the authority of Wakī', on the authority of Ismā'īl Abū Isrā'īl, from Fuḍail b. 'Umar, from Sa'īd b. Jubair, from Ibn 'Abbās, from al-Faḍl, or one of them from the other, that the Apostle of Allah—upon whom be Allah's blessing and peace—said: "If a man wants to make a pilgrimage let him make haste about it, for sickness comes to the sick man, and error leads astray, and necessities may come to stand in the way."

Muḥammad b. 'Abdallah b. Numair and 'Alī b. Muḥammad have related to us, on the authority of Manṣūr b. Wardān, on the authority of 'Alī b. 'Abd al-A'lā, from his father, from Abū'l-Bukhtarī, from 'Alī, who said: When the verse (III, 97/91) came down: "Due to Allah from the people is a pilgrimage to the House, from such as are able to make their way to it," they said: "O Apostle of Allah, a pilgrimage every year?" He kept silent, so again they asked: "Is it to be every year?" He answered: "No, but had I said 'Yes' it would have been obligatory." Then the verse (V, 101) came down: "O ye who believe, do not ask about things which, should they be declared to you, would annoy you."

Muḥammad b. 'Abdallah b. Numair has related to us, on the authority of Muḥammad b. Abī 'Ubaida, from his father, from al-A'mash, from Abū Sufyān, from Anas b. Mālik, who said: They asked: "O Apostle of Allah, a pilgrimage every year?" He answered: "Were I to say 'Yes' it would be obligatory, and were it obligatory ye would not accomplish it, and if you did not accomplish it you would be punished." Ya'qūb b. Ibrāhīm ad-Dawraqī has related to us, on the authority of Yazīd b. Ibrāhīm, on the authority of Sufyān b. Ḥusain, from az-Zuhrī, from Abū Sinān, from Ibn 'Abbās, that al-Aqra' b. Ḥābis asked the Prophet—upon whom be Allah's blessing and peace—"O Apostle of Allah, pilgrimage every year, or only once?" He answered: "Nay! only once, but should anyone be able let him do it oftener."

On the Merit of Circumambulating

'Alī b. Muḥammad has related to us, on the authority of Muḥammad b. Fuḍail, from al-'Alā' b. al-Musayyib, from 'Aṭā', from 'Abdallah b. 'Umar, who said: I heard the Apostle of Allah—upon whom be Allah's blessing and peace—say: "He who circumambulates the House, and prays two *rak'as,* has as [much merit accrue to him as from] the freeing of a slave."

Hishām b. 'Ammār has related to us, on the authority of Ismā'īl b. 'Ayyāsh, on the authority of Ḥamīd b. Abī Suwayya, who said: I heard Ibn Hishām ask 'Aṭā' b. Abī Rabāḥ about the Yamanī corner while he was circumambulating the House. 'Aṭā' said: Abū Huraira has related to me that the Prophet—upon whom be Allah's blessing and peace—said: "Seventy angels watch over it, who, whenever [they hear] anyone say: 'Allahumma! I ask of Thee pardon and well-being in this world and the next. O our Lord, grant us good in this world and the next, and preserve us from the torment of Hell Fire,' say: 'Amen.'" Then when he reached the black corner,[1] he asked: O father of Muḥammad, what have you heard about this black corner? 'Aṭā' answered: Abū Huraira has related to me that he heard the Apostle of Allah—upon whom be Allah's blessing and peace—say: "Whosoever comes over against it comes over against none other than the hand of the Merciful." Ibn Hishām then said to him: O father of Muḥammad, what about the circumambulation? 'Aṭā' replied: Abū Huraira has related to me that he heard the Apostle of Allah—upon whom be Allah's blessing and peace—say: "If anyone circumambulates the House seven times, not speaking save to say: 'Glory be to Allah! Praise be to Allah! There is no deity

1 The Ka'ba is roughly rectangular in shape and each corner has a special name. The "black corner" is the corner in which is inserted the famous "Black Stone" which has now been worn concave by the kissing and touching of generations of pilgrims.

save Allah! Allah is most great! There is no power and no strength save with Allah!' ten of his evil deeds will be blotted out, ten good deeds will be recorded to his credit, and by it he will be advanced ten degrees [in rank in Paradise], while if anyone circumambulates it but speaks while he is in that condition, he will wade with his feet in mercy as one wades in water."

THE LEGEND OF ZAMZAM

Sacred springs are known from the most ancient times in the Near East, their waters always having spiritual potency and sometimes also medicinal qualities. One such sacred spring was situated at Mecca, and the drinking of water from this well of Zamzam is still part of the ritual of the annual pilgrimage. To the present day pilgrims often bring their shrouds to have them dipped in its potent waters, and great numbers purchase flasks of it to carry home with them. With the Islamizing of the pilgrimage, the well and the nearby hills of Ṣafā and Marwa were associated with the Abraham story. The legend given here is that in Yāqūt's *Mu'jam al-Buldān*, ed. F. Wüstenfeld (Leipzig, 1866), II, 943.

Among the traditions [we read] how when Abraham—upon whom be peace—set Ishmael down at the site of the Ka'ba and turned to go back, Hagar said to him: "Into whose charge are you giving us?" "Into Allah's," he answered, and she said: "Allah is our sufficiency." Then she went back and stayed by her son until her water was finished and her milk was no longer flowing. This caused her distress and she was moved by pity for her child, so she left Ishmael where he was and climbed up Ṣafā to look out if haply she might espy a spring or some person, but she did not see a thing. At that she made supplication to her Lord asking Him for provision of water. Then she descended and made her way to Marwa, where she did the same thing, but hearing the voices of wild beasts she became filled with fear for her son, and so hurried in great haste to Ishmael. She found him looking at the water of a spring which had opened up beneath his cheek, or some say beneath his heels. It is said that it is because of this that there is a running [of the pilgrims] between Ṣafā and Marwa, imitating Hagar as she ran to seek her son when she was afraid of the wild beasts. They say that when Hagar saw the water she was happy and began to wall it in with earth lest it flow away and disappear. Had she not done this it would have been a flowing spring. It is about this that one of the poets has said

And she began to build for it retaining sides,
Had she left it it would have been water flowing to waste.

Some folk deny all this and say that Ishmael [when he was older] dug it with implements and with patient labor just as are needed for all other excavations, but Allah knows best.

THE ORIGINS OF THE KA'BA

From al-Azraqī's *Kitāb Akhbār Mekka,* in F. Wüstenfeld's *Die Chroniken der Stadt Mekka* (Leipzig, 1858), I, 4-5. This account has special interest as it shows the effort being made to transfer the "Navel of the Earth" from Jerusalem to Mecca.

Muhammad b. 'Alī b. al-Husain has related, saying: I was with my father 'Alī b. al-Husain (i.e., the great-grandson of the Prophet) at Mecca, and while he was circumambulating the House, and I was following behind him, there came to him a tall man who put his hand on my father's back. My father turned to him, whereat the man said: "Greetings to you, O child of the daughter of the Apostle of Allah. I want to question you." My father kept silent, so I and the man remained behind him till he had finished his seven circuits and had entered the Ḥijr and stood beneath the *mīzāb*.[1] The man and I stood behind him while he prayed the two *rak'as* pertaining to his sevenfold circuit. Then he settled himself in a sitting posture and turned to me, whereat I went and sat beside him. He said: "O Muhammad, where is this questioner?" I beckoned to the man, whereat he came and sat

1 The waterspout that carries the rain water from the roof of the Ka'ba. See Burton's *Pilgrimage,* II, 304.

before my father. My father said: "About what is it you wish to ask?" "I want to ask you," he replied, "about how the circumambulation of this House began, why and where and how it came to be." "Yes," said my father, "but from where do you come?" "I am," he answered, "of the people of Shām." "And where do you dwell?" he asked. "In Jerusalem," answered the man. "And have you read the two Books?" he asked, meaning the Torah and the Gospel. "Surely," replied the man. "O brother from the people of Shām," said my father, "take careful note of what I say and do not transmit from me anything but the truth.[2] As for the beginning of the circumambulation of this House, it goes back to when Allah—blessed and exalted is He—said to the angels (II, 30/28 ff.): 'I am going to appoint a vicegerent on the earth.' The angels said: 'O Lord, a vicegerent other than us? One of those who will cause corruption therein and shed blood, those who will be envious of one another, hate each other, tyrannize over one another? O Lord, why not appoint that vicegerent from among us? We would not cause corruption therein nor shed blood, and we would not be hating, nor envying, nor tyrannizing over one another. It is we who sing Thy praises with glory and hallow Thee, so we should be obedient to Thee and would not disobey Thee.' Allah answered: 'I know something ye do not know.' Thereat the angels thought that what they had said was a rejecting of what their Lord wanted and so He was wroth with them because of what they had said. So they took refuge at the Throne and raised their heads, making a sign of humility with their fingers and weeping because of their anxiety at His wrath. They went in circuit around the Throne for three hours. Then Allah looked at them and mercy descended on them. Then Allah established beneath the Throne a House on four columns of emerald encrusted with rubies and called that House *aḍ-Ḍurāḥ*. Then He said to the angels: 'Circumambulate this House and leave

[2] He was thinking of those who frequented Muslims who had been close to the Prophet that they might hear Traditions from them which they could transmit.

the Throne.' So the angels, leaving the Throne, circumambulated that House, which was much easier for them. That is the Frequented Fane (*al-Bait al-Ma'mūr*) of which Allah has made mention,[3] into which every day and night seventy thousand angels enter never to return to it again. Then Allah sent the angels forth, saying: 'Build for me a House on earth the shape and size of this.' [When that was done] Allah—glory be to Him—bade all His creatures on earth circumambulate that House precisely as the inhabitants of the heavens circumambulate the Frequented Fane."

Said the man: "You have spoken truly, O child of the daughter of the Apostle of Allah, that indeed was how it was."

THE BLACK STONE

This is perhaps the most famous object associated with the whole pilgrimage ceremonies at Mecca. Byzantine writers asserted that it was originally a black stone image of Aphrodite which was worshiped at the shrine in pre-Islamic days. The dissident Qarmaṭian sect seems to have considered that it was an idol of some sort, so when they took Mecca in 929 A.D. they carried it away and broke it up. It was said to have been broken at an even earlier date by the fire that burned down the Ka'ba in the days of Ibn az-Zubair (in 683 A.D.). When restored to their place, the pieces were cemented together and bound with a metal circlet. As it is today it has been worn concave by the constant touching of the annual visitors to the shrine. In Burton's opinion it is a meteorite, and so a "stone from heaven" as Tradition claims.

See Burton's *Pilgrimage,* II, 300-303; Gaudefroy-Desmombynes, *Pèlerinage,* pp. 208-210; Wensinck's article "Ka'aba" in *EI,* II, 585.

From the *Ṣaḥīḥ* of al-Bukhārī, ed. L. Krehl (Leiden, 1862), I, 406-407.

On Kissing the Stone

Aḥmad b. Sinān has related to us, on the authority of Yazīd b. Hārūn, from Warqā', who said: Zaid b. Aslam has related to us from his father, who said that he saw 'Umar b. al-Khaṭṭāb kiss the Stone, saying: "Had I not seen the Apostle

[3] He means Sūra LII, 4, though the reference there is almost certainly to the earthly shrine at Mecca.

of Allah—upon whom be Allah's blessing and peace—kiss you, I should not have kissed you." Musaddad said: Ḥammād b. Zaid has related to us, from az-Zubair b. 'Arabī, who said: A man asked Ibn 'Umar about touching the Stone, and he answered: "I saw the Apostle of Allah—upon whom be Allah's blessing and peace—touch it and kiss it." The man asked: "Do you think [one must do so even] if one is being jostled and forced along?" He replied: "Go and put your questions in the Yemen. I saw the Apostle of Allah—upon whom be Allah's blessing and peace—touch it and kiss it." Muḥammad b. Yūsuf al-Firabrī said: "I have discovered in the book of Abū Ja'far that he said that Abū 'Abdallah az-Zubair b. 'Arabī is a Baṣran and az-Zubair b. 'Adī is a Kūfan."

How One Should Make a Gesture Toward the Rukn[1] *when One Comes Over Against It*

Muḥammad b. al-Muthannā has related to us, on the authority of 'Abd al-Wahhāb, from Khālid, from 'Ikrima, from Ibn 'Abbās, who said: "The Prophet—upon whom be Allah's blessing and peace—made the circuit of the House on a camel, and each time he came over against the *rukn* (i.e., the Black corner in which the Black Stone is inserted) he made a gesture toward it."

On the Takbīr at the Rukn

Musaddad has related to us saying: Khālid b. 'Abdallah has related to us, on the authority of Khālid al-Ḥadhdhā', from 'Ikrima, from Ibn 'Abbās, who said: "The Prophet—upon whom be Allah's blessing and peace—made the circuit of the House on a camel, and each time he came over against the *rukn* he made a gesture toward it with something he had [in his hand] and pronounced a *takbīr*." Ibrāhīm b. Ṭahmān follows him in this Tradition from Khālid al-Ḥadhdhā'.

[1] A *rukn* is a corner, and as the Ka'ba is rectangular there are four corners, each of which has a special name, viz., the Black corner, the Yamanī corner, the Shāmī corner, and the 'Irāqī corner. See Burton's *Pilgrimage*, II, 208.

From al-Azraqī's *Kitāb Akhbār Mekka,* in F. Wüstenfeld's *Die Chroniken der Stadt Mekka* (Leipzig, 1858), I, 31-32.

The Legend of the Black Stone

[Al-Azraqī has related how the Stone came down to Adam from above, so white that it glistened, and Adam took it and embraced it, so delighted was he with it. Then he tells of Abraham and Ishmael rebuilding the House on the foundations of Adam's earlier structure. He continues.]

So Abraham was building and Ishmael was bringing him stones on his neck. Now when the building began to get a little high he brought him the *maqām* on which he would stand and go on with the building, while Ishmael would be working round about him in the vicinity of the House, till he finally came to the place of the black *rukn.* Then Abraham said: "O Ishmael, help me find a stone I can put here which will be a marker for the people that they may know from where to begin their circumambulation." So Ishmael went to seek such a stone for him. When he returned Gabriel had already brought him (i.e., Abraham) the Black Stone, which Allah—mighty and majestic is He—had deposited in Abū Qubais [2] when He submerged the earth under water in the days of Noah, and had said to him: "When you see My friend [3] building My house produce it for him." Ishmael came to him and said: "O my father, whence have you this?" He answered: "It was brought to me by one who would not let me use your stone. Gabriel brought it." So when Gabriel came with it and put it in its place, Abraham built upon it. At that time it was so intensely white it glistened, the light from it brightening up all to north, to south, to east, to west. Its light reached to the signs marking the boundaries of the sacred enclosure on all sides thereof. It became black only because it had suffered burning by fire time and again both in the pre-Islamic period and under Islam. It was burned in pre-Islamic days when once a woman, when the Quraish were ruling the

[2] A small mountain in the environs of Mecca.

[3] *Khalīl,* which is the special title of Abraham among the prophets.

city, was fumigating the Ka'ba and some sparks flew up and caught the cloth coverings, [causing a fire in which] the Ka'ba was burned. In this the Black *rukn* was also burned and became black, and the Ka'ba was so weakened that the Quraish were led to demolish it and rebuild it.

VI. DEVOTIONAL LIFE

Devotional life in Islam, the life of practical piety, expresses itself in both public and private devotional practices. Obviously the great feasts and festivals of the religious year are occasions not only of individual and corporate rejoicing but of stimulating religious fervor by sharing in devotional exercises. A similar stimulus is sought by supererogatory works, i.e., by adding voluntarily to the ordinary cult practices. Thus extra prayer services are added beyond the normal five daily prayers, extra days of fasting outside Ramaḍān, increase of almsgiving, or adding to the pilgrimage to Mecca pilgrimages to other sacred spots or to the tombs of famous saints or distinguished divines. The devotional reading or recitation of the Qur'ān is very commonly practiced. In all this, of course, there is the added motive of storing up merit, for a great many Traditions tell how good works can improve the status (*daraja*) the believer may have in Paradise, and this in spite of the doctrine of predestination.

In earlier days one prime method of gaining merit was to go out on Holy War (*jihād*) in the way of Allah, for to die sword in hand on the battlefield fighting against the infidels made one a martyr (*shahīd*), and innumerable Traditions tell of the highly favored position held by martyrs in the hereafter. Goodly numbers of Muslims find spiritual satisfaction in a kind of spiritual *jihād* by participating regularly or irregularly in the practices of the various dervish orders.

There is also in circulation in all Muslim countries a fairly extensive devotional literature. There are little books of prayers, invocations, litanies in honor of the Prophet, and volumes of what we might call sermons or hortatory addresses. There are manuals which, in a way, are an "examination of conscience," going over in detail the virtues that may be cultivated and the vices which must be rooted out of the heart. Then there are volumes of pious tales, concerning well-known figures of early Islam and inculcating pure religion. One special class of these is the rich hagiographical literature devoted to the lives and sayings of the Ṣūfī saints.

THE QUR'ĀNIC DESCRIPTION OF A PIOUS MUSLIM

LXX, 19-35.

Verily man was created a greedy person.
When evil touches him he is in grief.
But if good touches him he is one who grudges,
Except those who pray,
Those who are constantly at their prayers;
And those in whose wealth there is a right that is recognized
For the beggar and those who suffer deprivation;
And those who really believe in the Day of Judgment,
And those who are anxious about the punishment from their Lord,
For the punishment of their Lord is not something from which one can be secure;
And those who guard their private parts
Except with their wives and the slave girls they possess, for with such they are blameless;
But those whose desires go beyond that, they are the trespassers;
And those who are mindful of their trusts and covenants;
And those who stand by their testimony;
And those who pay careful attention to their prayers;
These [shall be] honored in [celestial] gardens.

XXV, 63/64-76.

Now the servants of the Merciful are those who walk humbly on the earth, and who, when ignorant folk address them, say: "Peace" (*salām*); those who devote the night to their Lord, making prostration of obeisance (*sujūd*) or standing up [to pray]; those who say: "O our Lord, avert from us the torment of Gehenna." Verily, its torment is a continuous one, and evil is it as an abode, an abiding place.

[The servants of the Merciful are those] who, when they contribute [alms], neither give lavishly nor are niggardly, for what is between that is proper; and those who call upon no other deity along with Allah, nor kill any person—a thing

Allah has forbidden—save where that is justified, and who do not fornicate, for whosoever does that involves himself in guilt, will have his punishment doubled on the Day of Resurrection, and will be thereby eternally in disgrace; save Him who repents, and believes, and performs righteous works, for Allah will substitute good deeds for the evil deeds of such. Allah is forgiving, compassionate. Now he who repents and works righteousness, it is to Allah that he turns in penitence.

[The servants of the Merciful are those] who do not bear witness to anything that is false, and who, when they pass by [and overhear] vain discourse, pass by in dignified manner; those who, when they are reminded of the signs of their Lord, do not fall down deaf and blind thereat. [Rather they are those] who say: "O our Lord, grant us from our wives and our progeny what will be a comfort to us, and make us an example to such as show piety." Such as these will be rewarded by an upper chamber [in Paradise] because of the way they have endured with patience, and therein they will meet with greetings wishing them life and peace. Therein will they abide, and good is it as an abode, an abiding place.

TRUE PIETY

From as-Sayyid al-Murtaḍā's *Itḥāf as-Sāda* (Cairo, 1311 A.H. = 1893 A.D.), X, 530.

Al-Khaṭīb[1] has related the following Tradition [which comes] on the authority of Ibn 'Abbās, namely [that the Prophet said]: "In Paradise there are Upper Chambers (*ghuraf*) whose inhabitants while they are therein fear for nothing that is without, and when they go out therefrom fear for nothing that is within." They asked him: "For whom are they, O Apostle of Allah?" He replied: "For whosoever

[1] I.e., Ibrāhīm b. Manṣūr al-Khaṭīb al-'Irāqī, who died in 596 A.H. = 1200 A.D.

keeps his speech good, makes his fasting continue, makes provision of food, spreads peace and says prayers at night when other folk are sleeping." They asked: "O Apostle of Allah, what is it to keep speech good?" He answered: "[To be using the phrases] Glory be to Allah! Praise be to Allah! There is no deity save Allah! Allah is most great! To Allah be the praise!, for these [pious ejaculations] will come along on the Day of Judgment, some going before, some following after, and some standing by the side." [2] They said: "And what is it to make one's fasting continue?" He replied: "It is to fast right through [the month] when Ramaḍān comes, and then look forward to fasting right through the next Ramadān." They asked: "And what is to make provision of food?" He answered: "To provide one's children with their daily food." They asked: "And what is spreading peace?" He replied: "Shaking hands with your brother when you meet him and wishing him well." They asked: "And what is it to pray when other folk sleep?" He answered: To pray the final evening prayer when the Jews and Christians are already asleep."

INTERCESSION AS HOPE FOR SALVATION

Translated from 'Alī al-Qārī's *Ḍaw' al-Ma'ālī* (Constantinople, 1293 A.H. = 1876 A.D.), p. 42.

Even those whose greater sins are of mountain size may hope for [salvation through] the intercession of the righteous (*ahl al-Khair*). Now righteousness is concerned with thought, with deed, with speech, with silence, for every thought which does not contain some element of warning is idle thought, and every deed that does not have in it some element of worship is remiss, and all speech that does not contain some mention [of Allah] is vanity, and all silence that does not contain some

[2] The meaning is that as each individual moves forward to Judgment, passing through the terrors of the Day, these will be like a protective bodyguard around him.

[religious] meditation is trifling. The intercession of the righteous means that such intercession by prophets and saintly persons for those who have been guilty of the greater sins, not to speak of the lesser sins, is something that may be hoped for. Greater sins, of course, means any sins save association (*shirk*),[1] for Allah Himself has said (IV, 48/51): "Allah will not forgive the association [of other deities] with Him, but anything other than that He will forgive to whomsoever He pleases." He will forgive them through intercession or otherwise. It is related by at-Tirmidhī and others that the Prophet —upon whom be Allah's blessing and peace—said: "My intercession is for those of my community guilty of the greater sins." In these words there is a reply to the Mu'tazilites[2] who do not believe that intercession can avail save for raising the rank [a man may merit in Paradise], for they teach that those who commit the greater sins must abide forever in the Fire. In the *Sunan* of Ibn Māja [there is a Tradition] on the authority of 'Uthmān b. 'Affān, who is transmitting directly from the Prophet [who said]: "Three groups will take part in the task of intercession on the Day: first the prophets, then the divines, then the martyrs." It may be thought that the phrase "may be hoped for" suggests that the effectiveness of intercession is merely a matter of opinion, but this is not so; it is something certain, for it is supported by famous Traditions which are almost sufficient to make it *mutawātura*.[3] Ibn al-Jamā'a[4] says: "Men fall into two categories, believers and unbelievers, and that unbelievers will be in the Fire is unanimously agreed. Believers also are of two categories, the obedient and the disobedient, and that the obedient will be in

1 On *shirk* see Glossary.

2 They were the rationalistic theologians of early Islam. See *EI*, III, 787-793.

3 A *mutawātur* Tradition is one with an uninterrupted and unchallengeable line of transmitters.

4 'Izz ad-Dīn Muḥammad b. Jamā'a, a Shāfi'ite savant who died in 819 A.H. = 1416 A.D.

Paradise is unanimously agreed. The disobedient again are in two categories, the repentant and the unrepentant. That the repentant will get to Paradise is unanimously agreed, but [the fate of] the unrepentant is as Allah—exalted be He—may will."

THE STORY OF FĀṬIMA'S HAND MILL

Qiṣṣat ar-Raḥā li's-Sayyida Fāṭima az-Zahrā', by Muḥammad Muṣṭafā al'Adawī (Cairo, n.d.), a little eight-page lithograph, very crudely produced for devotional reading in feminine circles.

The *raḥā* is the little hand mill in which the women grind the grain for some of the flour used for household purposes. Fāṭima was the daughter of the Prophet, the wife of his cousin 'Alī, and the mother of his beloved grandsons al-Ḥasan and al-Ḥusain.

In the Name of Allah, the Merciful, the Compassionate.

Blessings and peace from Allah be upon our Master Muḥammad, and on his family, and on his Companions. It is related from Abū Huraira—with whom may Allah be pleased—that he said: The Apostle of Allah—upon whom be Allah's blessing and peace—once entered to his daughter Fāṭima, the bright-faced one—with whom may Allah be pleased—and found her grinding barley flour and weeping. So the Prophet—upon whom be Allah's blessing and peace—said to her: "What is it makes you weep, O Fāṭima?" She answered: "O my father, it is because of overweariness from grinding the flour and the household needs. Would that you would ask the Imām 'Alī to buy for himself a slave girl. That would be a great reward for him." When the Prophet—upon whom be Allah's blessing and peace—heard her words his heart was touched with pity for her and his eyes overflowed with tears. Then the Prophet—upon whom be Allah's blessing and peace—took a seat near the hand mill, took a handful of barley in his blessed hand, and said: "In the Name of Allah, the Merciful, the Compassionate." Then he began to throw it into the hand mill, which then turned of itself, and he found it glorifying Allah—glorious and exalted is He—in a tongue most eloquent and a voice most sweet, which continued till the grinding of the flour was finished.

Then the Prophet—upon whom be Allah's blessing and peace—said to it: "Be silent, O mill!", whereupon Allah, who giveth speech to all things, gave it the gift of speech, so it said: "By Him Who sent you with the truth as a prophet, and with the message as a confidant, I will not keep silent till you guarantee me from Allah [that I shall have a place in] Paradise and escape from Hell Fire." The Prophet—upon whom be Allah's blessing and peace—said: "You are a stone, yet fear the Fire?" It replied: "O Apostle of Allah, I have heard [these words] from the great Qur'ān (LXVI, 6): 'O ye who believe, protect yourselves and your families from the Fire whose fuel is men and stones. Over it are angels, rough and violent, who do not disobey Allah in what He commands them, but do what they are bidden.'" So the Prophet—upon whom be Allah's blessing and peace—made supplication for it. When he had finished his supplication Gabriel, the Faithful One—upon whom be peace—came down and said: "O Muḥammad, the Lord—glorified and exalted is He—sends you greeting of peace and special salutation and honor, and says to you: 'Give to this stone the good tidings that Allah—glorified and exalted is He—has granted it freedom from the Fire, and appointed it to be among the stones of Paradise, in the palace of Fāṭima, the bright-faced, where its light will shine as the sun's light in this world.'" So he gave it these good tidings.

Then he turned to Fāṭima—with whom may Allah be pleased—and said to her: O Fāṭima, did Allah so will this hand mill would grind of itself every day, but Allah—glorified and exalted is He—desires to record to your credit [the merit of] good deeds and to raise your degrees (*darajāt*)[1] because of

[1] We have noted earlier the teaching that for each individual there is a record kept in heavenly places which will have to be faced at the Last Day, and also the teaching that there are degrees or ranks in the hereafter which may be increased by pious endeavor.

your grievous burdens. O Fāṭima, there is no woman who sweats at her baking but Allah will set seven trenches between her and Hell Fire, the distance between each trench and the next being the distance between heaven and earth. O Fāṭima, there is no woman whose eyes water as she cuts up onions for the family meal but Allah writes down to her record the reward of those who weep out of fear of Allah—may He be exalted. O Fāṭima, there is no woman who sets her hand to her spinning but for every thread thereof Allah writes in her record a good deed and blots out a hundred evil deeds. O Fāṭima, there is no woman who twists what she has spun but will have a specified place all for herself beneath the Throne on the Resurrection Day. O Fāṭima, there is no woman who spins and then clothes her children and little ones but Allah will write in her record the merit of one who has fed a thousand hungry persons and clothed a thousand naked. O Fāṭima, there is no woman who has oiled the heads of her children, untangled their hair, washed their clothes and deloused them but Allah will for every hair write in her record a good deed and for every hair blot out an evil deed, and will make her resplendent in the eyes of those who behold.

etc.

O Fāṭima, there is no woman who refuses her neighbors in their need but Allah will refuse her a drink from al-Kawthar on the Day.[2] O Fāṭima, there are five things which it is not lawful to refuse, viz., water, fire, leaven, the hand mill, and a needle, while for [liberality in the matter of] each of these there is a good deed [written to one's account]. O Fāṭima, whosoever refuses water Allah will afflict with the dropsy, and whosoever refuses fire Allah will afflict with enmity between him and his family, and whosoever refuses the hand mill Allah will afflict with illness. O Fāṭima, in Allah's sight the most excellent of your works is that which makes your husband well pleased with you. O Fāṭima, she with whom her husband is well pleased, and who dies while he is still well pleased with her, will have written for her by Allah a good

[2] This is a celestial stream, mentioned in Sūra CVIII, 1, which is said to be reserved especially for Muḥammad's community.

deed for every hair he has on his body, and she will not depart from this world till she has seen her abiding place in Paradise, nor will her spirit come forth from her body till her Lord is well pleased with her.

O Fāṭima, there is no woman who dies while obedient to her husband but Allah will write to her account a thousand good deeds. O Fāṭima, there is no woman without a husband but is like a tree without fruit. O Fāṭima, whenever a man looks on the face of his wife Allah writes to his account a hundred good deeds; if he goes on and has marital relations with her Allah writes to his account a good deed for every hair he has on his body, and if he washes himself thereafter Allah creates from every drop [of the water] an angel who will glorify Allah, Most High, and pray for his forgiveness till the Day of Resurrection, while the merit for all this [activity of the angels] goes to his account. O Fāṭima, should the woman become pregnant the angels in the heaven and the fish in the waters will pray for forgiveness for him, Allah will write to her account a thousand good deeds for every day of her pregnancy and blot out a thousand evil deeds, and [grant her] the merit of those who go out on Holy War in the way of Allah. Then when she is delivered of her burden she is made clean of her sins as on the day her mother bore her, while Allah writes to her account the merit of seventy acceptable pilgrimages. Should she suckle her child Allah, for every drop of milk, will write to her account a good deed and forgive an evil deed, while the Ḥūrīs in the Gardens of Delight will pray for forgiveness for her. O Fāṭima, whenever a woman is with child the angels in the heavens and the fish in the waters pray for forgiveness for her, while Allah writes to her account a thousand good deeds and blots out a thousand evil deeds.

O Fāṭima, there is no woman who puts on a cross face toward her husband but Allah is angry with her, as are all the angels, and should she forbid him her bed everything moist and everything dry curses her. O Fāṭima, there is no woman who says to her husband: "Shame upon you!" but comes under the curse of Allah and the angels and all men. O Fāṭima, there is no woman who lightens her dowry for her husband but Allah will decree that for every dirham [3] thereof she shall have a palace in Paradise. O Fāṭima, there is no woman who prays and makes a petition for herself yet no petition for her husband [4] but Allah will reject her prayer till she makes a petition for him. O Fāṭima, there is no woman whose husband is angry with her yet she does not seek to appease him so that he becomes well pleased with her, but comes under the anger and wrath of Allah.

O Fāṭima, there is no woman who dresses herself and adorns her person and goes out from her house without her husband's permission but every moist thing and every dry thing curses her till she returns to her house, and there is no woman who looks at the face of her husband and does not smile [at him] but Allah and the angels and all men will be angry with her. O Fāṭima, there is no woman who uncovers her face to anyone other than her husband but will be cast by Allah on her face into Hell Fire. O Fāṭima, there is no woman who enters a house of which her husband disapproves but Allah will send upon her [in her grave] seventy scorpions from the scorpions of Gehenna which will keep stinging her till the Resurrection Day. O Fāṭima, there is no woman who fasts without her husband's permission [5] but Allah will reject

[3] The *dirham,* a word derived from the Greek *drachma,* was a common unit of coinage in the early Islamic world. See the article "Dirham" in *EI*, I, 978-979. The *ṣadaq* or *mahr* is the dowry or bridal price paid to the woman on marriage. It is a remnant of the old pagan Arab purchase price paid for a bride which Muḥammad took over into his system and modified. It is wholly under the control of the wife, and is often a sore point with the husband, so that the lightening of it is magnified in the text as a virtue. See article "Mahr" in *EI*, III, 137-138.

[4] In the ritual for each of the five daily prayer services there is a place for *du'ā,* "petition" or "supplication," where the individual worshiper may insert his or her own particular petitions.

[5] The point is that fasting (*ṣaum*) is total abstinence from sex dalliance as well as from food and drink, so that a woman who vows fasts other than that of Ramaḍān is here considered as infringing on her husband's rights.

her fast and will accept from her no expiation or atonement. O Fāṭima, there is no woman who steals from her husband's house but Allah writes to her account the crime of seventy thefts. And Allah knows best. The end.

And may the blessings and peace of Allah be upon our Master Muhammad, and on his family and his Companions.

A SUPPLICATORY PRAYER TO BE USED FOR QUR'ĀNIC RECITATIONS

The prayer given here, a supplication to be recited before the Sevenths, is translated from the Sudanese Mahdī's *ar-Rātib ash-sharīf,* ed. Sulaimān Dāwūd Mandīl (Omdurman, 1342 A.H. = 1923 A.D.), pp. 19-29. For devotional reading or recitation the Qur'ān is commonly divided into thirty parts, one part to be read or recited each day of the lunar month, or into seven parts that the whole may be finished in a week.

Praise be to Thee, O Allah, such praise as is meet for Thy bounty and as may requite Thy provision given so richly. To Thee be praise, to Thy very Self, such praise as is due Thee for Thy being well pleased [with us]. May prayers and peace and blessing be upon our Master Muhammad, who is our means of access to Thee, and on his family and on his friends, who have labored according to Thy inspiration and followed the guidance of Thy Prophet—upon whom be Allah's blessing and peace.

I ask of Thee, O my Lord, O my God, O my Suzerain, O my Refuge, the One Who set up heavens and earth by His command, Who will raise the dead by His call, in Whose hand is sovereignty over everything, Who if He desires a thing only says to it "Be!" and it is (II, 117/111); I ask of Thee by the truth of the Chosen One, Thy Prophet, the one trusted, the trustworthy, that Thou cast into my heart [a sense of] Thy greatness, of Thy majesty, of Thy grandeur, and the completeness of Thy power over everything, so that Thou mayest charge my heart with reverence for Thy word as I read (or recite) it. Thus shall I find sweetness in it as I undertake to observe the elevated principles therein, and also [be led to] yearn for Thee because of Thy exceeding great love. O Thou in Whose hand is overpowering mastery and repute, O most merciful of those who show mercy, make me not of those who turn aside, the people of disobedience, nor of those who with hardness of heart address Thee. Amen. O Lord of Mankind.

O Thou Who dost answer the petitions of those in need, answer our petition, and accept us, broken and ephemeral though we be, in Thy mercy and Thy everlastingness, O Thou most merciful of those who show mercy. For I am in need of Thy mercy. If Thou dost not show mercy to me and save me I shall fall into the lowest state, that which causes one to drop down into al-Hāwiya,[1] by turning aside from the healing Thou hast provided in Thy word. Grant our requests, O Lord, that we may respond to Thy summons [made to us] in Thy Book, O Thou most merciful of those who show mercy.

O Lord of mankind, cause us to see the might of Thy word which was sent down from Him who created the earth and the high heavens, the Merciful, Who on the Throne has taken His seat. His is whatever is in the heavens, and whatever is on earth, what is between them and what is below the earth, He Who knows the secret and the most hidden things (XX, 4/3-8/7). There is no deity save Thee. Glory be to Thee. I was one of the wrongdoers by reason of the shortcomings in my knowledge of Thy might and my failure to stand by that which befits Thy majesty. O Thou Who dost help those who are in need, rescue me from the wickedness of mine own self, and honor me with that which will be worthy of Thyself. Make me not one of those deceived by their own ignorance, so that I fly for refuge to myself, have resort to my own senses, and stay away from my Holy One. O Thou in Whose hand I am, whether alone or in company, draw away my heart from being busied with my body and my senses [and draw it] to intercourse with Thee, that therein it may find pleasure in obeying Thy commands. Make me understand the secrets of

[1] One of the names of Hell, or of the deepest depth therein.

Thy Book, as Thou hast made the trustiest of those who love Thee understand them. Make me see therein what Thou hast set there for the guidance of those who will pay heed, those who will draw near, O Thou most merciful of those who show mercy.

O Mighty One, there is no one who gives what is really great save the Mighty One, and there is no one who magnifies the insignificant and gives him much, save Thee. I am an insignificant one who hopes for much from Thy great favor, that Thou shouldst honor me by [letting me learn] the secrets of Thy Book sublime. Make not my portion in it a mere recitation by the tongue like that of the generality, the heedless ones who only mouth senseless words, for Thou art watching not far off, and Thou lovest not vain display nor corrupt ways. My affair is in Thy hand, and my salvation is with Thee, O Lord of mankind. Unto Thee have I committed my affair, so improve my state into that which will be well pleasing to Thee, favor me with the [gift of being] strictly attentive to Thy word, send down into my heart Thy gifts which Thou dost grant to those honored ones who are attentive to Thee, and draw nigh to Thee. Make me one of them. Make me not one of those who are forsaken, O most merciful of those who show mercy.

I ask of Thee, O my God, O my Suzerain, since Thou didst create me when I was nonexistent, yet without any intermediary, do not confine me to the mere appearance of acts of obedience and supplication, nor with just looking at some individual thing out of the multiplicity of things Thou hast created, but draw me unto Thyself, content to be with Thee, preferring Thee above everything. O Thou to Whom nothing is impossible, make me a servant of Thine, content with Thee alone, busied with each command from Thee yet not allowing it to veil me from Thee. Thou art He Who brought me forth, so my affair is in Thy hand, and to Thee is my return and my final end. O my God, O my Refuge, reject not my supplication, but treat me with kindly treatment, as Thou hast brought me up in kindness, and put me in a true position in

Thy sight. Amen. O Lord of mankind. O Possessor of Majesty and Honor.

Allahumma! I seek absolution with Thee from myself, and with Thee do I take refuge from that and from all that would bar me from Thee. To Thee do I come back, freely choosing Thee, and preferring Thee because of what there is with Thee. Reprehend me not, O Lord, because of my faults, lest Thou put me in the power of one who would bar me from Thee and make me give up Thy wondrous promises and [cease from] being illumined by Thy light. Deter us not, O Lord, from coming forth to Thee, choosing that which is with Thee, and being content with what Thou dost desire. Thou art our Suzerain and our God, Lord of every creature, able to do whatever Thou dost desire. Turn not from me so that I should turn in vexation from the good Thou dost desire, choose what is vile, and by ill luck abandon that which is with Thee. With Thee do I take refuge, O best of refuge places, from the evil of all men and from the ill of the whisperer (Satan). O our God, O our Suzerain, O Lord of men, O Thou to Whom nothing is impossible, protect me from everything that might put me far from Thee, so that I may meet Thee without any defect, believing in Thee, well content with what Thou hast decreed, and thinking well of Thee. Take me to Thyself away from all enemies. Guard me from all that might make me fall. Thou over everything hast power, and Thou art well able to respond. There is no power or might save with Thee.

Now may the blessing and peace of Allah be upon our Master Muḥammad, and on his family and on his friends.

THE FEASTS AND FESTIVALS OF ISLAM

There are local feasts and holy days observed in almost every Muslim country. These differ widely from country to country, and even in different sections of the same country. There are, however, five feast days which are occasions of community rejoicing observed almost universally in Islam.

1. *'Id al-Fiṭr,* the day of feasting and merriment that marks the end of the great fast of Ramaḍān. It thus occurs annually on the first day of the month of Shawwāl, and is commonly called the "little feast."

2. *'Id al-Aḍḥā,* the Feast of Sacrifice, commonly called the "great feast," which falls seventy days later than the "little feast," on the 10th of Dhū'l-Ḥijja. In Turkey it is usually known as *Qurbān Bairām* and in India as *Baqar 'Īd.* It falls at the time the pilgrims outside Mecca, having stood at 'Arafāt, are sacrificing their animals ritually, and is said to commemorate in every Muslim home the redemption of Abraham's son by the ram miraculously provided.

These two are the canonical Feasts for which there are special prayer services in the mosques, and normally last three or four days.

3. *Muharram,* the Muslim New Year's Festival on the first and succeeding days of the first month of the year. Among the Shī'a it has become traditionally connected with mourning for the martyrs of the House of 'Alī, and the occasion for the celebration of a curious passion play. For them the 9th and 10th days are peculiarly significant.

4. *Mawlid an-Nabī,* the Festival of the Prophet's Birthday. This arose at a relatively late date and is traditionally celebrated on the 12th of Rabī' al-awwal. It is the occasion for reading and reciting various laudatory poetical pieces in honor of the Prophet, such as the *Bordah* of al-Būṣīrī in Egypt, the *Mevledi Sherīf* of Sulaiman Chelebi in Turkey, and the *'Iqd al-Jawāhir* of al-Barzanjī in India and Indonesia.

5. *Lailat al-Mi'rāj,* the Festival of the Prophet's Ascension, or Heavenly Journey, during which he had his vision of Paradise and Hell. It is traditionally celebrated on the night preceding the 27th of Rajab, when the mosques and the minarets are lighted and there is much devotional reading of popular accounts of the Mi'rāj.

HAGIOGRAPHY

Islam, like Christianity, has its *Lives of the Saints.* Saints' tombs are a characteristic feature of the landscape in most Muslim countries, where, whether associated with mosques or isolated, they are popular centers of visitation. The orthodox divines have spoken frequently and vigorously against this practice of visitation, but the consensus of the community has almost everywhere proved stronger than the condemnation of the theologians and the common folk still visit the tombs of saints to pray, to leave ex-votos, to seek blessing (*baraka*) and the intercession of the holy persons buried there. Some such tombs are thickly encircled with the graves of devotees whose last wish was to be buried in the proximity of the saint. The theologians are right in thinking that often enough this visitation becomes saint-worship such as is inconsistent with the spirit of Islam, and the student of comparative religion will not infrequently find that some famous shrine which now is visited as the tomb of a Muslim saint was a sacred site in the older religion of these lands into which Islam came, the "saint's day" being still the holy day associated with the pre-Islamic site.

A saint is called a *walī* (pl., *awliyā'*), i.e., a "friend" of Allah, and the attendant at a tomb will generally have there a *tadhkira* or account of the wonderful life and doings of that particular saint. There naturally has grown up in Islam a hagiographical literature, consisting for the most part of popular works recounting in great detail the sayings, the marvelous lives (*manākib*), and miraculous doings (*karāmāt*) of these saints, particularly those associated with Ṣūfism and the dervish orders. Several of these collections have come down to us, notably the *Nafahat al-Uns* of Jāmi' (d. 898 A.H. = 1492 A.D.), the *Tadhkirat al-Awliyā'* of Farīd ad-Dīn 'Aṭṭār (d. 627 A.H. = 1230 A.D.), the *Ḥilyat al-Awliyā'* of Abū Nu'aim (d. 430 A.H. = 1038 A.D.), while many such *Lives* are included in more general works on Ṣūfism, such as the *Risāla* of al-Qushairī (d. 467 A.H. = 1074 A.D.), or the *Kashf al-Maḥjūb* of al-Ḥujwirī, who died the same year.

See C. Trumelet, *Les Saints de l'Islam* (Paris, 1881); Ed. Montet, *Le Culte des Saints musulmans dans l'Afrique du nord* (Genève, 1909); I. Goldziher, "Le culte des Saints chez les Musulmans," *Revue de l'Histoire des Religions,* II (1880), 257-351, and "Die Heiligenverehrung im Islam" in his *Muhammedanische Studien* (1890), II, 277-378.

On Ṣūfism in general, see R. Hartmann, *Al-Kuschairis Darstellung des Sufitums* (Berlin, 1914); R. A. Nicholson, *The Mystics of Islam* (London, 1914) and *Studies in Islamic Mysticism* (Cambridge, 1921); Louis Massignon, *Al-Hallaj, martyre mystique de l'Islam,* 2 vols. (Paris, 1922) and *Essai sur la lexique technique de la mystique musulmane* (2nd ed., Paris, 1954); Miguel Asin, *El Islam cristianizado* (Madrid, 1931); E. Brögelmann, *Die religiösen Erlebnisse der persischen Mystiker* (Hannover, 1932); A. J. Arberry, *The Doctrine of the Sufis* (Cambridge, 1935) and *Sufism* (London, 1950); Tor Andrae, *I myrtenträdgården: Studier i sufisk mystik* (Stockholm, 1947); Margaret Smith, *Readings from the Mystics of Islam* (London, 1950).

On the dervishes see: Depont et Coppolani, *Les confréries religieuses musulmanes* (Alger, 1897); P. J. André, *Contribution à l'étude des confréries religieuses musulmanes* (Paris, 1956).

The following account of a Muslim saint, Shaddād b. Aws, is taken from Abū Nu'aim's *Ḥilyat al-Awliyā'* (Cairo, 1932), I, 264-270.

Among them [1] was that man so renowned for restrained yet clear understandable language, so prudent and so self-controlled, so given to weeping and humble entreaty, Abū Ya'lā Shaddād b. Aws, one of the Anṣār—with whom may Allah Most High be pleased.

Ibrāhīm b. 'Abdallah has related to us on the authority of Muḥammad b. Isḥāq, from Qataiba b. Sa'īd, from al-Faraj b. Fuḍāla, from Asad b. Waḍā'a, how when Shaddād b. Aws would go to bed and find himself restless therein because sleep came not to him, he would say: "Allahumma! [the fear of] Hell Fire has driven sleep from me," then he would rise up and perform prayers till the morning. My father and Abū Muḥammad b. Ḥayyān have related [2] how Shaddād b. Aws used to say: "You people see nothing of either good or evil but the occasions thereof. All the real good is within the borders of Paradise, just as all the real evil is within the borders of Hell. This world is but an accidental thing now presently existing, from which both the innocent and the guilty eat, but the next world is a promise in which one can put trust and where an all-conquering King will exercise authority. Each has its children, so be children of the next world, not children of this." Abū'd-Dardā' once said: "Among people are some who are given knowledge but not forbearance. Abū Ya'lā, however, was given both knowledge and forbearance."

Sulaimān b. Aḥmad has related to us how Shaddād b. Aws said: I heard the Apostle of Allah—upon whom be Allah's blessing and peace—say: "O people, this world is but an acci-

1 I.e., among the Ahl aṣ-Ṣuffa, who were reputed to be the early ascetic group of devotees in Islam. On them see *EI*, I, 185.

2 An *isnād* in the same style as that above is given by Abū Nu'aim here and similarly for every statement that follows, but to save space these *isnāds* have been omitted in the translation.

dental thing now presently existing, from which both the innocent and the guilty eat, but the next world is a promise in which one can put trust, where an all-conquering King will exercise authority, making the truth prevail and making the false of no avail. O people, be children of the next world not children of this, for every mother is followed by her children." Laith b. Abī Sālim has transmitted this same tradition though in somewhat different words. Abū 'Amr b. Ḥamdān has related how Shaddād b. Aws reported the like from the Apostle of Allah—upon whom be Allah's blessing and peace—but added [the words]: "Work away, keeping Allah ever in mind. Work away, for you will anon be brought face to face with your works. Without any doubt you are going to meet with Allah, and then whosoever has wrought an atom of good will see it, and likewise whosoever has wrought an atom of evil."

My father and Abū Muḥammad b. Ḥayyān have related how Abū'd-Dardā' used to say: "Every community has its *faqīh*,[3] and the *faqīh* of this community is Shaddād b. Aws." Abū 'Amr b. Ḥamdān has related on the authority of Thābit al-Banānī how Shaddād b. Aws one day said to one of his friends: "Bring the dinner table and let us occupy ourselves with it." Said that friend: "Never have I heard a word like this from you all the time we have been friends."[4] He replied: "[Hitherto] no word has slipped from me since the time I parted from the Apostle of Allah—upon whom be Allah's blessing and peace—save such as was restrained and bridled, and by Allah none save this ever shall so slip."

Abū Muḥammad has also related on the authority of Sulaimān b. Mūsā that Shaddād b. Aws one day said: "Bring along the dining table and let us concern ourselves with it." He was censured for this, whereat he said: "Look at Abū Ya'lā and

[3] A *faqīh* is literally one learned in *fiqh* (jurisprudence), but the word is popularly used of anyone specially versed in matters concerned with the religion of Islam.

[4] The point is that a saintly man should never have spoken of so worldly a thing as dining "occupying" their thoughts and attention to the exclusion of higher things.

what he has let slip. O children of my brother, this is the first time since I swore allegiance to the Apostle of Allah—upon whom be Allah's blessing and peace—that I have spoken a word which was not restrained and bridled. However, come along that I may relate to you some Traditions, and make ye this supplication from which you may receive benefit: 'Allahumma! we ask of Thee that we may stand firm in religion, continue steadfastly in the right way, be thankful for Thy bounty, and serve Thee well. We ask Thee for sound hearts and truthful tongues. We ask Thee for the good of that which Thou knowest, and take refuge with Thee from the evil of that which Thou knowest.' Take this and make this supplication."

Muḥammad b. Ma'mar has related that Shaddād b. Aws once came to a house and said: "Bring us the dinner table that we may busy ourselves therewith." Someone said: "O Abū Ya'lā, what is this?" and they found fault with him for it. He replied: "Never since I became a Muslim have I spoken a word without bridling it and restraining it save this one, so do not remember it against me, but remember rather from me that which I am going to tell you, for I heard the Apostle of Allah—upon whom be Allah's blessing and peace—say: 'While other people are busy storing up gold and silver, store ye up these words: Allahumma! I ask of Thee that I may stand firm in religion, continue steadfastly in the right way'; then he went on as above, but added: 'We ask Thy pardon for that which Thou knowest. Verily Thou art He who knows the unseen.' "

(Several further variants of the same Tradition are then given.)

'Abdallah b. Ja'far has related how Shaddād b. Aws reported having heard the Apostle of Allah—upon whom be Allah's blessing and peace—say: "The intelligent man is he who holds a reckoning with himself and labors with a view to that which comes after death, whereas the man lacking in intelligence is he who follows his own desires and hopes the best from Allah—mighty and exalted is He."

Abū 'Amr b. Ḥamdān has related how he heard az-Zuhrī say to the people one day: "Sit ye down while I relate to you Traditions," though before that day I had never heard him tell them to sit down. [He said]: Maḥmūd b. ar-Rabī' has informed me that when death drew near Shaddād b. Aws he said: "The thing I fear most for you people is hypocrisy and secret lusts." [5] Abū 'Alī Muḥammad b. Aḥmad has related how 'Ubāda b. Nasī once said: "Shaddād b. Aws one day passed by, took me by the hand and led me to his house. There he sat weeping till I too wept because he was weeping. When he recovered his composure he asked: 'What made you weep?' 'I saw you weeping,' I answered, 'so I too wept.' Said he: 'I was remembering something I heard the Apostle of Allah—upon whom be Allah's blessing and peace—say. I heard him say: The thing I fear most for my comunity is *shirk* [6] and secret lusts.' 'Well,' I replied, 'there is one of the two of which there is no danger.' He retorted: 'That is what I said at the time to the Apostle of Allah, but he said to me: Yet I want to have you fear both; and then went on: It is true they will not worship sun or moon, nor will they set up idols, but they will perform works for the sake of other than Allah—majestic and exalted is He.' "

Sulaimān b. Aḥmad related that 'Ubāda b. Nasī said: I entered to Shaddād b. Aws, who was weeping, so I said: "What makes you weep, O father of 'Abd ar-Raḥmān?" He answered: "It is because of something I heard the Apostle of Allah—upon whom be Allah's blessing and peace—say. [He said:] 'What I fear most for my community is their associating anything with Allah, and secret lusts. A man will begin his morning fasting, but then he will see something he lusts for and will fall because of it. *Shirk* is not that they will worship stones or idols but that they will act hypocritically.' " 'Abd ar-Raḥmān b.

[5] Shaddād is here quoting what the Prophet said he feared for the Muslim community after his death.

[6] *Shirk* is the sin of "association," i.e., of associating anyone or any thing with Allah in such a way as to imperil His uniqueness.

Ghanam said: When Abū'd-Dardā' and I entered the mosque at al-Jābiya [7] we met there 'Ubāda b. aṣ-Ṣāmit. While we were there together Shāddad b. Aws and 'Awf b. Mālik came upon us and sat down with us. Shaddād said: "The thing I fear most for you folk is something I heard from the Apostle of Allah—upon whom be Allah's blessing and peace—namely, *shirk* and secret lusts." 'Ubāda and Abū'd-Dardā' said: "Allahumma! forgiveness. Did not the Apostle himself tell us that Satan despaired of ever being worshiped in the land of Arabia? As for secret lusts, we are aware of them, they are the lusts of this world, for its women and their desires, but what is this *shirk* of which you would make us afraid, O Shaddād?" Shaddād answered: "What think you? If you should see one performing prayers for the sake of some man, fasting for the sake of some man, giving alms for the sake of some man, would you judge that he was guilty of *shirk?*" "Surely," they replied, "any man, by Allah, who gives alms, or fasts, or prays for the sake of some man is guilty of *shirk*." Thereat 'Awf b. Mālik said: "Does not Allah—mighty and majestic is He—pay close attention to all such works used as a means to seek His face, so that He accepts what thereof is unadulterated and rejects that in which there is *shirk?*" Shaddād said: "I heard the Apostle of Allah—upon whom be Allah's blessing and peace—say: 'Allah Most High saith: I get the best share even from him who associates another with Me. When anyone associates anything with Me it is his body and his works, whatever he has whether little or much, [that he gives] to the partner he has associated with Me, and I can do without it.' "

Ibrāhīm b. 'Abdallah has related that Maḥmūd b. ar-Rabī' told how one day Shaddād b. Aws went out with him to the market place. Then he went and lay down, covering himself with his garment, and said repeatedly: "I am still a stranger. Islam is still new [to me]." When he stopped I said to him: "Today you have certainly done something I had never thought you would do." Said he: "I fear for you *shirk* and secret lusts." "Do you fear *shirk* on our part after Islam?"

[7] Jābiya is a place in the environs of Damascus.

I asked. "May your mother be bereft of you, O Maḥmūd," he replied. "Is there any other *shirk* than your setting up another deity beside Allah?"

Muḥammad b. 'Alī has related to us on the authority of Maḥkūl how Shaddād b. Aws reported that the Apostle of Allah—upon whom be Allah's blessing and peace—once said: "Repentance washes away sin, and good deeds cancel evil deeds. If a man remembers Allah when things are going well, He will deliver him when they are going badly. That is because Allah says: 'Never will I combine for My servant two securities, nor will I combine for him two fears. If he considers himself secure from Me in this world he will fear Me on the Day when I assemble My servants, but if he fears Me in this world I will give him security in Ḥazīrat al-Quds [8] on the Day when I assemble My servants, and make his security a lasting thing, not annihilating him among those whom I annihilate.' "

A PRAYER FOR USE WHEN VISITING THE TOMBS IN AL-BAQĪ'

From Muḥammad al-Ḥawarī's *Al-Kawkab al-Muḍiy* (Cairo, 1927), pp. 74-76. *Al-Baqī',* or more accurately *Baqī' al-Gharqad,* is the ancient cemetery of Madina, which is still today a place for pious visitation. Muḥammad's little son Ibrāhīm was buried there, and later his daughters and his wives, along with several of the Old Believers and kinsfolk of the Prophet. Once it was renowned for the magnificent mausoleums erected over these tombs, but they were mostly smashed by the iconoclastic Wahhābī reformers.

Let [the visitor] say as follows when he enters the gate of al-Baqī':

"Greeting of peace to you, O abode of believing people. Ye are those who have gone ahead, and we, if Allah so wills, will some day be joining you. Allahumma! grant forgiveness to the inhabitants of al-Baqī', Baqī' al-Gharqad. Allahumma! grant

[8] One of the names of Paradise or of a portion thereof.

forgiveness to us and to them. Allahumma! deprive us not of their reward, and after them let us not be led astray. Greetings of peace to you, O ye inhabitants of these dwellings, ye believers, ye Muslims. May Allah show mercy to both the former among you and the latter. May Allah's friendliness companion your loneliness, and His mercy temper your sense of strangeness. May He double your good deeds and pardon your evil deeds. O our Lord, grant forgiveness to us, to our parents, to our teachers, to our brothers and our sisters, to our children and our grandchildren, to our kinsfolk and our friends and those we love, to those who do good to us, to anyone who has a claim upon us, to anyone who has given us a trust, to the believers both male and female, to the Muslims both male and female, whether living or dead.

"O our Lord, grant forgiveness to us and to our brethren who have preceded us in the faith, and set not in our hearts any rancor against those who believe. O our Lord, Thou art kindly and compassionate. Allahumma! Lord of the bodies that waste away, of the bones that crumble, and of the spirits that depart from this world and are in safety with Thee, send upon them cheer from Thee and a greeting of peace from me. Allahumma! send blessing on the spirit of our master Muḥammad among the spirits; send blessing on the body of our master Muḥammad among the bodies; send blessing on the tomb of our master Muḥammad among the tombs. O our Lord, cause us to die Muslims, have us join the righteous, and cause us to enter Paradise in safety, by Thy mercy, O Thou most merciful of those who show mercy. Amen. Send blessing on all the prophets and messengers, and on Thy angels who draw near [Thy Throne]. Have mercy on us along with them, make their intercession a provision for us, and raise us up with them. Praise be to Allah, Lord of the worlds."

Then it is most appropriate for the visitor to recite Sūra CXII eleven times, for the recitation thereof is customary, and there is good Tradition for some folk reciting it that number of times at a cemetery.

THE MUGHNĪ OF THE SANŪSIYYA

Every dervish order has its peculiar forms of nonliturgical prayer for devotional use. Such a form of prayer is called a *wird* (pl., *awrād*) and this *wird*, known as *al-Mughnī* (that which suffices), is taken from pp. 25-30 of the collection *Jumlat Awrād munīfa* (Stambul, 1342 A.H. = 1923 A.D.) by the Sheikh Aḥmad Idrīs as-Sanūsī, and is in current use among the members of the Sanūsiyya order.

Allahumma, it is from Thee that I seek help, so help me; it is with Thee that I seek satisfaction, so satisfy me; in Thee have I put my trust, so be my sufficiency. O Great Provider, provide for me whatever it is important for me to have in this world and in the next. O Thou who art the Merciful, the Compassionate, in this world and the next, I am Thy slave at Thy door, Thy humble one at Thy door, Thy unfortunate one at Thy door, Thy prisoner at Thy Door, Thy guest at Thy door. O Lord of mankind, [I am] the weary one at Thy door. O Succorer of those who seek for help, [I am] the anxious one at Thy door. O Thou who dost uncover the grief of all the grief-stricken, I am the one who has rebelled against Thee. O Thou who dost seek those who seek forgiveness, [I am] the one who stands constantly at Thy door. O Thou who dost forgive sinners, [I am] the one who is submissive at Thy door. O Most merciful of those who show mercy, [I am] the guilty one at Thy door. O Lord of mankind, [I am] the evildoer at Thy door, the unhappy one, the humble one at Thy door. Have mercy upon me, O my Lord.

O my God, Thou art the One who forgives, I am the one who does evil, and will anyone have mercy on him who does evil save Him who forgives? My Lord, my Lord, my God, Thou art the Master and I am the slave, and will anyone have mercy on the slave save the Master? My Lord, my Lord, my God, Thou art the Possessor and I am the possessed, and will anyone have mercy on the possessed save the Possessor? My Lord, my Lord, my God, Thou art the Mighty One, and I the one of no account, and will anyone have mercy on him who is of no account save Him who is mighty? My Lord, my Lord, my God, Thou art the Generous One and I am the mean one, and will any have mercy on the mean one save the Generous? My Lord, my Lord, my God, Thou art the Provider, I am the one provided for, and will any have mercy on the one provided for save Him who provides? My Lord, my Lord, my God, I am weak, I am humble, I am a paltry thing, but Thou art the High One, Thou art the Pardoner, Thou art the Forgiving, the One good at pardoning. Thou art the All-Merciful, the Great Benefactor, I am the culprit, I am the fearful, I am the feeble one.

O my God, [grant me] safe protection in the darkness and narrowness of the grave. O my God, [grant me] safe protection at the questioning of Munkar and Nakīr [1] and their awful presence. O my God, [grant me] safe protection in the loneliness and dreadfulness of the grave. O my God, [grant me] safe protection on the Day whose length is fifty thousand years (LXX, 4). O my God, [grant me] safe protection on the Day when the Trump will sound and all in heaven and on earth will be in terror save those whom Allah wills (XXVII, 87/89). O my God, [grant me] safe protection on the Day when the earth with a quaking will quake (XCIX, 1). O my God, [grant me] safe protection on the Day when the sky with all its clouds will be rent asunder (XXV, 25/27). O my God, [grant me] safe protection on the Day when the heavens will be rolled up like a scroll of writing (XXI, 104). O my God, security, security, on the Day when the earth will be changed to another earth and the heavens likewise, and [men] will appear before Allah, the One, the All-Conquering (XIV, 48/49). O my God, security, security, on the Day when a man will see that which his hands have sent forward, and the unbeliever will say: O would that I were dust! (LXXVIII, 40/41). O my God, security, security, on the Day when a call will come from the midst of the Throne: "Where are the re-

[1] For these questioners of the dead in the grave, see *EI*, III, 724, 725.

bellious? Where are the sinful? Where are those who went astray? Let them come to the Reckoning."

Thou knowest my secret and my open state, so pray accept my excuses, O my God. Alas for the abundance of sin and disobedience! Alas for the abundance of wrongdoing and worthlessness! Alas for the soul of him who is rejected! Alas for the soul of him who has been fashioned according to desire from desire! Cover me, O Thou who dost succor. Cover me when my state is being changed. Allahumma! I am Thy guilty, wicked, sinful servant. Save me from the Fire, O Thou who dost protect. Save me from the Fire, O Thou who dost protect. Save me from the Fire, O Thou who dost protect. Allahumma! shouldst Thou show me mercy that is Thy right, and shouldst Thou punish me that is what I deserve. O Thou who deservest to be feared! O Thou who art entitled to grant pardon! O most merciful of those who show mercy! O best of helpers! O most wonderful of forgivers! Allah alone is my sufficiency. It is in Thy mercy, O most merciful of those who show mercy.

And now may Allah bless our lord Muḥammad, his family and his Companions, and give them peace. May He bless also all the prophets and messengers along with their families and companions and followers, and [bless] us along with them in Thy mercy, O Thou most merciful of those who show mercy, O Lord of mankind. Amen.

SOME FAMOUS INVOCATIONS

From al-Ghazzālī's *Iḥyā' 'Ulūm ad-Dīn* (Ḥalabī edition; Cairo, 1348 A.H. = 1929 A.D.), I, 284-287.

Adam's Invocation

'Ā'isha said that when Allah—mighty and majestic is He—willed to turn [in kindliness again] to Adam—upon whom be Allah's blessing and peace—Adam circumambulated seven times around the House [at Mecca]. In those days it had not yet been built but was a red hillock. Then he stopped and prayed two *rak'as*, and said: "Allahumma! Thou knowest what I keep secret and what I reveal, so accept my excuse. Thou knowest my need, so grant me what I ask. Thou knowest what is in my soul, so forgive me my sins. Allahumma! I ask Thee for a faith that will enliven my heart, and a perfect assurance so that I may know for sure that nothing will ever befall me save what has been written for me and be well pleased with what Thou hast appointed for me, O Thou possessor of majesty and honor." Thereupon Allah—mighty and majestic is He—spoke to him by revelation, saying: "I have forgiven you, and no one of your progeny will ever come to Me and invoke Me with the like of this invocation of yours but I shall pardon him, remove his anxieties and cares, and remove poverty from between his eyes."

Abraham's Invocation

When Abraham arose in the morning he used to say: "Allahumma! this is a new creation, so may it open with my being obedient to Thee, and may it close with Thy pardoning me and being well pleased with me. Provide for me in it some good Thou wilt accept from me, increasing it and multiplying it for me, and forgive me for whatever evil I do therein. Thou art the Forgiving, the Merciful, the Beloved, the Generous." He said: "Whosoever makes this invocation when he gets up in the morning has really given thanks for his day."

The Invocation of Jesus

Jesus used to say: "Allahumma! I have become one in such a state that I cannot ward off that which I detest nor seize upon the benefit of that for which I hope, and the matter is in hands other than mine. I have become worn out by my labors and there is no poor person poorer than I am. Allahumma! let not my enemy rejoice over me, and let not my friend be in any evil because of me. Suffer me not to meet with mishap in my religion. Let not this world be my greatest care, and put me not under the authority of one who will show me no mercy, O Thou Living, Self-subsistent One."

Al-Khiḍr's Invocation

It is said that when al-Khiḍr and Elias meet each other every harvest time they do not separate without saying these words: "In the Name of Allah! What Allah has willed! There is no strength save with Allah! What Allah has willed! Every blessing is from Allah! What Allah has willed! All good is in the hand of Allah! What Allah has willed! No one can deter evil save Allah." Whoever says this three times when he gets up in the morning will be secure from fire, from drowning, and from being robbed—if Allah wills, exalted be He.

'Ā'isha's Invocation

The Apostle of Allah—upon whom be Allah's blessing and peace—said to 'Ā'isha—with whom may Allah be pleased: "O 'Ā'isha, avoid ostentation and say: 'Allahumma! I ask of Thee every good thing, what thereof comes early and what thereof comes late, what I know of and that of which I know not. And I take refuge with Thee from every evil thing, what thereof comes early and what thereof comes late, what I know of and that of which I do not know. I ask Thee for Paradise and for that whether of word or of deed which draws one near to it, and with Thee I take refuge from Hell and from that whether of word or of deed which draws one near to it. I ask of Thee that good which Thy servant and Thy Apostle, Muḥammad—upon whom be Allah's blessing and peace—asked of Thee, and I take refuge with Thee from that from which Thy servant and Thy Apostle, Muḥammad—upon whom be Allah's blessing and peace—took refuge with Thee. Also I ask Thee that no matter what it be Thou hast decreed for me Thou wilt make its final outcome be right direction, by Thy Mercy, O Thou most merciful of those who show mercy.' "

Fāṭima's Invocation

Said the Apostle of Allah—upon whom be Allah's blessing and peace: "O Fāṭima, what hinders you from hearkening to that with which I charge you, namely, that you should say:

O Living One! O Self-subsistent One! To Thy mercy I turn for succor. Entrust me not to myself for even the twinkling of an eye, but set Thou Thyself aright for me in my state."

Abū Bakr's Invocation

The Apostle of Allah—upon whom be Allah's blessing and peace—taught Abū Bakr—with whom may Allah be pleased—the trusty one, that he should say: "Allahumma! I ask of Thee, for the sake of Muḥammad Thy prophet, and Abraham Thy friend, and Moses Thy confidant, and Jesus Thy word and Thy spirit, and for the sake of the Torah of Moses, of the *Injīl* of Jesus, of the *Zabūr* of David, and of the *Furqān* of Muḥammad—upon whom and upon all of whom be Allah's blessing and peace—and for the sake of every revelation Thou hast revealed, or decree Thou hast decreed, or petitioner to whom Thou hast given [what he asked], or rich man Thou hast made poor, or poor man Thou hast made rich, or one astray whom Thou hast guided, and I ask Thee for the sake of Thy Name which Thou didst reveal to Moses—on whom be peace—for the sake of Thy Name by which Thou dost exercise toward men Thy Providence, for the sake of Thy Name which Thou didst place upon the earth and it settled firmly, for the sake of Thy Name which Thou didst set in the heavens and they were raised aloft, for the sake of Thy Name by which Thy Throne was raised, for the sake of Thy Name undefiled, purifying, one, eternal, unique, which has been revealed in Thy Book [which came] from before Thee from the Light that makes clear, for the sake of Thy Name which Thou didst set upon day so that it is bright and upon night so that it is dark, for the sake of Thy greatness and Thy grandeur, for the sake of the light of Thy noble face, that Thou grant me the Qur'ān as my portion, and knowledge thereof, that Thou cause it to intermingle with my flesh and my blood, with my hearing and my seeing, and that my earthly body be fully occupied therewith, by Thy might and Thy power, for there is no might and no power save with Thee, O Thou most merciful of those who show mercy."

'Utba's Invocation

The slave boy 'Utba was seen in a dream after his death, and he said: "I entered Paradise because of [my use of] these words: 'Allahumma! Thou who guidest those who go astray, Thou who showest mercy to those who sin, Thou who dost overlook the slips of those who fall, have mercy on Thy servant who stands in such grave peril, and on all Muslims without exception. Set us among the good, those well provided for, to whom Thou hast been gracious, namely, the prophets, the just, the martyrs, the righteous. Amen. O Lord of Mankind.' "

GLOSSARY

adhān, the call to prayers made by the muezzin daily from the mosque.

'aqīda (pl., *'aqā'id*), a statement of religious beliefs or tenets, a credal statement.

bait, house, and then in a restricted sense a temple or shrine as God's House. *Ahl al-Bait,* "the people of the House," sometimes means the people of Allah's House at Mecca, sometimes the family of the Prophet.

baraka, blessing.

bid'a, innovation, and then, in a derived sense, heresy.

daraja (pl., *darajāt*), a step, degree, rank, grade. It is used of the ranks or degrees of eminence humans may attain in the Hereafter.

dīn, religion, more particularly religion as expressed in practice. The same word means also judgment, so *yaum ad-Dīn* is Day of Judgment.

dīnār, a unit of coinage. It is derived from the Latin *denarius* and came through Greek and Syriac into Arabic.

dirham, a unit of coinage derived from the Greek *drachma.*

diya, blood-wit: compensation to be paid to the family or tribe of a man who has been slain.

du'ā, supplication, invocation, spontaneous extempore prayer.

farā'iḍ, the pl. of *farḍ,* an incumbent duty of religion the performance of which is not optional but obligatory.

al-Fātiḥa, the Opener. The name of the first Sūra in the Qur'ān.

fiqh, jurisprudence. A *faqīh* is properly a jurist whose professional interest is in *fiqh.*

fiṭra, a natural disposition of the soul.

furqān, that which distinguishes or separates. A name for the Qur'ān.

ghusl, bathing, ablution, the greater lustration for purifying the body.

ḥādith, something new, a novelty, a phenomenon.

ḥadīth, news, a story, then a Tradition embodying the *sunna* of the Prophet.

ḥāfiẓ, one who has memorized the Qur'ān. A professional Qur'ān reciter.

ḥajj, pilgrimage. Technically it is the greater pilgrimage to Mecca as contrasted with the *'umra* or lesser pilgrimage. So a man who has completed the duty of pilgrimage is a *Ḥajjī.*

ḥanīf, a striver after true religion.

ḥarām, forbidden, particularly a sacred area which must be kept inviolate.

ḥūrī, one of the *ḥūr 'īn* or celestial damsels of Paradise.

'ibāda, service, and then in a particular sense an act of worship.

Iblīs (from *diabolos*), a Qur'ānic name for Satan.

iḥrām, sanctification, i.e., putting oneself in a sacral state for cult purposes. It is also used for the sacral garb assumed by pilgrims approaching Mecca.

i'jāz, miraculousness. So *mu'jiza* is a miracle.

ijmā', consensus, more particularly the consensus of the Muslim community as to the rightness or wrongness of certain things.

imām, leader. It is used in a general sense, as, e.g., the prayer leader, and in the particular sense of a community leader. Among the Shī'a the *Imāms* take the place that the Caliphs have among the Sunnī Muslims.

īmān, faith, belief, and in particular the beliefs of religion as opposed to *Dīn,* which refers to the cult practices.

'iṣma, preservation, and in particular preservation from the committing of sins, so that, as used of the prophets, it means impeccability.

isnād, the chain of authorities through whom a Tradition has been handed down from the days of the Prophet.

jāmi', a cathedral mosque, i.e., a larger mosque in which Friday prayers may be held.

janāba, ritual impurity which must be removed before certain cult practices may be performed.

jihād, Holy War, i.e., fighting against infidel peoples for the spread of Islam.

jinn, spirits, sprites.

Ka'ba (cube), the central shrine in the holy city of Mecca.

kāfir, an unbeliever. It is the opposite of *mu'min*, a believer.

kalām, speech. It is used of the *Word* of God, and later came to mean scholastic theology which discussed dialectically questions of religion.

kalima, a word. Technically it means the short credal statement of Islam that there is no deity save Allah, whose messenger Muhammad was.

karāmāt, the charismata or wonders often associated with Allah's saints.

khalīfa, successor, vicegerent. Technically it means the Caliph as successor of Muḥammad.

khuṭba, address, sermon, hortatory speech.

kitāb, writing, document, book, in particular Scripture.

Kunya, name telling personal relationship.

madhhab, way of acting: a system of rules to be followed to assure right living.

majlis, sitting, assembly, place of sitting.

majnūn, possessed by the jinn, crazed.

malā'ika, angels (sing. *malak*).

maqām, a standing place. The *maqām Ibrāhīm* is a structure near the Ka'ba at Mecca.

masjid, a place for doing prostrations of obeisance (*sujūd*), and so a place of worship, a mosque.

miḥrāb, the niche in the wall of a mosque which indicates the *qibla*, direction to be faced during prayers.

mi'rāj, ladder, way of ascent: the Ascension of Muḥammad.

muezzin (*mu'adhdhin*), the man who gives the *adhān* or call to prayers.

muḥtalim, a youth who has reached puberty.

mu'jiza, a miracle granted to a prophet in confirmation of his mission.

mu'min, one who believes, a true believer as opposed to an unbeliever (*kāfir*).

mursal, one sent on a mission, an envoy, a messenger.

muṣḥaf (pl., *maṣāḥif*), a codex, and exemplar of the Qur'ān.

mutakallimūn, the scholastic theologians who specialized in *kalām.*

mutawātur, a Tradition handed down by many lines of unimpeachable transmitters.

muṭawwif, one who directs the *ṭawāf* or circumambulation, a pilgrim guide.

nabī, a prophet sent by Allah with His message.

nāfila, a good work undertaken voluntarily in excess of what is required by the religious law.

namāz, prayers: the word commonly used in India for the daily *ṣalāt.*

nāsikh, that which abrogates, so *mansūkh* is that which is abrogated.

niyya, intention. It is customary at the commencement of any cult act to express intention of performing such and such an act.

qadar, the decreeing of good and evil.

qadīm, ancient, from of old, eternal in the sense that it always has been.

qibla, the point toward which a worshiper faces in prayer.

qiyās, analogical reasoning.

Qur'ān, Scripture lesson: then the name for Muḥammad's Scripture.

rak'a, bowing, prostration. Technically it means a complex of bodily genuflections accompanied by the repetition of liturgical formulae in ritual prayer. A certain number of these make up one *rak'a,* and a normal prayer service consists of a varying number of *rak'as.*

rasūl, messenger, Apostle, one sent on a mission from Allah.

rūḥ, spirit.

rukn, a corner, a cornerstone, a pillar, and then the principles on which anything is based.

ṣadaqa, charitable alms.

sajda, a prostration of obeisance. *Sujūd* is the act of so prostrating oneself in obeisance, and a *masjid* is a place set apart for such prostrations.

salām, peace, and then the greeting of peace.

ṣalāt, liturgical, ritual prayers.

ṣaum, fasting.

shahīd, a witness, and then a martyr as one who by his death has borne witness to his faith.

sharī'a, the body of regulations which makes up the religious law.

shirk, association, in particular the sin of associating any other with Allah in any way that would impugn His absolute uniqueness.

ṣuḥuf, sheets. It is sometimes used for the earliest Scriptures sent to mankind.

sunna, custom, the customary way of acting, particularly that of the Prophet.

sūra, a section or chapter of the Qur'ān.

ta'awwudh, the act of taking refuge with Allah, or using the formula: "With Allah do I take refuge."

tahajjud, vigil, special prayers said during the watches of the night.

tahlīl, to raise the *hallel,* i.e., to praise Allah by using the formula: "There is no deity save Allah."

taḥmīd, to praise Allah by using the formula: "Praises be to Allah."

takbīr, to praise Allah by using the formula: "Allah is very great."

tamjīd, to utter pious phrases in glorification of Allah.

tanāsukh, the belief in reincarnation and transmigration of the soul.

tartīl, cantillation, particularly the cantillation of the Qur'ān.

tasbīḥ, to praise Allah by using the formula: "Glory be to Allah."

taṣdīq, putting full trust in the reliability of someone or something.

tasmiya, the devotional use of the phrase: "In the Name of Allah."
tatawwu‘, the performance of works of supererogation.
tathniya, to praise Allah by using expressions of eulogy.
tawḥīd, the maintaining of the Divine unity.
tayammum, purification by fine sand instead of water.
‘Ulamā’, teachers of religion, theologians, divines.
umma, a community, party.
‘umra, visitation, the lesser pilgrimage to Mecca.
waḥy, revelation, inspiration where the very words are dictated to the messenger.
wakīl, a trustee, agent, executor.
walī (pl., *awilyā’*), a saint.
wildān, youths, in particular the youthful attendants in Paradise.
wird, a form of nonliturgical prayer.
witr, an odd number, a word used for extra prayers with an odd number of *rak‘as.*
wuḍu’, ablution, the lesser lustration necessary before prayers.
zakāt, legal alms.
Zamzam, the sacred well at Mecca.

INDEX OF QUR'ĀN CITATIONS

HOBBES, T., Leviathan, I and II
HORACE, The Odes of Horace *and* The Centennial Hymn
HUME, D., Dialogues Concerning Natural Religion
Inquiry Concerning Human Understanding
Inquiry Concerning the Principles of Morals
Of the Standard of Taste, and Other Essays
Philosophical Historian
Political Essays
KANT, I., Analytic of the Beautiful
Critique of Practical Reason
First Introduction to the Critique of Judgment
Foundations of the Metaphysics of Morals
The Metaphysical Elements of Justice, Part I of *Metaphysik der Sitten*
The Metaphysical Principles of Virtue, Part II of *Metaphysik der Sitten*
On History
Perpetual Peace
Prolegomena to Any Future Metaphysics
LEIBNIZ, G., Monadology and Other Philosophical Essays
LUCIAN, Selected Works
LUCRETIUS, On Nature
MACHIAVELLI, N., The Art of War
MILL, J. S., Autobiography
On Liberty
On the Logic of the Moral Sciences
Utilitarianism
MOLIÈRE, Tartuffe
PAINE, T., The Age of Reason
PICO DELLA MIRANDOLA, On the Dignity of Man, On Being and the One, *and* Heptaplus

PLATO, Epistles
Euthydemus
Euthyphro, Apology, Crito
Gorgias
Meno
Phaedo
Phaedrus
Protagoras
Statesman
Symposium
Theatetus
Timaeus
Commentaries:
BLUCK, R., Plato's Phaedo
CORNFORD, F., Plato and Parmenides
Plato's Cosmology
Plato's Theory of Knowledge
HACKFORTH, R., Plato's Examination of Pleasure
Plato's Phaedo
Plato's Phaedrus
POPE, A., An Essay on Man
PLAUTUS, The Menaechmi
QUINTILIAN, On the Early Education of the Citizen-Orator
REYNOLDS, J., Discourses on Art
Roman Drama, Copley and Hadas, trans.
RUSSELL, B., Philosophy of Science
Sappho, The Poems of
SCHLEGEL, J., On Imitation and Other Essays
SCHOPENHAUER, A., On the Basis of Morality
SHELLEY, P., A Defence of Poetry
Song of Roland, Terry, trans.
TERENCE, The Woman of Andros
VERGIL, Aeneid
VICO, G. B., On the Study Methods of Our Time
XENOPHON, Recollections of Socrates *and* Socrates' Defense Before the Jury